The
Charismatic
Century

The
Charismatic Century

The Enduring Impact of the Azusa Street Revival

Jack W. Hayford
and S. David Moore

WARNER Faith®

NEW YORK   BOSTON   NASHVILLE

Warner Faith
Time Warner Book Group
1271 Avenue of the Americas, New York, NY 10020
Visit our Web site at www.twbookmark.com

The Warner Faith name and logo are registered trademarks of the Time Warner Book Group.

Printed in the United States of America

First Warner Books edition: August 2006

10 9 8 7 6 5 4 3 2 1

Library of Congress Cataloging-in-Publication Data

Hayford, Jack W.
The charismatic century : the enduring impact of the Azusa Street Revival / Jack Hayford and David Moore.—1st ed.
p. cm.
ISBN-13: 978-0-446-57813-4
ISBN-10: 0-446-57813-4
1. Pentecostalism. I. Moore, S. David (Seth David) II. Title.
BR1644.H39 2006
270.8'2—dc22   2005034264

Dedicated to all who welcome God's Holy Spirit into their hearts and lives as they reach toward and serve human loss, pain and need with the love and power of Jesus Christ.

Contents

Contents

Preface

Commemorating the Azusa St. Revival centennial, this book tells the story of the modern Pentecostal and Charismatic Renewal. Our emphasis is on the United States but we are not ignoring the Renewal's far broader expressions. Our aim is to explore the rich textures and fabric of the Pentecostalism made visible in its people and institutions. We write as two participants in the Renewal, both Classical Pentecostals. The story is told with a prophetic and interpretive eye seeking to understand why the movement has impacted so many.

There are no claims of objectivity here since we are both too immersed in the world of Renewal to suppose we could somehow make ourselves aloof observers. No, we care very deeply about what we write and cannot dismiss our conviction that God is at work renewing His church. Nevertheless, we seek to avoid idealism and pride and do our best not to gloss over controversies or excuse the problems and peculiarities of the Renewal, since there are many. There is no intention to sound like parochial partisans because we cherish the invaluable heritage found in varying Christian traditions and hope this work will foster mutual appreciation.

The story has been told well by many capable scholars. Why then another book on Pentecostalism? Our answer is that this book adds to the discussion through its unique blend of historical and theological sensitivity coupled with pastoral and prophetic passion. Also, we are writing to a general audience in hopes of expanding the vistas of readers, in and out of the Renewal, who have an interest in the rather remarkable story of modern Pentecostalism. Since we have the non-specialist in mind, whenever necessary we define terms. Generally, footnotes/endnotes are only used when making direct quotes.

The story that follows is told chronologically. At times the narrative takes turns or stops for pastoral and prophetic perspectives and interpretations. All and all it is a journey through the extraordinary "charismatic century."

Authors' Acknowledgments

It is a privilege to be trusted by any publisher of repute, and I don't know an author who does not feel indebted to those who are interested, gifted, and sensitive enough to put him or her in print. Accordingly, I am more than *formally* grateful for the phone call Rolf Zettersten made to me a year ago, inviting me to consider this project: I am *fraternally* grateful. His brotherly trust in my ability to deliver, especially when the patience of others would have been taxed by reason of my difficulties answering our deadline, occasions my deep gratitude. Gary Terashita, the editor who literally waltzed this project through to completion, is a new friend: thank you, Gary, for your wonderful assistance.

The primary person who made this book possible, however, is my respected friend David Moore. David is a longtime fellow pastor—one who has answered the Holy Spirit's call on his ministry to give the rest of his life teaching ministry keys to others.

David, who is presently completing his Ph.D. at Regent University (USA), is one of the most knowledgeable persons concerning the events covered in this book. His willingness to partner in this project is not only appreciated beyond words but, as I told Rolf Zettersten when he first contacted me, "I can only pursue this if David Moore joins me in the task." So, to you and (his wife) Patty, David, I extend thanks from the depths of my heart. While you and I both join to give glory to God for anything of His blessing that is spread or compounded by reason of our joint effort, I here and now give the credit for its publication to you.

Finally, as with everything I do in any aspect of ministry Jesus privileges me to serve, I want to thank the team of co-laborers who serve as my immediate staff: Russ Davis and Bill Shumate, my executive assistants (at the Foursquare Church's central offices and The King's College and Seminary, respectively), and Lana Duim, whose immeasurable help as my personal assistant is among Anna's and my greatest gifts.

And, of course, my Lady Anna—my bride, wife, and mother of our wonderful kids, grandkids and now great-grandkids (!), has not only been my partner for over half of the past century, she is the first reader and trusted critic of every book with my name on it. I love you, Babe.

There is an extended tribute at the end of this book—something of an acknowledgment as well, but actually far more. I trust you will find it, and all between here and there, enriching, enlightening, and spiritually igniting to your soul.

—Jack Hayford
Los Angeles, California
November 2005

I was thrilled at the invitation of Jack Hayford to co-write this book. With it came the opportunity to share with a wider audience the remarkable stories contained in these pages. It truly has been a unique century as the Pentecostal and Charismatic movements have reshaped global Christianity. I was also humbled by Pastor Jack's invitation, for no one has more shaped life and my philosophy of pastoral ministry. There is no one I respect more deeply; what an honor to team with him in this endeavor. Together I believe we have forged a narrative that is both pastoral and prophetic while historically interesting.

My aim throughout has been to be as biographical as possible. I believe this is the best way to write popular history. All through Christian history God has chosen to extend His kingdom through ordinary folk who were willing to surrender their lives to His purposes. Despite the human condition with all its flaws and sins, this is how God gets His work done on the earth.

There are many people whose voices echo on these pages, none more than that of Dr. Vinson Synan, Dean of Regent University's School of Divinity, who has been a friend, advocate, and mentor of my scholarship. His master storytelling made history a living thing not a collection of obscure facts. He has lived a sizable piece of the history he tells! Thank you for being an example of a Godly man as well a great historian. I owe you a great debt.

My academic study has focused on the history of neo-Pentecostalism over the last five decades of the twentieth century. Consequently, I owe a great debt to several scholars whose research and writings were an invaluable resource for the chapters that predate WWII. I wish to express my gratitude to William Faupel, Edith Blumhofer, Cecil Robeck, Gary McGee, and Donald Dayton. They not only informed my writing tremendously but were an inspiration as well.

To a few others I extend personal thanks. Steven Land, Grant Wacker, David Edwin Harrell, and Frank Macchia have been models of superior scholarship and have inspired me to think more deeply. Special thanks to Ralph Iervolino, the best pastor I ever had, who taught me that pastoral work was about loving people. I want to thank Jim W. Adams, Guy Romito, and Jack Coldren for being true friends.

To my children, Emily, Jonathan, and Anna, I want to say how much you mean to me and how proud I am of each of you. You have had to live with all my idiosyncrasies (my obsession with books for one).

Of course, no one deserves greater thanks than the love of my life, dear Patty. She has encouraged me in multiplied ways; her belief and trust in me is a constant inspiration. Though she is a behind-the-scenes person, I would never do what I do without her. Thank you for so graciously and sacrificially making room for Christ's work in my life. You are the real hero in this family!

In the end words are never adequate to fully express my gratefulness to God for granting to a "two bit hippie" the privilege to be called His son and co-worker.

—David Moore

Manteca, California

November 2005

Note: The authors also wish to thank Selimah Nemoy for reading the manuscript and offering insights we believe will make this work a better one for the reader.

Perspective on
a "Latter Rain" Storm

The streets of Tel Aviv were three inches deep in rainwater everywhere, and sheets of torrential rain swept across the windshield of the van taking us to Ben Gurion Airport for our departure. My thoughts ran back to the prayer meeting I had led near Galilee two days before, where passionate intercession sought an intervention of God's hand. Ten years of drought had Galilee at its most desperate level in modern history—now on the brink of actually being unable to maintain its internal flora and fauna. The lake's fish population as well as its in-water plant and other life forms were at risk if water levels dipped any lower below the red line marking the beginning of its self-destruct mode.

Within three months, the water level was at its peak, subterranean aquifers were beginning to refill, and Mt. Hermon had a blanket of snow twenty-four-feet deep in places. What had been expected to take three years of good rainfall to restore had been restored within the first three months of 2004. Our prayers were privileged to be among the final ones offered, uniting with those of so many who had for so long invoked God's grace upon His Land: Israel, the only nation on earth to which God lays claim as uniquely His.

And as though He intentionally dramatized the point, the season surrounding the meteorological phenomenon of the "latter rain" storm of restoration coincides with the present season of God's hand at work in *spiritual* restoration. Without elaboration—and certainly, with no claim to have led the decisive prayer meeting that brought the blessing of the rain or the present move of God's Spirit among Israelis today—suffice to say the principle is well illustrated: *rain and restoration travel hand in hand!*

This is a book about a century-long rainfall—about a storm of divine proportions prophesied by God's Spirit, pointing to His own intention of climaxing history with a global outpouring of spiritual awakening, restoration and redemptive blessing. It's a look at the greatest revival in history: the last one hundred years.

Question: Who cares about the last 100 years?
Answer: Anyone who cares about the next 10 years!

That's what moved me to accept the invitation of the publisher to engage the project resulting in this short work on the Charismatic Century: because I believe the immediate decade before us is destined to become, at once, the most sociologically traumatic and the most spiritually dynamic ever known.

Those equipped for this future immediately upon us will *live it*—living a life of *hope with power*, while experiencing a dimension of divine grace unseen since the first century. Those unequipped will, at best, *undergo it*—constantly reacting or struggling through changing circumstances in an effort to *merely survive*. The contrast will not be produced by human wisdom or mechanics, but simply by reason of the difference between humanly *temporal* resources and divinely *eternal* enablement, between the strength of "the flesh" and the power of the Spirit. However we look at ourselves—as individuals or as a race, as believers in Christ or as spiritually undecided, as the Church or as the World—history has ushered us into the twenty-first century and thus we have been *brought to this moment.*

Those four words have gripped me as I have worked in partnership with a friend to place this book in your hands. What for some causes history to be associated with the musty, dusty or disinteresting will find no place in this volume. The brisk flow of past events and personalities, racing before your eyes in ten short chapters covering key features of God-at-work through the twentieth century, is condensed here for one reason: to focus on today! To do what Jesus commanded, saying, "He that has ears to hear, let him hear what the Spirit is saying . . . " (Rev. 2:7). And, as in no other 100-year span since creation, God's Holy Spirit has swept like rain and spoken like thunder—both restoring and stirring those who will listen . . . and those who will respond.

The possibility that you might find help toward making *a timely response to timeless truths*, standing before us on the landscape of the past century, is what motivated my passion for these pages. Joining me with equal zeal is David Moore, the man I immediately turned to when I was asked to write this book. I felt the *prophetic pulse beat* of the present, set by the tempo of the increasing magnitude of the tide of the Holy Spirit's working through recent decades, but I needed a scholar to relate the *historic drama* that has unfolded. *To see the future clearly the past must be assessed wisely.* Alexander Solzhenitsyn said, *"Dwell on the past and you'll lose an eye . . . Forget the past and you'll lose both eyes!"* More contemporarily, Ken Burns notes, *"History is really about defining the present and who we are,"* and with his words joined to Solzhenitsyn's you have David's and my intention here.

Having been "brought to this moment," what does the past teach us about how to live in it? Indeed, how to win in it!

There are victories waiting to be won! And, as God's Word says, "The battle will not be to the strong (humanly speaking) . . . ," but to those who learn and live life on terms that win, "not by might, nor by power, but by My Spirit, says the Lord!" (Zec. 4:6)

Join us in a quest to discern the pathway into the future by looking at the milestones of the past. Let's look together at "What God hath wrought," and open to hear together "What the Spirit is saying."

Our work is structured briefly, to the point, and with a specific strategy: First, to look at the unfolding of an unprecedented season in history—the twentieth century, as God's Holy Spirit was unleashed through the lives of simple but profoundly enabled people. Then, listening to the echoes of God's voice, remaining open to listen to His Holy Spirit preparing us for *now*—the "now" of "this moment" to which He has brought each of us.

The
Charismatic
Century

1

The New Shape of Christianity

On January 1, 1901, the first day of the new century, from the Vatican, Pope Leo XIII invoked the Holy Spirit by singing the hymn "Veni Creator Spiritus" (Come Holy Spirit, Creator Blest) dedicating the twentieth century to the Holy Spirit.[1] That same day on the other side of the world, a group of students in Charles Parham's tiny Topeka, Kansas, Bible school, experienced a Pentecostal outpouring when a young woman was filled with the Holy Spirit and spoke "in tongues."

What made this so unique was not that she spoke in tongues. Others had done that. The uniqueness was for her, and those who soon experienced the same thing, that it served as evidence of a renewal of the New Testament "baptism in the Holy Spirit." When she spoke "in tongues" (to supernaturally speak in a language never learned), she did so believing that it was a biblically based, empowering experience that is distinct and subsequent to conversion. Parham and his followers saw their experience just like that of the apostles on the day of Pentecost as described in Acts 2. This, they were convinced, was a restoration of New Testament power for ministry in the latter days. The Charismatic Century had begun.

Five years later, another outpouring occurred in Los Angeles when William J. Seymour, influenced by Parham, moved to California and preached the Pentecostal baptism with the Holy Spirit. There, through Seymour's preaching, a small group of believers, mostly African-Americans, were filled with the Holy Spirit and as in Topeka, they spoke with tongues as a biblical evidence of that experience. Under Seymour's leadership, it became a full-fledged revival.

Within weeks people were flocking to hear Seymour at the tiny old mission building in the heart of the city. Within months "Azusa Pilgrims" were coming from all across the country to experience "their Pentecost."

Early Pentecostals often likened the Los Angeles revival to the birth of Jesus Christ. He was born in a humble stable in Bethlehem to common people, and Pentecostalism was born among common folk in a building once used as a stable. And so the story became part of Pentecostal folklore, as 312 Azusa Street became an immortalized address in their collective history.

This amazing revival was one of many Holy Spirit awakenings around the world at about the same time, and though scholars debate whether the Azusa Street revival was *the* beginning, it was and *is*, at the very least, the popular beginning point. Pentecostalism, with its emphasis on the presence and power of the Holy Spirit, was erupting.

Though the crowds were never huge, they defied the racial taboos of their day as Blacks, Whites, Latinos, and a smattering of Asians worshipped together. Daily meetings continued for three years. The Apostolic Faith Mission, as it was known, became the catalytic birthplace of the modern Pentecostal movement.

From these commonplace beginnings just a century ago, the Pentecostal/Charismatic Renewal began changing the landscape of global Christianity. Marginalized and dismissed by the larger church and the secular media for much of the twentieth century, the sheer size and dynamic vitality of the movement have brought growing recognition and appreciation. No longer ignored, it is often spoken of with sweeping superlatives. In 1998, the evangelical publication *Christian History* called Pentecostalism "the most explosive Christian movement of the twentieth century." In 2000 it ranked Azusa Street founder William Seymour as one of the most influential leaders of the twentieth century and called the Azusa Street Revival "the most phenomenal event of twentieth century Christianity."[2]

GROWTH EXAMINED, TERMS DEFINED

Not only the fastest-growing segment of the Christian faith, the Pentecostal and Charismatic movements are far and away the most widespread and diverse expressions of the church, comprising roughly twenty-five percent of all Christians in the world. The numbers are astounding by any measure. With estimates as high as 600 million adherents in 2005, the Renewal is the second largest distinct grouping of Christians in the world; only the Roman Catholic Church is larger. The movement is expanding by 9 million new participants a year (twenty-five thousand per day) and Pentecostals and Charismatics are found in large numbers on every continent and in 236 nations.[3]

The Renewal's makeup reflects its global character with 71 percent non-white with women outnumbering men and children outnumbering adults. While in the West, Pentecostals and Charismatics are now a part of the middle class, a majority of its members in the developing world are poor and cluster in the mega-cities of the world. And although growth of the Renewal has slowed in North America, it continues unabated outside the West. The grassroots and egalitarian character of the Renewal is deeply appealing to the disenfranchised. It is here that the message of the dynamic power and presence of the Holy Spirit heralds hope for the marginalized and downtrodden.

Pentecostalism is far from being a monolithic movement. It is extremely diverse and cannot easily be defined theologically. Some believe the baptism of the Holy Spirit follows conversion and that speaking with tongues is the "initial physical evidence" of that experience. Others see the baptism of the Spirit as part of conversion or confirmation. Still others think tongues is an important gift but not essential as evidence.

The fact is Pentecostals come in all shapes and sizes that reach across the broad spectrum of the larger church. Some embrace the name "Pentecostal" and others refuse it. Some are in Pentecostal denominations while others are spread throughout all denominations. The largest group by far is the independent Pentecostals who span the globe. In the Pentecostal potpourri only one thing is the same for all: *the passion they share to experience the presence and power of the Holy Spirit.* This is the common denominator.

This emphasis on the Holy Spirit, the third person of the Trinity, is what defines the "charismatic century."[4] Neglected in theological reflection over the centuries, as other doctrinal issues took center stage, the twentieth century became the "century of the Holy Spirit." From theologians to pastors, from denominational leaders to the people in the pews, there has been an unprecedented new focus on the person and work of the Holy Spirit in the last 100 years. It continues into this new millennium.

For the purposes of our study, and given the rich diversity among Pentecostals, several terms need to be clarified. Generally, when unmodified, we use *Pentecostal(s)*, *Pentecostalism*, the *Pentecostal/Charismatic movements*, and simply *the Renewal*, as broadly inclusive terms referring to all Pentecostals irrespective of their differences. Whenever we use any of these or similar terms to name groups or movements we capitalize them, as in the Charismatic Renewal or Classical Pentecostals. Sometimes when they are used as modifiers, as in *the charismatic gifts*, we do not capitalize them.

We also use the terms *baptism in the Holy Spirit*, *filled with the Spirit*, *Spirit filled*, and *Spirit baptism* synonymously in reference to receiving an empowering fullness of the Holy Spirit. We acknowledge and respect the differing perspectives on the particular nature of this experience and seek to engender as much mutuality as possible.

THREE "WAVES" OF THE RENEWAL

As is common now in the study of Pentecostalism, we follow the approach that delineates three distinct categories within the Renewal. First, there are the Classical Pentecostals or denominational Pentecostals. This is the first wave of Pentecostals whose origins are found in the first decades of the twentieth century. Most acknowledge the Azusa Street revival—though not exclusively—as an essential part of their history.

Classical Pentecostals frequently identify speaking with tongues as evidence of the baptism of the Holy Spirit (sometimes referred to simply as "initial evidence"). This group is quite diverse on other points of doctrine and while the majority believe in initial evidence even here there are those who believe tongues is only "a sign" of Spirit baptism and not the only sign.

These first Pentecostals were primarily from the working class and a number were poor and on the margins of society. People outside the movement saw them as uneducated and given to emotionalism and excess. It was a stereotype that would take decades to overcome. Drawing on an epithet that dates back to the nineteenth-century Holiness movement, Pentecostals were frequently called "holy rollers" because of their enthusiastic meetings where worshippers joyfully and full-heartedly sang, clapped, shouted, danced, and celebrated "before the Lord." In the midst of progressivism's heyday, these ordinary folk found identity and purpose in the "end times" revival. Casting off the "threat" of the modern age they were seeing a restoration of the New Testament Christian experience.

As Duke University historian Grant Wacker points out, these early Pentecostals could not be dismissed in hopes that they would simply fade away. On the one hand, while they were passionate about getting back to the New Testament patterns, these folk were not a "head in the cloud" group. Rather, they were sensitive, discerning, and flexible leaders with an ability to adapt and adjust their message to their cultural contexts, traits that have contributed to the success and longevity they have achieved.[5]

The second wave of Pentecostals emerged after the Second World War. Although its earliest origins are in the 1940s and 1950s with the healing movement associated with Oral Roberts, and the latter rain movement of the 1940s and 1950s that started in Canada, it was an event in 1960 that marked the popular beginning of this second wave of the Charismatic Renewal. Neo-Pentecostalism, as it is also called, is usually associated with Episcopalian priest Dennis Bennett. While pastoring St. Mark's Episcopal parish in Van Nuys, California, a large, affluent congregation, Bennett was filled with the Holy Spirit and spoke in tongues. After telling his congregation of his Pentecostal experience in April of 1960, the uproar that followed drew national attention. Here was a respectable, highly educated Episcopalian acting like a Pentecostal. What was most striking is that Bennett chose to remain an Episcopalian and he believed his Holy Spirit baptism would serve to renew his denomination.

This is what marked the Charismatic Renewal. Where in the early decades of the century people almost always left non-Pentecostal churches after experiencing a Pentecostal-like Spirit baptism to join Pentecostal churches, the emphasis in this second wave was renewal of existing structures rather than creating new ones. Characteristic of the Charismatics was that they stayed in the denominations and became a breath of Holy Spirit refreshing. The Charismatic Renewal of the 1960s and 1970s touched almost every denomination in America and many of the historic denominations of Western Europe.

The "third wave" of renewal has been popularized by church growth specialist and missiologist C. Peter Wagner. He has used the term to describe those Christians outside the first two waves who experience the Spirit's power and presence yet prefer not to be called either Pentecostal or Charismatic. In this volume we join with others in broadening the term. Along with Stanley Burgess, editor of *The New International Dictionary of the Pentecostal and Charismatic Movements*, we identify the third wave with the huge throng of independent, indigenous churches that do not carry direct connections with Classical Pentecostalism or the Charismatic Renewal.[6] These churches and believers have Pentecostal-like experiences yet do not identify themselves as Pentecostal/Charismatic. They simply believe they are practicing biblical Christianity and acknowledge the place and power of the Holy Spirit in ways of which many were unaware. They accept the gifts and workings of the Holy Spirit and see them as normal to the church today as in the first century.

"Neo-Charismatics" are found in their greatest numbers in the developing world and are far and away the largest expression of the modern work of the Holy Spirit. Together, the twentieth-century composite of these three surges of renewal is changing the shape of the Christian faith.

CHRISTIANITY'S CHANGING SHAPE

Consider that at the beginning of the twentieth century, notwithstanding even then its broader character, Christianity was primarily seen as an Anglo, Western phenomenon centered in Europe and North America. Largely because of the explosive growth of Pentecostals and Charismatics, Christianity has experienced a dramatic seismic shift to the East and South in the last 100 years. Growing centers of the Christian church are burgeoning in Africa, Latin America, and in regions of Asia.

This reach and impact of the Pentecostal/Charismatic Renewal is in many ways a recovery of the shape of the Church over much of Christian history. The tendency to tell the Church's story with the focus on its European and North American dimensions often ignores or overlooks the vigorous and dynamic Christian history in the East. In fact, it was the Greek-speaking Orthodox Church in Asia Minor and Palestine that had the more robust theology of the Holy Spirit and saw the exercise of the supernatural gifts of the Spirit from the New Testament period all the way through the medieval centuries.

The worldviews and interpretive frameworks (ways of perceiving and deciding what is real) of people in the developing world are far more akin to biblical realities than those of people living in the West. Perhaps one of the most significant contributions of the Renewal is the confrontation it makes to the edifice of western rationalism which, despite Post-Modernity's growing influence, still dominates the educational and political structures of Europe and North America. The assumption that religion is just a private matter, so embedded in western thought, makes little sense to those outside the West, who regularly cry out for supernatural intervention in their affairs in the face of often corrupt, civil authorities. Modern man's arrogant dismissal of the supernatural world has little resonance with people who assume that the invisible world offers gods, spirits, and supernatural activities.

A story told by a Pentecostal missionary who worked churches on the island nation of Papua New Guinea illustrates this reality well. A young evangelist was sent into a remote area to plant a church. After arriving, he was asked to go to a nearby village to pray for the family of a woman who had died and was being readied for burial. When he got there he found family and friends still in deep grief over the woman's death. As he began to comfort the mourners he heard God speak and say, "do not bury her but raise her up." He prayed over the corpse and the woman woke up. The people were in awe of the power of God and a church was started as many in the village turned to Christ. On the very site that was to be her grave, a church building was erected to house a congregation that was named "Resurrection Foursquare Church."[7]

This amazing account is not unusual or unbelievable to Christians in Asia, Africa, and Latin America. These believers heartily affirm this kind of supernatural intervention as part and parcel to the message Jesus proclaimed in the New Testament. Matthew writes in his Gospel:

> And Jesus went about all Galilee, teaching in their synagogues, preaching the gospel of the kingdom, and healing all kinds of sickness and all kinds of disease among the people. Then His fame went throughout all Syria; and they brought to Him all sick people who were afflicted with various diseases and torments, and those who were demon-possessed, epileptics, and paralytics; and He healed them. Great multitudes followed Him—from Galilee, and [from] Decapolis, Jerusalem, Judea, and beyond the Jordan. (Matthew 4:23-25 NKJV)

The offer of hope, healing, and spiritual liberation is a significant reason for the great attraction to Christianity and its explosive growth around the world. All the more remarkable considering that much of the twentieth century pronouncements were made about the demise of Christianity.

In view of the vitality and expansion of Christianity one would think it would receive more media notice. Yet since September 11, 2001, the attention has focused on the growth of Islam with little mention of the growth of the Christian

Church. While there is little question about the growth of Islam, what is sometimes missed is that in many regions of the world, Christianity is outpacing Islam. Africa dramatically illustrates this. At the beginning of the twentieth century there were 10 million Christians, roughly 10 percent of the African population. In 2000, there were 360 million Christians, about forty-six percent of the continent's population. In pure numerical terms this is the largest regional religious change that has ever happened.[8]

Another example is Nigeria. In 1900 Christians comprised one percent of the population in the territories that would become Nigeria, with Muslims at thirty-three percent. Yet by 2000, the two faiths were roughly balanced at about forty-five percent each in the country.[9] Leading this growth throughout Africa are the Pentecostals, particularly the independents. Similar figures could be given for South America where ninety percent of all non-Catholic Christian conversions are Pentecostal. Harvard University professor Harvey Cox has said the growth of Pentecostals in the Southern hemisphere is "so astonishing as to justify claims of a new reformation."[10] Some say it will be "the next Christendom."

NORTH AMERICAN IMPACT

Though less dramatic, North American Christianity, particularly the United States, has been impacted by the Pentecostal/Charismatic movements as well. Estimates on the number of Pentecostals and Charismatic Christians in the United States vary from 40 to 75 million.[11] Several distinct constituencies that did not exist a century ago now have membership in the millions. A 1980 survey found that "about twenty percent of mainline Catholics and Protestant Church members identified themselves as 'charismatic.' "[12]

Perhaps the fastest growing sector of the Renewal is among African-Americans and Latinos. T. D. Jakes' Dallas-based church, the Potter's House, has over twenty thousand members and is just one example of a number of large independent African-American Pentecostal churches. Currently, the largest attended church in America is Lakewood Church located on the outskirts of Houston, Texas. Pastored by Joel Osteen, the church is multi-ethnic and has a weekend attendance of over twenty-five thousand. The congregation recently purchased the eighteen thousand seat Compaq Center to accommodate its rapid growth.

The growth of Classical Pentecostalism throughout the twentieth century, coupled with the emergence of the Charismatic Renewal in 1960, has ushered in a new era of acceptance and respectability. Pentecostals are no longer on the margins of American society. Notable sociological analyses have acknowledged the upward socioeconomic improvement that religious conversion effects in whole cultures. Many Pentecostals had moved beyond poverty and prospered by mid-century. Their churches moved from storefront meeting halls into high-tech, beautiful buildings, often in the nicest neighborhoods. They built colleges and universities. Some ran large successful businesses and became reputable community leaders. Joined by educated, socially sophisticated Episcopalians, Presbyterians,

Roman Catholics, and the like, all speaking with tongues and excited about the Holy Spirit's work, the stereotypes associated with Pentecostalism have slowly faded.

In the United States the influence of the Pentecostal and Charismatic Renewal goes far beyond growth and cultural acceptance. In many ways it is contributing to a radical transformation of the American church.

In the early part of the twentieth century much of the Christian community were cessationists: those who believed the miraculous gifts of the Holy Spirit were no longer necessary once the New Testament Canon was completed. Basing their cessationism on an interpretation of 1 Corinthians 13, many of the early opponents of the Pentecostal movement vigorously attacked the movement's claims of healing, prophecy, supernatural knowledge and wisdom, and other spiritual gifts calling them counterfeits at best and Satanic manifestations at worst. The abrasive and strident criticisms of Pentecostalism have largely ended—though some remain.

Particularly in the last four decades more and more sectors of the non-Pentecostal church are acknowledging the continuation of spiritual gifts and the miraculous. A major factor in this reappraisal has come from seeing how crucial the supernatural manifestations of the Holy Spirit are on mission fields in the developing world. Without question the reception of the gospel is aided by the presence of healings and other spiritual gifts. This has contributed to greater acknowledgement and partnership between non-Pentecostals and Pentecostal/Charismatics.

One rather striking change in the topography of the American church is in the area of worship style. In the last twenty years more and more churches have put significant emphasis on contemporary and expressive worship. Admittedly this is a generalization that is not true everywhere, but in many communities it is hard to distinguish between the non-Pentecostal churches and the Pentecostal ones. There is a confluence of reasons for this. Ministries like Promise Keepers and March for Jesus have modeled more enthusiastic worship expression and in doing so have helped bridge the divide between non-Pentecostals and Pentecostals since many of the worship leaders of these groups were Pentecostals/Charismatics. The plethora of worship resources, like Integrity Music, birthed out of the Charismatic Renewal, have fostered more heartfelt experience of devotion to God for worshippers across a wide spectrum of the church. In addition, many non-Pentecostal churches are recognizing the remarkable growth of the Pentecostal/Charismatic churches and are pragmatically seeking to provide a worship environment that is more experience-based.

In the last few decades the American church has gone through a prayer renewal. In many cities across the country pastors from various denominations are meeting together regularly to pray. In some cases they meet in a retreat setting for several days to pray and fellowship and cultivate genuine good will and mutuality. Prayer meetings are again becoming a meaningful part of church life, and community concerts of prayer are not uncommon. As with worship, books and resources to encourage corporate and individual prayer abound. While this emphasis on prayer is not a unique contribution of Pentecostals, they certainly have been at the forefront of this renewal both in leadership and participation.

It is a fair assessment to say that Pentecostal/Charismatic Christianity is helping supply new vitality to the Christian church in the United States and is profoundly rearranging the landscape of global Christianity. Most demographers and futurists believe its worldwide impact will only grow over the coming years. And to think that most Pentecostals trace it all back to one revival in Los Angeles some 100 years ago. The Azusa Street revival is more than an "ideal" symbol. Led by an African-American pastor and embracing a vision to evangelize the world before the return of Christ, the revival's ethnic diversity signaled the emergence of a movement that leapt across cultural barriers. More than any expression of the church since the first century, it is creating a church from "every tribe and language and people and nation" (Rev. 5:9). It is a revival that has changed the church.

BROUGHT TO THIS MOMENT:

In Light of the Beginning of the Charismatic Century

There is an inescapable dynamic inherent in the fact that the century literally began with the most visible and ecclesiastically powerful person in the world issuing a distinct invitation to the Holy Spirit to "Come!" Irrespective of how any particular protestant may feel about the Pope, God seems to have sovereignly moved upon the man as a means of providing His own invocation. At that time, global Christianity held a *creed*

regarding the Holy Spirit but lacked *confidence* in how to partner with Him—how *to personally relate* to the third person in
The Trinity.

In reality, so much of the vital life of the early Church was
overtaken by apathy, pride, spiritual blindness and biblical
ignorance, empty tradition and ecclesiastical power struggles,
that only with the Reformation (c. 1500 AD) did a *beginning* of
recovery occur. Starting with the foundational concept of the
authority of God's Word and the truth of justification (human
salvation) by faith in Christ alone, a century-to-century process
was launched.

Degrees of reform effected the restoration of the Church's
concepts of and approach to (1) the great commission, (2) personal sanctification, (3) practical devotion, (4) social responsibility, and (5) forthright evangelism reappeared—often within
both protestant and catholic circles, and thus each generation
brought to its "moment." But it wasn't until the turn-of-the-
century, global outpouring of the Holy Spirit that a growing
familiarity with His *fullness, works and power* began to spread,
bringing the Church to *this* moment.

As remains the case today—God responds to an increased
hunger for, and full hearted openness to *Him*; recognizing that
The Holy Spirit of God is poured out at the hand of The Son
of God (John 1:33; Acts 2:33-39). Indeed, to this day there
are many who seem mystified by the very fact of God's three-
in-one-ness, almost preferring to avoid too direct an exposure to the Holy Spirit Himself. There is something about
our oft-human insistence that seeks either information or *an*

explanation about the Holy Spirit, rather than opening our hearts as Jesus commanded—to *an experience*—saying, *"Receive the Holy Spirit . . . and you shall receive power"* (John 20:22; Acts 1:8).

Especially in the Western world, intellect—which is never demeaned or insulted by our Creator—too often is made a sub-stitute for *Him*. But the Living God, Who knows that our finite minds will never be able to fully comprehend His greatness, grandeur or the breadth and scope of His being, comes to us as a Father. He invites us to experience a relationship with Him—to the One Who is responsible for our life's existence, and Who offers to bring us, through knowing Him personally and intimately, to understand our life's purpose and potential through His love and power.

Like children being taught to walk again, each step with our Creator's call to experience His redemptive graces calls us to the next "moment"—bringing us to points of decision as to how much we really want to know Him. He calls us:

- to the moment we *repent* and ask His forgiveness for hav-ing mishandled the life-trust He has given us; then, with that "moment," to bow . . .
- in that moment we receive Jesus Christ, God the Son, to acknowledge Him as our Savior—whose death for our sins provides the one way for our return to the Father. And then, to answer His call . . .
- to that moment *beyond* our *spiritual rebirth* by the Spirit's power, to our entry into *Spirit-fullness*, opening to His

overflowing us with His resources of enabling power for service and ministry in Jesus' Name.

These steps highlight how God—Father, Son and Spirit—prioritizes His ever deepening call for our openness to Him as His creatures. At each step, He invites us to open and know Him in the sense of *intimate "knowing"* rather than *intellectual knowledge*. Such a summons never dishonors His gifts to us of intelligence or intellect, but rather calls us *first* to humble ourselves with the recognition that God can only be known by *revelation* and not by *reason*. That "revelation" to our hearts begins as His glory shines to us in creation and His righteousness whispers to our conscience—both affirming He is *there*. With these, the revelation of His Word testifies to us of the gift of His Son—His ultimate revelation—and all this calls us to bow to receive Christ. Because this decision brings us *into Christ's life*, relatively few believers between the Reformation and the 20th century pursued more of the Holy Spirit than His incoming which each receives when they are born again.

The passion that birthed the twentieth century awakening to the Spirit's *overflowing* answered to the step *beyond*; beyond receiving Christ's saving life from the *well* of salvation (John 4:14), to opening freely to the *rivers* He wants to overflow through us and unto a needy world (John 7:37-39). And now, as we stride into the twenty-first century, the "charismatic century" has brought us all to *this moment*. You and I are called to answer to this stage of the Church's reformation and restoration. The handful in Topeka and the tens of thousands at

Azusa Street represent millions more who are opening to a deeper hunger to *know* Him; to "hunger and thirst" for that overflowing which Jesus calls us to, and into which He is ready to immerse us (Matthew 5:6; John 1:33). But here, as at each preceding step in following Him, our powers of *reason* will be called to surrender to the simplicity of His *revelation*. Only the childlike enter into the fullest dimensions of His Kingdom life and power, without which limits us to what we can achieve or explain on our own rather than what He invites us to experience by *His grace alone*.

We've been brought to *our* moment—100-plus years later. Let us say as well, "Come, Holy Spirit!"

The Road to Topeka

As the nineteenth century drew to a close, many Christians yearned for a revival of New Testament dynamism that would prepare the church for the last days. Using Scripture references to the rainfall patterns of the Holy Land, they likened the Holy Spirit's coming on the day of Pentecost to the spring rains that watered the freshly planted fields. Now they awaited eagerly the "latter rains" that came in the fall just before harvest. This was a metaphor for the coming revival that would ready the church for a great evangelistic ingathering right before the consummation of the age.

Early Pentecostals felt their movement was the fulfillment of this expectation. Drawing on the phrase in Acts 2:2, they believed their movement was born "suddenly . . . from heaven," jumping over the centuries to connect them to the same power the Apostles and early church received on the day of Pentecost.

These Pentecostal pioneers saw much of church history as a chronicle of decline that started after the Apostles died.

The Holy Spirit and His gifts had been neglected and rejected as the church put more emphasis on organization. The Roman emperor Constantine's conversion and the emergence of "Christendom" in the fourth century brought an even more dramatic loss of charismatic activity. Some acknowledged that God had started to restore New Testament Christianity through Martin Luther and the Reformation and saw John Wesley, founder of Methodism, as another important step in God's plan of restoration. But more than any other movement before, Pentecostals believed their movement was the "latter rain," a final restoration of the church just before the end. For most Pentecostals this made the rest of church history irrelevant. With Christ's second coming so close at hand, why look back? There was too much work to do reaching a lost world.

This a-historical orientation was not completely unique to Pentecostals at the time. It typified many evangelical Christians' interpretation of church history through a restorationist lens. Restorationism is the quest to recover a pristine, primitive, "New Testament Christianity" and almost every new Christian renewal movement aims to this ideal (some claim their movement embodies it). From the Puritans to Pentecostals this impulse has been central to American Protestantism since the colonies were founded in the seventeenth century. These groups understood the past in a way that made them averse to traditions that emerged from what they believed to be a largely corrupt church from the New Testament times to their day.

RENEWAL OVER THE CENTURIES

Roman Catholics and Eastern Orthodox Christians see church history much differently. For these traditions, the church has experienced cycles of decline and renewal over the centuries but has always embodied apostolic teaching and authority despite its problems. For them there is an unbroken connection that reaches back to the New Testament church. And while admittedly imperfect, it is a rich tradition to be cherished and embraced for the lessons and solid foundation it provides. They see the restorationist model as an attack on their institutional heritage and integrity.

The Christian story after the close of the New Testament suggests that both perspectives have merit. As the young expanding Christian church struggled to define and defend itself amidst the surrounding confusion of mystery cults and competing philosophies in the Greco-Roman world, it became increasingly organized. Particularly, facing internal heresies, the church had to determine which leaders could speak authoritatively in doctrinal matters. This significantly contributed to the practice of having a single bishop over a city, one who had authority over other church bishops, pastors, and leaders in that particular city. City bishops in larger cities often received greater respect and exercised authority over entire regions, eventually leading to the prominence of cities like Rome, Alexandria, Antioch, and later Constantinople.

Church leaders courageously fought for a biblical understanding of Christ's nature as both God and man. They vigorously defended the full deity of Jesus Christ while not losing sight of the implications of the incarnation. God had truly entered human history to live and die in order to secure the forgiveness of sinful mankind. The creator of the world became a man. As some sought to subordinate Christ by arguing He was only a created being, leaders like the church father Athanasius suffered rejection and exile to stand for Christ's full equality with his Father. Doctrinal formulas that continue to serve the church today were hammered out during those first Christian centuries.

This growing emphasis on formalized leadership coupled with the development of creeds in answer to theological disputes created inevitable tension between the church's institutional nature and its charismatic character. The formulation of a clear and agreed-upon definition of the Person of Christ Himself was understandably given primary focus, and thereby the role and work of the Holy Spirit was not given much attention. There was a loss of focus on the empowering presence of the Spirit of God that was so central to the New Testament Christian experience.

This does not mean that there was a complete cessation of supernatural healings or the exercise of other spiritual gifts. Throughout the second and third centuries, Justin Martyr, Cyprian, Tertullian, and other church fathers of the early Church tell of demonic deliverance and divine healings. Irenaeus spoke of the dead being raised. Yet, as in all eras of the Church, the preoccupation with structure and political power contributed to a significant erosion of emphasis on the experiential activity of the Holy Spirit.

This is unquestionably the case in the Western Church after St. Augustine, another early church father. Over the centuries that follow, spiritual gifts fade from practice in the west and become rare, sporadic manifestations among a spiritually elite class of Saints. This inactivity of the spiritual gifts in everyday church practice fostered the notion of cessationism that slowly grew in the Western Church and was popularized especially by Reformation leaders like John Calvin.

Since so much of the focus in Church history among North Americans and Europeans has been on the western church, little attention has been paid to the ongoing charismatic activity in the Eastern Church. The East's tendency toward the mystical, along with a greater emphasis on the Holy Spirit made them more receptive to the spiritual gifts and they continued to be encouraged and practiced. The Cappadocian church fathers, Basil of Caesarea, Gregory of Nazianzus, and Gregory of Nyssa, all spoke of healings and miraculous spiritual gifts. Even in the East, however, most of this activity was confined to the monasteries and not central to church life after the first few centuries.

Early on, renewal groups arose to challenge what they saw as a decline of vitality of the New Testament Christian experience. In the mid-second century, Montanus, a leader in Asia Minor, and his followers challenged the mainline church for not emphasizing charismatic leadership or exercising spiritual gifts. Emphasizing particularly the gift of prophecy, the Montanists attacked what they saw as the moral laxity of the institutional church and called for complete separation from the world. Montanists were given to extremes. They were legalistic and intolerant of all other Christians not embracing their views. Critics of the movement made many accusations of heresy about what the Montanists taught and destroyed almost every written document they produced. This has made it difficult to determine how serious their errors were.

The Montanist controversy illustrates the struggle that the church had in dealing with emerging groups who offered critique. Was God speaking prophetically through these groups? This struggle between the established, more mainstream church and movements emphasizing the more charismatic dimensions of the church has been an ongoing feature of Christian history. Some renewal movements were anathematized by the formal church. Dissenters were sometimes horribly persecuted and even martyred for reformist views. Occasionally more moderate voices won out. The Roman Catholic Church sometimes created special orders that incorporated these groups into the formal church, as with monastic movements like the Benedictines.

The extremes were on both sides. In many ways the Montanists were emblematic of the tendencies of other renewal movements over the coming centuries. Often, the excesses of these groups caused their legitimate concerns to be ignored and dismissed. Their criticisms were often harsh, condemning, and uncompromising. Their extremism made dialogue difficult or impossible.

One thing is certain. Whether it was on the margins of the church or within its mainline, the Holy Spirit has never ceased His renewing, empowering activity. In monasteries and religious orders men and women experienced Pentecostal-like manifestations, speaking in tongues and prophesying. Throughout Europe and Britain, a continued experience of spiritual gifts is reported. Admittedly some groups were unorthodox, but not all of them.

All through the centuries the Holy Spirit was at work in the lives of His people preserving the church and enabling its stewardship of His purposes. Despite human carnality and ignorance with all the failings that naturally follow, God's Kingdom reign would not be thwarted. The church father Origen once said that the church is filled with the "ragtag and bobtail of humanity." It is that very reality that shows the remarkable ability of God to redeem fallen humanity and invite them as partners in accomplishing His will on this earth. He truly is a sovereign God.

PENTECOSTAL TRIBUTARIES

The tributaries of modern Pentecostalism that reach back into the eighteenth and nineteenth centuries were many and varied. Together they helped create the religious ferment from which the movement would emerge.

Pentecostal historian Vinson Synan has argued for the Wesleyan roots of Classical Pentecostalism. He has called John Wesley the "spiritual and intellectual father of the modern holiness and Pentecostal movements."[1] He certainly was one of the most significant.

JOHN WESLEY AND METHODISM

John Wesley is best known as the founder of Methodism. A product of seventeenth-century English Anglicanism, Wesley passionately pursued a devout and holy life. He read widely and was especially drawn to the Catholic mystical tradition. For example, the books of eighteenth century English spiritual writer William Law, particularly *A Serious Call to a Holy and Devout Life*, deeply influenced him. Extremely methodical, Wesley's "Holy Club" at Oxford University epitomized his quest for holiness. Believing that the Christian life required both rigorous discipline and sacrificial service, Wesley and club members gave much of their income away and called for regular "good works" to validate their faith. They were called "methodists."

Wesley's quest to serve God brought him to the American colonies in 1735 as a missionary where he spent two unfruitful and disappointing years of ministry. While returning to England, he was deeply impressed by a group of Moravians, German Christian pietists, and a group who calmly prayed and sang hymns during a violent storm at sea while Wesley feared for his life. He realized that he had no assurance of salvation. Not long after, Wesley had his famous Aldersgate experience. While listening to the reading of Luther's Preface to Romans in May of 1738, his famous words "I felt my heart strangely warmed," expressed his having discovered peace with God.

Wesley continued to seek a holy life and deeply desired to be saved not only from outward sin but "inward sin" as well. This led to his conviction that there was a second work of grace that was distinct and subsequent to conversion. This crisis experi- ence of sanctification enabled the believer to live free from the bondage of the sinful nature. The "second blessing" empha- sized the necessity of a transformed Christian life in answer to the Reformed scholasticism that influenced the Anglicanism of Wesley's day. The clergy were overly concerned with precise doctrine to the neglect of personal holiness. Wesley was not out to start a new denomination. His intention was to renew the Anglican Church. A master organizer and gifted innova- tor, Wesley formed a "church within the church," utilizing new kinds of meetings and structures that fostered discipleship and lay participation. His small groups of bands, classes, and soci- eties provided a venue for many to grow in grace.

Wesley seemed to have limitless energy. He campaigned against slavery and argued for the education of unschooled children. Over the course of his ministry, he made numerous journeys to and from America and his tireless crisscrossing of England totaled an estimated 250 thousand miles on preach- ing and ministry tours, much of it riding a horse. Along with revivalist George Whitefield he helped pioneer field preaching that took the gospel message to the poorer classes. John Wes- ley lived in a time of rapid change economically and politically and he gave great leadership to the church at a hinge point in history. Wheaton College historian Mark Noll has said that the innovations of the brothers John and Charles Wesley (who was also a Methodist minister), along with George Whitefield, were "probably the most important single factor in transform- ing the religion of the Reformation into modern Protestant evangelicalism."[2] Important for Pentecostalism was Wesley's focus on a crisis encounter with God's transforming power that was distinct and subsequent to conversion.

Also significant to the eventual development of Pentecostalism, John Fletcher, Wesley's chosen successor, taught that the second blessing was the "baptism of the Holy Spirit." Although it is true that he did not endorse Fletcher's view, Wesley and Methodism helped provide a new vocabulary that put fresh emphasis on the Holy Spirit. Many of the nineteenth century religious movements would pick up on this and express it in their own ways. The Holy Spirit's place in the church was being rediscovered.

The enthusiastic and experiential faith of missionary Methodists from England proved particularly appealing to the young United States in the late eighteenth century. The optimism and victorious promise of sanctification found a ready audience among the poor and marginalized in the cities and backwoods of early America. Circuit riding Methodist preachers spread the Methodist message around and by the early nineteenth century it was far and away the fastest growing Christian group in America. Worshippers in Methodist meetings often wept, shouted, shook, and some fell down "as if they were dead."

As Methodism continued to grow and prosper in nineteenth century America, some Methodists became concerned that church leaders were neglecting the sanctification message to accommodate success and social acceptance. In 1835, Sarah Lankford, a Methodist church member, began holding the "Tuesday Meeting for the Promotion of Holiness" in the parlor of the New York City home she shared with her sister and brother-in-law Phoebe and Dr. Walter Palmer. The meetings continued weekly for over 60 years. They were patterned after Wesley's class meetings and were used to reemphasize the doctrine of sanctification.

By 1839 Phoebe Palmer, the more capable leader of the two women, had taken over leadership. Palmer taught crisis sanctification, that one could be instantly sanctified by the "baptism of the Holy Spirit" when one completely surrendered to the Lord. Rather than tarrying for a long period, people were encouraged to receive the second blessing by faith whether they felt anything or not. This was the "shorter way" as they called it. Also in 1839 a group in Boston began publishing *The Guide to Christian Perfection*, a journal that promoted the sanctification doctrine. This periodical carried testimonies from the Tuesday meetings and was a significant voice for the holiness camp for the rest of the century.

REVIVALISM

Another tributary was the revivalism that developed in the nineteenth century. In 1801 a revival broke out in Kentucky. Barton Stone, a Presbyterian pastor of the Cane Ridge and Concord churches, visited a nearby revival and after returning planned meetings for August of that year. Stone and others were amazed when over ten thousand (some estimates say twenty-five thousand) came out for the meetings, some traveling all the way from Ohio and Tennessee to attend. The revival continued for more than a year. The "camp meetings" were just that. Seekers would live in tents or wagons for the week or more that they stayed to attend the revival meetings. Echoing the phenomena associated with the First Great Awakening 150 years before, people would run, roll, sing, dance, convulsively jerk, cry out, fall down, groan as they were touched by the power of the Holy Spirit. During the meetings, sinners would be so deeply convicted of the sins that they would cry out for mercy and then once sensing God's forgiveness they would leap and dance for joy. There were as many as three thousand conversions.[3]

Barton Stone's eyewitness accounts are colorful. Describing what he called the "running exercise" he said that sinners "feeling something of these bodily agitations, through fear, attempted to run away and thus escape from them. But it commonly happened that they ran not far before they fell down or became so greatly agitated they could proceed no farther." Of so-called barking, Stone said that people "affected by the jerks would often grunt, or bark, if you please, from the suddenness of the jerk."[4]

The revival spread from Kentucky over much of the South. The unusual manifestations drew much attention and criticism and were significant in sensationalizing revivalism. The 1801 awakening ignited revival fires that would burn off and on for the next two hundred years.

Charles G. Finney is the most identifiable figure associated with nineteenth century revivalism. An attorney, Finney was powerfully converted in 1821. In the evening of the day he was saved, he testified of a dramatic "baptism in the Holy Spirit" in which he was overwhelmed by "waves and waves of liquid love," so much so that he cried out for it to stop. "I shall die if these waves continue to pass over me," he prayed.

Though on the way to a career in Presbyterian parish ministry, he changed course in 1825 after conducting several evangelistic meetings in upstate New York in which there were many conversions. This convinced Finney to begin holding revival meetings in cities on the East coast, and so began his famous revival ministry. One of the high points came in 1830-31 in Rochester, New York, when the whole region was stirred by the revivalist. Business owners closed their stores and urged their customers to attend Finney's meetings and many were saved.

His "new measures" were highly controversial at the time. He allowed women to pray publicly in mixed meetings and his use of the "anxious bench" put people who felt deep concern for their souls in front of the church. His "protracted meetings" would go on for days and many were taken back by his confrontational pulpit manner. These innovative methods attracted even more seekers to his revival meetings. Finney became the "father of modern revivalism" paving the way for other evangelists of the nineteenth and twentieth centuries. Christian leaders still study his revival methods.

In 1835 Finney was appointed as a professor of theology to Oberlin College in Ohio. Along with Asa Mahon, Oberlin's president, Finney led a movement toward social reform that emphasized temperance, education for immigrants, and most notably the abolition of slavery. They called their students to "live worthy of the Kingdom of God" and the school served as a model. The college was coeducational with men and women and whites and blacks learning together. When a group of white students wanted African-American students to have a separate table for meals, the Oberlin administration refused and said that a table would be made available for white students if they chose to separate themselves. It was a brilliant response that forced those students to publicly defy the college's egalitarian vision if they wanted to eat separately.

Symbolic of the school's vision for racial equity was the 1862 graduation of Mary Jane Patterson, a former slave, who became the first African-American woman to receive a bachelor's degree in the United States. After graduation Patterson taught school until her death in 1894.[5]

Finney's Reformed roots joined with Mahon's second blessing perfectionism created a curious mix theologically. Finney came to embrace the terminology of entire sanctification and believed it was a state entered into through the baptism of the Holy Spirit. He became a most important voice, drawing attention to the Spirit's cleansing and empowering work that not only initiated a holy life but brought periodic refreshings subsequent to sanctification. "Oberlin Perfectionism" taught that the believer could break the power of sin through the Holy Spirit and that the believer could live in perfect obedience to God. Although the terminology of the Oberlin group sounded almost identical to the Wesleyan holiness stream, most of the Oberlin faculty remained committed to Reformed theology. Much like the Keswick holiness groups, that would emerge later in the century, Finney and the faculty at Oberlin did not believe that the sin nature was eradicated through an instantaneous sanctification experience. Rather, the power of the old nature was broken when believers yielded their lives to the Holy Spirit.

REVIVAL AND THE CIVIL WAR

In 1857 and 1858 a prayer revival swept the Northeast. In New York City, Jeremiah Lamphier, a businessman turned urban missionary, started a weekly prayer meeting in September 1857. Within days a bank failure shook the American financial community. This along with talk of Southern secession troubled many. So many people flocked to the prayer meeting that they were forced to meet daily. As the financial crisis spread so did the growing passion for prayer. In early 1858 over ten thousand people met throughout New York for daily prayer. Touching the major cities first, the revival continued to spread to smaller communities as well. The YMCA, only newly started, was an important part of spreading the prayer revival. Historian J. Edwin Orr has pointed out that this revival seemed to prepare many people in the nation for the trauma that lay ahead with the Civil War.

The mid-century quest for perfectionism fueled a strong anti-slavery movement that eventually split the Methodist Church in America between the Northern group who ardently opposed slavery and the Southern group, who passionately defended it. The nation was increasingly divided politically and religiously; it seemed to divide everywhere. Secession and war were inevitable. The Civil War's horrors affected the entire nation and dimmed religious fires as the United States struggled to survive. Church attendance waned. In 1860 nearly a quarter of Americans were church members, a figure that would not recover for another thirty years. In the years that followed the war all Americans were forced to adjust to changing times. Darwinism, urbanization, industrialization, and general social upheaval created many challenges. Reconstruction, the "Gilded Age," and progressivism all impacted the church and contributed to the development of many radical movements during the last three decades of the century.

Following the war a significant shift became evident in many religious groups. Before the war many Christians believed that the church's growing influence was preparing the way for Christ's triumphal return. Typical of the positive outlook of this view, Charles Finney had suggested that if the church got busy doing God's work the second coming could happen in just a few years.

The Civil War dashed this optimism. In its place came a more pessimistic eschatology, one that believed times were getting worse and the only hope was God's cataclysmic intervention at Christ's return. This was counter to how most mainstream church leaders responded to the post-war era. For them the issue was reinterpreting the Christian faith in ways that congealed to modern thought. Influenced by the dramatic social and intellectual changes, this paved the way for the emergence of liberal Christianity with its embrace of higher critical methods coming out of many of the German schools. Understandably this alarmed conservatives and fueled all the more their concern that these were the last days. This helped set the stage for premillennial dispensationalism.

DISPENSATIONALISM

Coming to America John Nelson Darby's "dispensational" teachings found a ready audience. Darby divided history into seven dispensations, each expressing a different aspect of how God was dealing with His creation. Darby emphasized the importance of the nation of Israel in Bible prophecy. He taught that God would restore the Jewish nation before the end of the age, a seemingly impossible idea given the centuries that the Jews had been without a homeland.

A notable distinctive of Darby's teaching was the idea of a "secret rapture" in which Christ would come invisibly to "catch away" the church. This would be followed by seven years of great tribulation and then Christ would visibly and victoriously return. In the decades that followed the Civil War, Darby made several trips to America. This, along with the Bible Prophecy Conference movement, helped stir great interest in Bible prophecy. When the dynamic Chicago evangelist D. L. Moody joined the dispensational bandwagon, it quickly became the prevailing view of much of conservative grassroots Christianity.

HOLINESS RESURGENCE

Among the Methodists a separation between more radical voices and the mainstream widened in the last half of the nineteenth century. The more conservative leaders were increasingly disheartened by the "worldliness" of the Methodist clergy and the loss of practices they saw as central to their Wesleyan heritage, like the class meetings, camp meetings, and emphasis on crisis sanctification. Coming out of the 1867 camp meetings held in Vineland, New Jersey, a fresh emphasis on holiness began to grow in post-bellum America. Led by a small group of Methodist pastors and other lay leaders, the National Holiness Association's aim was to renew the Methodist Church. Helped by a large number of small holiness publications across the nation, the movement's influence spread.

While the holiness movement found a significant hearing among grassroots Methodists, its independent character and critical stance began to provoke reaction from leading pastors and denominational leaders. An ever larger group within the holiness associations talked about the necessity of leaving a church they believed was becoming cold and formal. The rhetoric of these "come-outers" only heightened the perception of extremism and made them seem a serious threat to the institutional cohesion of Methodism. This growing rejection of radical holiness folk made a split inevitable. By the 1890s there were more and more defections from the Methodist church and many new holiness denominations were born. Vinson Synan has pointed out that the holiness movement's break with Methodism was part of a growing populist protest within America against the Eastern establishment that had become associated with big business "monopolies." The financial struggles of the 1890s made the masses distrustful of any perceived hierarchy, whether secular or religious. The independence of the American people was evident.

THE KESWICK MOVEMENT

Another essential expression of Christian renewal in the nineteenth century was the Keswick movement born out of an annual conference in England. Named for the small English village where the conference was held, the movement was focused on the "higher life" in Christian experience. Influenced by the U.S. holiness movement, Keswick perfectionism did not emphasize crisis sanctification yet still affirmed a usually subsequent dynamic experience with the Holy Spirit. Though adopting holiness terminology, their view of sanctification was progressive in nature. The kinship between the two movements came in the emphasis of a distinct experience with the Holy Spirit that followed conversion. Keswick followers saw this experience as essentially an act of full surrender to God wherein the Lord had full control of the believer. The Keswick movement put much more emphasis on the idea of empowerment and preferred the terms "filled with the Holy Spirit" or the "fullness of the Spirit" for the experience. Between 1875 until the end of the century Keswick holiness teachings were popular in Great Britain, continental Europe, and the United States.

Evangelist D. L. Moody was a proponent of the Keswick movement along with others, including Hannah Whital Smith, whose book *A Christian's Secret of a Happy Life* is still read today by thousands. R. A. Torrey, an associate of Moody whose influence was rapidly increasing, championed Keswick's ideas and utilized the term "baptism of the Holy Spirit" in reference to the experience. Keswick views had a significant influence on A. B. Simpson, founder of the Christian Missionary Alliance, which became a denomination by that name. His formulation of a fourfold gospel, Jesus as Savior, Sanctifier, Healer, and Coming King paved the way for later expressions of the "full" or "foursquare gospel."

THE RADICALS

The late nineteenth century quest of NT dynamism continued with the emergence of the more radical "third blessing" proponents. B. H. Irwin, a former Baptist minister, embraced the holiness doctrine after studying the works of John Wesley. Also influenced by John Fletcher, Irwin taught that there was a third crisis experience that followed regeneration and sanctification. This baptism of the Holy Spirit or "baptism with fire," as he often called it, was an empowering for service and mission. Highly critical of denominational holiness leaders, Irwin strongly denounced what he saw as the worldliness of most churches of his day, particularly Methodists. His third blessing message found a ready audience among holiness folk who were yearning for a deeper experience of God's power beyond sanctification.

The "Fire Baptized" churches that formed under Irwin's leadership initially saw significant growth. But by 1900 he was teaching that there were additional "baptisms of fire" beyond the third blessing, naming these subsequent spiritual baptisms "dynamite," "lyddite," and "oxidite." Irwin's strident anti-denominational rhetoric along with his increasingly eccentric teachings brought suspicion and concern in holiness circles and his influence began to fade. Finally, he was forced to resign as overseer of the Fire-Baptized Holiness Church when he acknowledged moral failure. J. H. King was appointed in his place and would lead the Fire-Baptized Holiness Church into the Pentecostal movement a few years later.

Among the profusion of radical Christian groups at the end of the nineteenth century were the restorationist utopian visionaries. Two of these visionaries were direct antecedents to the emergence of Pentecostalism.

John Alexander Dowie, a Congregational Church pastor, became convinced of divine healing and left the denomination in 1878 to start an independent ministry. In 1895, Dowie established and became the leader of the Christian Catholic Church and in 1900 founded Zion City in Illinois, a utopian community. Dowie hoped, through education, to develop an egalitarian, classless society. Pacifism and concern for the poor and needy were essential values to the new city. Drama, music, and the arts were valued as well as a concern for sports and recreation. Key to everything at Zion was a commitment to the Christian faith and divine healing. Dowie taught his followers to renounce all medical remedies and instead to exercise faith in God for healing.

Dowie became increasingly extreme and in 1901 made the claim that he was the promised Elijah sent to restore and prepare the church for the Lord's coming. After suffering a stroke in 1906, he eventually lost control of his leadership of Zion City and died in disgrace in 1907.

Deeply influenced by A. B. Simpson's teaching on divine

healing, former Free-will Baptist minister Frank Sandford, driven by a vision to recover "apostolic life and power,"[6] founded in 1895 the "Holy Ghost and Us" Bible school near New Durham, Maine. Sandford sought to form a community around his college that would serve as a base for world evangelization. This evangelization would be accomplished by signs, wonders, and spiritual gifts just as the Scriptures taught. Over the next few years the growing Shiloh community built a children's home, a hospice, and a dormitory to fulfill the vision. Several hundred residents also gathered around Sandford for training to accomplish the task. In addition, as Sandford's notoriety grew, many traveled to Maine to spend anywhere from weeks to months at his college.

In November of 1901, Sandford told his followers that he was the promised Elijah. Sandford was long rumored to be given to extreme authoritarian rule over his followers and in 1911 he was convicted of manslaughter and sentenced to a ten-year prison term after the death of several followers on an ill-planned ship voyage. Sailing ostensibly to seek God's direction for world evangelization, the befuddled voyage and later conviction ended Sandford's influence.

Both Dowie and Sandford influenced the birth of Pentecostalism in that many of their followers became Pentecostal after their downfall. In addition Charles F. Parham, the subject of the next chapter, traveled to both Zion and Shiloh during the time leading to the Topeka revival. Dowie and Sanford's emphasis on healing, their anti-institutional character, and end time restorationism undoubtedly affected Parham and other early Pentecostal leaders.

PERSPECTIVES

This nineteenth century cacophony of voices actually shared several points of harmony. First and foremost, all these radical groups emphasized Christ as Savior of all people. There was no other way to be saved and this fueled the fires of mission. A second overarching theme of revivalism in the holiness and Keswick movements, and in utopian restorationists, was the ministry of the Holy Spirit to cleanse and empower Christians. In their view this was to be the normal Christian experience. Third, there was a deep desire for a restoration of New Testament Christianity, including the signs, wonders, and spiritual gifts so vital to the spread of the Gospel. This is in part why there was such emphasis on divine healing. And finally, these groups, joined with the dispensationalists, saw time drawing toward a sudden and cataclysmic end with Christ's soon return. This perspective along with their sense that Jesus was the only way to salvation supplied a heartfelt urgency to evangelize and missionize the lost.

These groups were the streams that would contribute to the Pentecostal river whose headwaters are the subject of our next two chapters. Their restorationist vision with its emphasis on Pentecost and the Holy Spirit created a vocabulary easily adopted by Pentecostals. Many of these nineteenth century movements initially aimed at church renewal. In the end most abandoned existing church structures to form new organizations to carry their messages. This brings to mind the words of Jesus in the Gospels about new wine needing new wineskins.

Today the question remains: is it possible for a renewal of church structures without creating new ones?

If the twentieth century was the century of the Holy Spirit, then the nineteenth century was the century that "prepared the way." The emphases and ideas of so many groups became the seedbed from which modern Pentecostalism emerged. The nineteenth century reveals a God at work renewing and moving His church along in His purposes just as He has done for the last two thousand years. The Pentecostal and Charismatic movements are not new; they are just the most recent manifestations of God's activity in human history. As the nineteenth century drew to a close the stage was set for a fresh drama to begin.

BROUGHT TO THIS MOMENT:

In Light of Twenty Centuries of Pursuing God

Augustine's words continue to resound over the centuries since they were first spoken. Addressed to God, they declare, "You have made us for Yourself, and our souls find no rest until they find it in You." When searching souls seek, they find—and the diligent will never be satisfied to live at a superficial level of merely being "religious." Their answer to Jesus' call, "Follow me," will take them beyond an encounter with His salvation at The Cross, to an encounter with the Holy Spirit in the Upper Room.

Often referred to as "the pursuit of God," or as a quest for "the knowledge of the Holy," or simply as a plain desire to "walk with God," the personal spirituality the Bible describes is neither mystical nor fanatical. Jesus Himself, irrespective of how He might be depicted by actors or portrayed by Hollywood, shines from the pages of Scripture as a warm, human and touchable person. He is approached and is approachable by children, who are undoubtedly the least likely to be attracted to a mystic's aloofness. He is trusted by women, whether broken by moral failure having been exploited by other men, or whether secure and confident by reason of gifting or established heritage. And strong men, established in their vocations and successful at their trade, choose to follow Him—and later, to die as witnesses to His resurrection and provision of salvation for mankind.

In short, the real Jesus was a person who healed the sick, confronted demon presences, spoke words of divine forgiveness, manifested God's love and justice with a beautiful balance, and at the same time was welcome at social events as a desired guest and was comfortable in virtually any setting. The point: He clearly modeled a "pursuit of God" that demonstrates a good-sense, gracious manner of life among others that is equally ready to enjoy a dinner or extend a healing touch.

This chapter's accompanying review of God's miracle grace, alive and well throughout two thousand years (though often ridiculed by the religious community, just as Jesus was Himself), is another summons to our "moment." We have not rehearsed the truth of the unchanging, timeless availability of the Holy Spirit's gifts and power as a theological argument. Their potential functionality as a day-to-day part of your life and mine is what Jesus has in mind for every twenty-first century disciple. He calls us to fullness that He might equip us unto effectiveness. The "Spirit-filled, Spirit-formed" life is intended to beget neither pretentious mystics nor bizarre bigots. Receiving the fullness of the Holy Spirit, and learning to enter into a simple exercise of His gifts, has one goal in view. It is that you and I become replicas of the life, grace, love and ministering touch of Jesus Christ—Who wants to express Himself through every member of His Body . . . each of us who believe in Him and receive of His fullness.

The common denominator of first century believers was not a mystical way of life, but a practical, on-the-job order of life in the power of the Spirit. They moved from their introductory relationship with Jesus, unto and into their "moment" of destiny in History, engaging a call to "be filled with the Holy Spirit" (Eph. 4:18, 19). They changed their world, not by an aura of religiousness but by a lifestyle of credible practicality ignited by the powerful works and loving ways of Christ Himself. Today's "moment" calls for the same—for a supernaturally empowered people who know how to relate to a society in need. The hour calls for people who are more than simply believers—we need disciples—people who not only know who Jesus is, but who are equipped to do what Jesus did (John 14:12).

As we process the flow of a century of the Holy Spirit's spreading a power-filled witness to Christ unto our day, the reason for the dynamic increase of their number is not related to platformed stars, but to deployed saints—"saints" being the Bible's designation of every person who receives Christ, follows Him and wants to pursue His fullness in and purpose for their lives.

The world is never so dark that people like that won't be welcomed by the multitudes that are tired of or locked in darkness. The darker the hour, the brighter our "moment." Let's pursue His purpose in it. We've been brought here for that!

3

The Enigma of Charles Fox Parham

According to Charles Parham it happened on December 31, 1900. A teacher, he had left the students at his small Topeka Bible school with an assignment. They were to study the second chapter of Acts to see "what was the Bible evidence of the baptism of the Holy Ghost."[1] For the last ten years various radical Christian groups were making various claims for proof one had received Spirit baptism and Parham felt it was critical to search the Scriptures for an answer. After giving the assignment, he traveled to Kansas City for three days, returning on New Year's Eve. Parham said that to his "astonishment" the students had all arrived at the same conclusion: "that while there were different things [which] occurred when the Pentecostal blessing fell, that the indisputable proof on each occasion was, that they spoke with tongues."[2]

In Parham's account it was at around 11 p.m. on New Year's Eve that Agnes N. Ozman, a student at the school, asked for prayer to receive the baptism with the Holy Spirit, with the biblical evidence of speaking with tongues. Parham laid his hands on Ozman and "scarcely had repeated three dozen sentences when the glory fell upon her." Parham said he saw a halo on Ozman's head and she began speaking in a language they thought was Chinese. It was reported, though disputed by some accounts, that Ozman could not speak in English for three days and that when she tried to write, it came out in odd, scribbled letters.[3]

Interestingly Agnes Ozman herself tells a different story. She says it was actually the next day, January 1, that these events occurred and she did not believe tongues were the only evidence of the baptism of the Holy Spirit.[4] Whatever the case, all agreed that two days of prayer followed and no one else received the same experience until the third day when Parham and several others spoke with tongues. Parham said he worshipped God in tongues into the morning hours.

James Goff, Parham's biographer, has argued that Parham's telling of the story is a product of romanticized memory, wanting to have Ozman speaking in tongues as the new century dawned. The idea that Ozman was speaking in tongues at the precise moment the twentieth century begins, is for him, a bit hard to believe. He also thinks Parham expected the students to come to the conclusion about tongues as Bible evidence of the Spirit baptism, having already come to that conclusion himself, well before December 31, 1900.

In Ozman's version, she began to study the Bible in depth on the issue of evidential tongues only after her January 1 experience. And she also says it was not until several months later that she independently concluded that tongues was the initial evidence of the baptism of the Holy Spirit. Ozman claims she had no part of any Bible study assignment by Parham prior to her tongues speaking experience. In fact she says she pointed students to Acts 2 in answer to their questions about her glossolalic experience.[5]

This very confusion is just one part of the enigma that surrounds the life of Charles Fox Parham. Conflicting reports like the above, along with his eccentric beliefs and accusations of moral failure, have left historians wrestling with Parham's role in the founding of modern Pentecostalism. Most of the early attempts to record Pentecostal origins ignore Parham, at least in part because they were embarrassed by him. But his role cannot be ignored for, at the very least, he is central to the genesis of the theological formulation that made Pentecostals distinct from other radical Christian groups of the early twentieth century. The formula, that speaking with tongues is the Bible evidence of the baptism with the Holy Spirit, gave rise to Pentecostalism as a movement. Parham so exemplifies the nexus of early Pentecostalism. Drawing from the multifarious religious streams at the end of the nineteenth century, he mixed them together and then added the initial evidence formula to create a distinctly Pentecostal stew.

PARHAM'S LIFE AND MINISTRY

Charles F. Parham, the middle child of five sons, was born on June 4, 1873, in Muscatine, Iowa. An early childhood illness left him weak and frail for years and when he was nine he contracted rheumatic fever, a chronic, progressive disease he struggled with all his life. Parham was very close to his mother and took her 1885 death hard. Vowing to see her in heaven, he was converted that same year. Parham felt an early call to preach and held his first public service when he was fifteen. He began attending Southwestern Kansas College in 1890 and struggled over his call to preach for the next two years. During his college years he continued to have physical problems. Parham saw this struggle as a way God was pushing him toward his call to preach and proclaim divine healing. He would continue for the rest of his life to attach spiritual significance to times of illness and deep personal struggle, often believing that God was speaking to him in the midst of crisis.

Parham quit college in 1893 and was appointed as a supply pastor for a small Methodist congregation in Eudora, Kansas, where he served for two years. He was young, unmarried, and energetic and he held evangelistic meetings in nearby communities while pastoring the Eudora church. He helped start a church in Linwood, Kansas, and was a "circuit-riding" pastor for both congregations for a season. Despite the apparent fruitfulness, Parham chafed under what he perceived to be narrow and restrictive attitudes of denominational leaders and he left Methodism in 1895 to begin an independent ministry. For the next four years he conducted evangelistic meetings and had moderate success. Reflecting the restorationistic tendencies of many of his contemporaries, Parham believed the traditional denominations were not conducive to the practice of biblical Christianity, the "Apostolic Faith" as he called it. After leaving Methodism Parham at first associated with the various holiness groups but withdrew because he thought they were too organized. He was an independent through and through.

In late 1896 Parham married Sarah Thistlewaite, who became "a valuable partner and his most loyal defender."[6] At the end of 1897 Parham again faced failing health along with his infant son's sickness. He felt God was judging him for his reliance on doctors and medicine and failure to boldly preach divine healing. After committing himself to preach the healing message both he and his son recovered. Consequently, the proclamation of God's healing power became central to Parham's message.

In 1898 the Parhams established the Bethel Healing Home in Topeka, Kansas, to serve as a healing and training center. Adopting the theme "a living Christianity,"[7] the ministry offered an array of services throughout the day. The Bethel Home was a live-in ministry where the sick could nurture their faith until healing came. The ministry had a Bible school, an orphanage, and other services for the needy. Beyond the Bethel ministry, Parham was involved in serving the broader needs of Topeka, working with others to serve the poor and the destitute. He sought to work with other churches in the city in these efforts but was largely rebuffed by them. This only reinforced his distrust of more formally organized churches. Parham's message was "salvation by faith; healing by faith; laying on of hands and prayer; sanctification by faith; the (premillennial) coming of Christ; the baptism of the Holy Ghost and fire, which seals the bride and bestows the gifts."[8] Parham also began publishing *The Apostolic Faith* newspaper which became an important expression for his message. In keeping with many other ministries of the time, the Bethel Healing Home was a "faith work" supported solely by gifts and contributions.

From 1895 through 1900 Parham began to eclectically put together what would become the Pentecostal gospel. Problematic for many Pentecostals later on was Parham's amalgamation, which continued to evolve, containing assorted beliefs that would prove to be an embarrassment. From a Quaker friend Parham picked up the notion of annihilationism with its belief that an eternal hell is unbiblical. Rather, the lost are simply annihilated. At times he flirted with a modified universalism, believing that most of humankind would receive "everlasting human life" and that hell was reserved for the "utterly reprobate."[9]

Parham was a proponent of the restoration of a Jewish homeland and lectured in support of the Zionist cause frequently. Influenced by Frank Sandford, he also embraced British-Israelism, believing that the Anglo-Saxon race is the ten lost tribes of Israel. This view of Anglo superiority reinforced many of the racist stereotypes in America at the time and likely fueled the racism that Parham displayed in later years.

Parham also came to believe that Spirit baptism gave entry of believers into the "bride of Christ," putting them in a special category from other Christians. These Spirit baptized saints would be raptured by Christ before the tribulation while other Christians would be left on the earth to endure its hardships, albeit with God's help. He later moderated his view but it was another example of his sometimes unusual convictions.

More positively, Parham's role in shaping a Pentecostal message is seen in his borrowing from different sources the various parts that later become central to the "full gospel." Beginning

with Jesus Christ as Savior, Parham embraced from Methodism the "second blessing" idea of entire sanctification and like
B. H. Irwin, he added a "third blessing:" the baptism of the
Holy Spirit. Influenced by A. B. Simpson and from his own
experience, he emphasized divine healing as part and parcel to
the gospel message. As with so many of his radical Christian
contemporaries, the premillennial soon return of Jesus Christ
was a gospel essential to Parham and motivated his deep eschatological passion for evangelism.

It was this emphasis on end time evangelism that helped add
the Pentecostal distinctive of evidential tongues to the above
amalgam. For several months in 1900, Parham left Topeka to
travel and investigate "the latest truths restored by latter day
movements."[10] Visiting ministries in the Midwest and Northeast,
Parham, more than ever, became convinced of the urgency to
prepare for the work of evangelism. He was particularly influenced by his visit to Frank Sandford's Shiloh ministry in
Maine. Parham stayed there for several weeks and attended
the Holy Ghost and Us Bible School. He returned to Topeka
in September excited to start a new Bible school like Sandford's, where the only text was the Bible. What Parham found
in Topeka was that his ministry had been taken over in his
absence by the holiness workers he left in charge. Undeterred,
he saw the loss of Bethel Healing Home as an opportunity to
start over afresh.

Parham rented a large, ornate, vacant mansion just outside
Topeka. The unusual looking turreted structure had bankrupted
its builder and many locals thought it was haunted. Parham was
pleased to secure "Stones Folly," as the mansion was known, and

it provided an ideal setting for a live-in school. With a handful of students, the Bible school opened on October 15, 1900. The students were required to "forsake all" and brought their families and possessions with them to begin their studies. The highly regimented schedule was built around daily prayer, class study, routine chores, evangelism, and community service. Parham was the sole teacher and he taught both verse by verse through the Bible as well as topically by taking a subject and finding verses that addressed it. A twenty-four-hour prayer chain was established with each student taking a three-hour shift.

By December 1900, the Bible school had 34 students and after finishing several weeks of teaching on the basic doctrines of salvation and holiness, Parham began teaching on the Holy Spirit. Agnes Ozman later said that Parham set out to convince his students that they had not yet fully received the baptism of the Holy Spirit. He told the class "that it was our privilege to have it fulfilled to us here and now."[11]

For at least a year Parham had been especially curious over stories about the Holy Spirit giving the gift of "xenoglossa" (supernatural ability to speak in a foreign language without formal training) and was writing about it in his newspaper, *The Apostolic Faith*. In 1899 Parham told his readers about Jennie Glassey, a woman associated with Frank Sandford's Shiloh community. Glassey said that God had given her the ability to speak in several African dialects after deciding to be a missionary. To Parham this was a wonderful example of "a holy, consecrated woman, filled with the Holy Ghost." He praised God "for the return of the apostolic faith."[12] By April of 1900 Parham seems to have concluded xenoglossa was essential for world evangelization and hopeful missionaries under his ministry were eagerly expecting the gift.

On his previous trip to Shiloh he heard more reports about scattered instances of missionaries having this xenoglossalalic ability and for the first time he witnessed people speaking in tongues. Since Parham was convinced that a Holy Spirit-empowered evangelistic revival was key to the last days and the coming of the Christ, he saw xenoglossa as a harbinger of things to come. He saw this gift as a proof of Holy Spirit baptism, fulfilling Acts 1:8 in that it made instant missionaries of all who received xenoglossalalic tongues. This was the part of the Holy Spirit's "power" that enabled Christians to be Christ's witnesses to the ends of the earth and this was Parham's conviction in December 1900. Sadly, the idea of xenoglossalalic tongues would later prove an embarrassing failure as Pentecostal workers went off to mission fields with their gift of tongues and found their hearers did not understand them. But in 1900 it was Parham's great hope for world evangelization.

And so in the closing days of December, Parham gave the assignment to the students to search Acts 2 for the Bible evidence of the baptism of the Holy Spirit. Did he set them up to come to the same conclusion he already held? Or was Parham himself still wrestling with the idea? His account of the events suggests the latter. James Goff, his biographer, believes the former. The historical record suggests the former but is not conclusive. What is clear, according to James Goff, is that "Parham wanted to prove to his students that the baptism of the Holy Spirit should have some tangible evidence—something unmistakably biblical and functional . . . . It was especially noteworthy that the first glossolalic outbreak in Acts included what appeared to be xenoglossic tongues."[13]

The days that followed the January 1 outpouring were exciting. On January 3, Parham spoke at a church in Topeka and told of what had just happened at his Bible school. That same evening when Parham went back to Stone's Folly he saw a remarkable sight in the upstairs room where students had gathered to pray.

The door was slightly ajar, the room was lit with only coal oil lamps. As I pushed open the door I found the room was filled with a sheen of white light above the brightness of the lamps.

Twelve ministers, who were in the school of different denominations, were filled with the Holy Spirit and spoke with other tongues. Some were sitting, some still kneeling, others standing with hands upraised. There were no violent physical manifestations, though some trembled under the power of the glory that filled them.

Sister Stanley, an elderly lady, came across the room as I entered, telling me that just before I entered tongues of fire were sitting above their heads . . . . I fell to my knees behind a table[,] unnoticed by those upon whom the power of Pentecost had fallen[,] to pour out my heart to God in thanksgiving. . . .

After praising God for some time, I asked Him for the same blessing. He distinctly made it clear to me that He raised me up and trained me to declare this mighty truth to the world, and if I was willing to stand for it, with all the persecutions, hardships, trials, slander, scandal that it would entail, He would give me the blessing. And I said "Lord I will, if You will just give me this blessing." Right then there came a slight twist in my throat, a glory fell over me and I began to worship God in the Sweedish [sic] tongue, which later changed to other languages and continued so until the morning.[14]

Some accounts of this night along with other events create an image of a kind of "second Pentecost" and since many of the stories were written much later than the actual events and differ at times in the details of what happened, there have been questions as to what really occurred. The Marxist historian Robert Mapes Anderson rather cynically says Parham's story is "too pat to be true."[15] What seems to be missed by many historians is that the same accusations are made about biblical accounts. Whatever the case, something significant was happening at Topeka.

Over the next few weeks more of the students and their family members experienced Spirit baptism along with what they all thought was xenoglossa. This remained the focus for Parham and his followers and besides Chinese and Swedish, students were said to have spoken in "Japanese, Hungarian, Syrian, Hindi, and Spanish."[16] Before long, the press caught word of the unusual happenings at the Bible school. The claims of xenoglossa were met with obvious skepticism and to most hearers the tongue speech sounded like "gibberish."[17] Some critics felt that if these people were speaking actual languages it was a kind of cryptomnesia where the speaker, though unaware, is actually speaking words heard sometime in the past from exposure to people speaking another language. Parham and his students stood steadfastly by their claim that this was a gift from God to help missionize the world. They were all certain this was a true restoration of New Testament Christianity.

Some students left immediately in disgust thinking Parham and the others were deceived. Yet Parham, still exhilarated by the whole affair launched out to convince supporters and the public that this was a sign of Christ's imminent return. At first the response was positive, with people being saved, receiving healing, and experiencing the baptism of the Holy Spirit, speaking with tongues. Despite Parham's initial proclamations that great growth lay ahead, the momentum did not last long as more and more students, many disillusioned by recent events, left the school. Parham's supporters dropped off and the school struggled to survive. His son Charles Fox Junior died in the spring and Stone's Folly was sold in the summer of 1901, leaving what was left of the school with no home.

Parham fell into a season of deep despair and soul-searching. He decided to take the emphasis off missionary tongues and again preach boldly the message of divine healing. In view of his son's death this may seem odd, but as his wife later wrote, "we felt to give up our faith in healing, we would also lose our hope in salvation and all would be lost."[18] Parham felt the press were enemies out to destroy him and that "my wife, her sister and myself seemed to stand alone."[19] But as before he showed his resilience and weathered the storm. In 1903, he was again on the evangelistic circuit holding meetings in Kansas, Oklahoma, and Missouri drawing large crowds with his message of divine healing.

In the summer of 1903, after a woman from Galena, Kansas, reported a miraculous healing at one of Parham's meetings, he was invited to Galena. Over the winter of 1904/1905, Parham preached there twice daily to large crowds, with many testimonies to salvation, healing, and Spirit baptism. He became a sensation of sorts in the region and again found committed supporters. Parham's Apostolic Faith movement had found a home. Heartened by the swelling support, he decided to expand his movement into Texas and in 1905 Parham began planting Apostolic Faith congregations in the Houston area.

Much like the success he experienced in Galena, Parham's meetings attracted a following as people heard his message of divine healing. Parham's methods were unique. He and his followers would march through the streets dressed in biblical garb, carrying signs and banners. By the end of the year Parham had several thousand supporters in Texas with a concentration in Houston. In December, with the growing numbers, he decided to start a short-term Bible school in the Houston area to train missionaries. The school continued to catalyze support as teams went out from the school to evangelize the surrounding communities. Though Spirit baptism and tongues were not center stage they were still very much a part of Parham's ministry in Texas, and tongues speech was regularly reported in his meetings.

Without doubt Parham later became a racist, with racism so common in his time. This makes it all the more notable that a few African-Americans were influenced by Parham during his time in the Houston area. Most important to our story is William J. Seymour, the focus of the next chapter. Seymour attended some of the classes Parham taught at the Bible school. Because of segregation laws he was not allowed to sit in the same room with the white students, but Parham let him sit just outside the room in the hallway, with the door open enough for Seymour to listen in. Parham had been reluctant to even allow for this but he was impressed by Seymour's humility. It was here that Seymour was introduced to the teaching on Spirit baptism and xenoglossa/tongues as the Bible evidence of the experience and fully embraced the Apostolic Faith message. Parham also ministered with him in African-American sections of Houston. When Seymour received a call early in 1906 to pastor in California, Parham, despite wanting him to stay in Texas, went ahead and blessed his decision to accept the invitation.

In March of 1906 Parham closed the Bible school sending his students out to spread the work. Shortly after closing the school he began credentialing gospel workers and he established various leaders over regions. In the summer of that year Parham traveled extensively through the Midwest. All the while he denied any intention of starting another sect or denomination. It was during this time that James Goff says Parham experienced his greatest success with as many as ten thousand followers. At the end of the summer of 1906 Parham believed God was calling him to new horizons in the North.

In obedience to this sense of divine guidance Parham traveled to Zion, Illinois, at the very time city founder John Alexander Dowie was struggling with Wilbur Voliva to recapture leadership over the city he had founded. Parham saw an opportunity to expand his influence into a confused and divided community. At first Parham seemed heartily received as he proclaimed himself sent by God to help rescue the troubled city. He quickly gained hundreds of committed followers as thousands attended his meetings in Zion City. It became clear that Parham was now a real player in the battle for control of the city. Voliva began to openly oppose Parham, calling him "an intruder intent on destroying the city."[20] Voliva did everything possible to prevent Parham from teaching in the city, trying to shut off his influence. Nevertheless, Parham's influence continued to be felt. In the midst of his growing success he announced his convictions on Spirit baptism and speaking with tongues as evidence. Voliva seized on this in order to discredit him and Parham was "no longer a serious contender for leadership of Zion City though he still had a sizable following."

Parham was aware since April that William Seymour was now leading a Pentecostal revival in Los Angeles. Seymour regularly wrote Parham keeping him updated on events and asking him to come and help lead the revival. The Midwest travels and the events in Zion had delayed his going to Los Angeles until October. That trip, chronicled in the next chapter, was another turning point for Charles F. Parham. There his racism became fully visible and the decline of his influence began.

From Los Angeles, Parham returned to Zion City but left soon to travel to the Northeast. Some think Parham had his sights on gaining influence or control of Frank Sandford's Shiloh community while Sandford was away on a three-year global voyage.[21]

Parham's base in Texas suffered from his absence and echoing his loss of the Bethel Healing Home while he traveled in

1900, one of the leaders in Texas sought to take control of the Apostolic Faith movement there. Parham traveled to Texas but ran into even more trouble. Long the target of rumors of homosexual activity, he was arrested in San Antonio and charged with sodomy. Oddly Parham did little to defend himself, expecting that his followers would simply trust that the charges were false. While the charges were eventually dropped, some of Parham's associates thought they were true and the incident left a shadow over Parham's ministry that he could never escape. Along with concerns over financial management, his eccentric doctrines, and racist attitudes Parham became an embarrassment to the Pentecostal movement as it grew in the first decades of the twentieth century.

Parham's reaction was both one of retreat and accusation. He withdrew to his one remaining stronghold, the Galena area of Kansas, establishing a base in nearby Baxter Springs. From there he bitterly denounced Seymour and other Pentecostal leaders. He became an ardent segregationist and in his later years offered praise to the Ku Klux Klan. For over twenty years until his death in 1929, Parham was alienated from and ignored by the movement he helped start.

PERSPECTIVES

The debate as to Parham's role in the founding of modern Pentecostalism continues. Biographer James Goff argues that Parham, more than Seymour, deserves recognition as the father of the movement. It is certainly true there would have been no Pentecostal movement as we know it today without him. Just how then are we to consider Parham?

Charles Fox Parham's single greatest contribution was his fashioning of the Pentecostal formula that asserted tongues speech (in his mind always xenoglossa) as the "Bible evidence" of the baptism with the Holy Spirit. This distinction separated Pentecostals from the other radical Christian groups who were all very similar in many ways. Initial evidence as it would be called, though not embraced by every Pentecostal group, became the most identifying characteristic of the emerging new movement born in the first decade of the twentieth century. Parham was its architect.

Parham displays the complex mix of the human condition. Oneness Pentecostal patriarch Howard Goss, who worked closely with Parham in the Houston area, summarized the Apostolic Faith message that Parham proclaimed was centered in Jesus Christ and that everything else—healing, holy living, and the like—flow from this focal point.[22] Some described him as a humble man and even the press acknowledged Parham as "a right good fellow and is earnest in his life's work."[23] His wife stood by him to the end. Still, it is easy to see, at various times, his unbridled ambition, his racism, and his headstrong independence. As to his alleged sexual indiscretions, nothing is certain. Parham displays both the virtues and flaws that lace the human race.

Importantly, as James Goff has argued, Parham mirrors the religious milieu of his times and the "complex origins" of the

Pentecostal movement.[24] Parham fused the many pieces together into a kind of whole that became the heart of early Pentecostalism. As he reacted to the rapidly changing era, he helped fashion a response that struck a chord in the hearts of many people who were longing for the transcendent and were yearning for some solace and hope in troubled times. Parham displayed a missionary passion for a last-days proclamation of the full gospel.

So was Parham the true father of the Pentecostal movement? Was he ignored by Pentecostal historians and leaders because of his eccentric ways and possible failings? The first question is a matter of perspective. If the question is more ideological, concerning who was the theological founder of the movement, then the answer is Parham. The patriarchal Pentecostal researcher Walter Hollenweger has pointed out another way of looking at the question. If rather, the question is: who most embodies the ethos of Pentecostalism with its egalitarian character and its ability to break stereotypes and social barriers? The answer then is William Seymour.[25]

Perhaps Vinson Synan finds a fair assessment. He argues that both men are essential to the founding of Pentecostalism. He sees Parham as the theological founder and Seymour as the catalytic founder, the one who popularizes the movement. Central, however, is that both made Jesus Christ the center of their message.

It is true that for decades Parham was overlooked in the Pentecostal story for obvious reasons. He was easy to ignore as was any human founder. Pentecostalism after all was not founded by any man but as a sovereign work of the Holy Spirit, and so the story went in Pentecostal folklore. But Parham was not the only person written out of the story. William Seymour, the focus of our next chapter, was also ignored but for a much different reason. Seymour was a black man in a white man's world.

BROUGHT TO THIS MOMENT:

In Light of Miscalculating Leaders

There are probably few things that more disturb thoughtful and sensitive believers than the apparent prominence some leaders find notwithstanding their doctrinal unpredictability or moral dalliances. To read any account of the "springboard" event of the Pentecostal revival—the episode at his Topeka, Kansas, Bible school on the first day of the twentieth century—is to find the name Charles Parham at the middle of it. Yet to discover the accumulated miscalculations and misjudgments he made over the ensuing years of his ministry, not to mention some preceding, tempts us to inquire, "God, why do You seem to allow the things You do—especially when Your truth is at stake and Your holy standards and values are vulnerable to being tainted in the eyes of multitudes?"

The most immediate answer is in the Bible: It is filled with God's patience with people—people like Abraham, David, Peter and others who stumble, fumble and occasionally fall. That answer doesn't suggest God is casual about either moral behavior or His own high standards and values. What it does reveal, however, is two things.

- God's sovereign workings are His to exercise, and He doesn't feel obligated to ask us our opinion before He decisively takes steps to advance His purposes. "How unsearchable are His ways, and His judgments past finding out!" (Romans 11:33b)
- God's viewpoint is always from the inside out—He looks on the heart more than the outward appearance (I Samuel 16:7). We may not like it, but there are apparently times He finds enough "heart" like His to risk using a human vessel whose behavior doesn't meet your or my style, preference or standards.

As a pastor and Church leader I have often been assailed through the years—not for moral, ethical or doctrinal compromise on my part, but because of my frequent unwillingness to pass judgment on leaders who irritate or offend many other leaders. I've learned the price of "being slow to speak," especially when my reticence suggests to some that I thereby must "approve" of the errant leader.

But my hesitation is born neither of a lack of conviction or of courage. In fact, there are many situations in the Church which demand decisive confrontation and redress, and when discernment has dictated immediate action, I've taken it—or called for it, even at a national level.

But there is an appropriate call to all of us who are living in this "moment"—this season just inside the twenty-first century as the Holy Spirit brings Christ's Church to what very possibly is her last season of service: the End seems so very near. And in this hour, God is still as limited as ever by reason of His sovereign choice to make Himself dependent upon "earthen vessels"— mere, fallible, sincere-though-oft-mistaken, devoted yet-so-often-blinded-to-pitfalls, humans! This being the case, and in view of the fact that not one of us can "read" the true, inner "heart" of leaders who gain recognition though we don't judge them "worthy" of their fame or following, you and I must arrive at a determination. We face questions like:

- When do I speak, and have I honestly evaluated my own motive?
- Am I self-verifying—more anxious to prove myself right than to note another's wrong?
- What risk is there that I am a twenty-first century Pharisee rather than what I prefer to be—i.e., a servant in the spirit of God's ways to "in wrath remember mercy," and mindful that "His mercy endures forever" (Habakkuk 3:2; Psalm 136:1-26)?

Whatever shadows blight the historical record of Charles Parham this much can be said to his credit: (1) His primary passion was for revival and his essential focus was not on revival "blessings," but on world evangelism. (2) In the face of criticism leveled at him, for what was in reality a breakthrough of divine grace launching an awakening, he persisted beyond despair and tirelessly sought to win the lost to Christ and advance the spirit of revival in the Church.

Today, each of us in His Church is wise to remember Jesus' words: "God did not send His Son into the world to condemn the world." And while judgment (correction and discipline) is to take place in "the house (family) of God" (I Peter 4:17), there is a balance required that we "take heed"—remembering our vulnerability to failure (Galatians 6:1), and our inclination to be blinded by self-righteousness (Matthew 7:3-5).

To scrutinize history is to be reminded of both, triumphs and failures, of stalwart heroes and, on occasion, of fallen heroes. Then, to examine ourselves in this, our "moment" will be to discover that this is a constant feature of history—unto this moment. Accordingly, we will likely find occasions and settings that may not always have representative leaders who suit our tastes, and we will face the need to balance grace with wisdom, human fallibility with divine mercy. It calls all who refuse to rush to judgment to learn humility and, in the light of God's Word and of God's sovereign grace across history, to be "slow to anger and slow to speak." Such wisdom is not cowardly or devoid of discernment, but it is more likely to maintain an openness to God (notwithstanding His will to pursue His purposes on His terms, not ours) and open to being more patient and forgiving than otherwise. And that will put us squarely in position to enjoy what God is up to in our moment, and make us available as instruments in His hand to model His truth and ways without self-righteousness or mercilessness.

William J. Seymour and the Azusa Street Revival

On February 22, 1906, William J. Seymour arrived by train in Los Angeles unaware that he was walking into the annals of history.[1] A son of former slaves, Seymour was invited to pastor a small holiness church in the heart of the rapidly growing Southern California city. He could not have imagined that in just two months the Apostolic Faith Mission, housed at 312 Azusa St., would become the wellspring of the North American Pentecostal and Charismatic movements.

That first Sunday, February 24, Seymour stood before the Ninth and Santa Fe mission congregation and taking Acts 2:4 for his text, he preached the Pentecostal message he learned from Charles Parham in Houston: Speaking in tongues was the "Bible evidence" of being baptized in the Spirit, just as it was in the beginning of the book of Acts. This, Seymour declared, is a recovery of New Testament Christianity. He told the little flock that sanctification was not the baptism with the Spirit; rather, after salvation it was the second step that cleansed the heart, preparing it for a mighty Spirit baptism, with tongues as evidence. Seymour said that unless they had spoken with tongues they were not filled with the Spirit. He may have meant well, but the congregation's leadership did not agree with the message.

Julia Hutchins, the little group's elected pastor who had invited Seymour to pastor the church, arranged a meeting with Southern California Holiness Association leaders. They listened to Seymour but in the end decided his teachings were counter to holiness doctrine. By the next Sunday Seymour found himself locked out of the church he had traveled halfway across the nation to serve. He had come sensing a special call and destiny yet now he was without a flock or a place to stay.

Seymour found temporary lodging in the home of Mr. and Mrs. Edward Lee, members of the church. While the Lee's initially were not in support of Seymour's message they wanted to help him out, realizing his predicament. Over the next few days Seymour prayed earnestly for God's direction. Impressed with Seymour's humility and sincerity, the Lee's gradually opened to his teaching of Spirit baptism. Invited to attend a cottage prayer meeting in the home of Richard Asberry,[2] a friend of the Lee's, Seymour continued to preach his message.

The small group was receptive and asked Seymour to lead the prayer meetings. Over the next few weeks Seymour, and those with him, earnestly prayed for a Los Angeles-based revival. In April the group entered a ten-day season of prayer and fasting, meeting nightly leading up to Easter. Before the meeting on Monday, April 9, Seymour prayed for Mr. Lee who was ill and did not want to miss the prayer meeting. Fulfilling a vision Lee saw earlier, he broke out speaking in tongues. That evening at the prayer meeting, as the two men told of Lee's experience, several listeners fell to the floor and began speaking with tongues. One young woman went to the piano and sang in a tongue she thought was Hebrew.

News spread quickly of the events at the 214 (now 216, where the house still exists) North Bonnie Brae Street home and crowds began to gather. Some reports said that people were coming and going twenty-four hours a day for three days and that the porch collapsed under the weight of visitors. People in and around the house testified to being baptized in the Holy Spirit.[3] Seymour himself never possessed the experience he taught that others should have, until finally on Thursday evening, three days after the first outpouring, he spoke with tongues.

Recognizing they were going to need more room, the group secured the site that would be immortalized in history: 312 Azusa Street. Located in the black section of the city near downtown, Azusa Street was a scant two blocks long. The two-story, 40 by 60-foot building they leased was dirty and in disrepair with broken doors and windows. The building originally housed the Stevens African Episcopal Church that had relocated. Since then it was used for many purposes including serving as a stable with the upstairs rooms rented out. In the spring of 1906 it was used as storage for construction materials. Seymour and the others got to work cleaning up the place, spreading sawdust over the exposed dirt first floor, and hastily building makeshift furniture. "They cleared space for about a hundred persons, laying redwood planks across nail kegs, old boxes, and chairs."[4] A small platform was placed in the center of the room with a pulpit made of two stacked crates. Windows and doors were repaired and the building was readied for Easter Sunday services. The second story was cleaned up and designated as an "upper room" for prayer to seek Spirit baptism. The upstairs also became Seymour's residence. It did not look like much at first but the Azusa Street revival was underway.

WILLIAM J. SEYMOUR

William Joseph Seymour, like many African-Americans of his day, has a history with little public record and few known details of his early life. We know he was born in Centerville, Louisiana, on May 2, 1870, the oldest child of Simon and Phyllis Seymour, both former slaves. Raised a Baptist, Seymour had some schooling and learned to read and write. As a young man Seymour lived in Indianapolis from 1894 to 1900, where he worked as a railroad porter and waited tables at several hotel restaurants. He was converted sometime while living in Indianapolis where he attended a Methodist Episcopal Church. He moved to Cincinnati around 1900.

In Cincinnati, Seymour associated with the Methodist evangelist, Martin Wells Knapp and likely attended classes at God's Bible School and Missionary Training Home run by

Knapp. He was also involved with the Evening Light Saints, a Church of God (Anderson, Indiana) group where he was "sanctified." Seymour struggled with a call to preach and contracted smallpox while living in Cincinnati, losing sight in one eye. Much like Parham did with his illnesses, Seymour attached spiritual significance to the sickness and felt God was judging him for not entering the ministry.

In 1902 or 1903 Seymour moved to Houston where he held evangelistic meetings in Texas and Louisiana. In 1904 or 1905 Seymour believed he was called by a revelation to go to Jackson, Mississippi, to obtain direction from Charles Price Jones, an influential African-American leader. Jones and fellow African-American pastor and church leader Charles H. Mason had founded the Church of God in Christ in 1897. (Jones and Mason later split over the Pentecostal experience, with Mason assuming leadership of COGIC). After Seymour returned to Houston in 1905, Lucy Farrow, an African-American pastor of a small holiness church, asked him to take over her church while she traveled as governess for the Parham family who had only recently moved to the area. It was through Farrow that Seymour met Parham. He was inspired by Parham's Pentecostal message and after Parham's Bible school opened in December, as already noted he arranged with him to listen in on the classes, from outside the classroom. Seymour embraced the notion that Spirit baptism was distinct from sanctification and evidenced by tongues.

Seymour continued to preach and minister in the Houston-area African-American holiness missions. At one of the meetings where Seymour preached he met a young woman named

Neeley Terry, who was visiting from Los Angeles. When she returned home to the little holiness mission she worshipped at, she encouraged the group to invite Seymour to assist with the work. So Julia Hutchins contacted Seymour in early February with an invitation to come to Los Angeles and against the advice of Parham who urged him to stay in Houston, Seymour left for California.

THE APOSTOLIC FAITH MISSION

With all the attention to the events overwhelming the little Bonnie Brae Street house, the Apostolic Faith Mission—a name reflecting Parham's influence—likely held their first meeting at the Azusa Street location on Sunday, April 15. The revival started slowly with only a small number of enthusiastic worshippers in the first meetings. Three days later *The Los Angeles Daily Times* carried the banner headline "Weird Babel of Tongues" and gave an eyewitness, although negative, account of one of the mission's first meetings.

> Breathing strange utterances and mouthing a creed which it would seem no sane mortal could understand, the newest religious sect has started in Los Angeles. Meetings are held in a tumble-down shack on Azusa street, near San Pedro street, and the devotees of the weird doctrine practice the most fanatical rites, preach the wildest theories and work themselves into a state of mad excitement in their peculiar zeal.

Colored people and a sprinkling of whites compose the congregation, and nights are made hideous in the neighborhood by the howlings of the worshippers, who spend hours swaying forth and back in a nerve-racking attitude of prayer and supplication. They claim to have "the gift of tongues," and to be able to comprehend the babel.[5]

The report described Seymour as an "old colored exhorter, blind in one eye . . . " and was sharply critical of the "wildest of meetings." The article ended by telling of a prophecy given at the meeting that "prophesied awful destruction to this city unless its citizens are brought to belief in the tenets of the new faith." Given this prophecy many of the Azusa Street worshippers saw *The Los Angeles Daily Times* headline of the next day as a warning to the city. Reading "Heart is Torn from Great City," the paper reported on the devastating San Francisco earthquake of April 18.[6] The Azusa Street congregants interpreted this as a confirmation that God was moving mightily in their midst and that the end of the age was near.

The journals and writings of Frank Bartleman, a holiness minister, who attended many of the early Azusa Street meetings, give us a vivid, though sometimes overstated, glimpse into the revival. In March of 1906 Bartleman attended a few of the cottage prayer meetings at the Asberry's home on Bonnie Brae Street and heard the early reports of the April 9 meeting when the Spirit fell on the group. He was greatly encouraged that Jesus was "showing himself alive."[7]

Bartleman, echoing the sentiment of so many early Pentecostals, said the Azusa Street revival was an example of "the

Spirit born again in a humble 'stable,' outside ecclesiastical establishments as usual."[8] Bartleman first attended a meeting at the Azusa mission on April 19. He found only "about a dozen saints there, some white some colored." This small beginning is important and the Azusa Street historian Cecil Robeck has pointed out that "this was a revival that was not immediately apparent."[9] While sometimes the mission's services had crowds, other meetings were small.

If the revival's gatherings at first lacked large numbers they never lacked enthusiasm. An early report said the "meetings begin about ten o'clock in the morning and can hardly stop before ten or twelve at night, and sometimes two or three in the morning, because so many are seking, [sic] and some are slain under the power of God."[10] Several altar calls were made each day with people being "saved, and sanctified, and baptized with the Holy Ghost."[11] Seymour would preach sometimes for an hour, though usually much shorter and the preaching was preceded by testimonies, singing, and prayer. People jumped, shouted, shook, jerked, danced, sang, spoke and sang in tongues. Sometimes the whole congregation was just silent. Seymour led the meetings but did his best to make room for the Holy Spirit's leading. He often sat behind the pulpit of two stacked boxes, sometimes putting his head inside the top box. (Apparently, Seymour did not want to interfere with the work of the Holy Spirit by asserting too much control.) Bartleman said an air of humility was present in the services.[12] Seymour even occasionally gave critics time to speak.

Seymour was the main preacher but regularly opened the pulpit to guests. After the sermon people would "rise and flock to the altars," one report said. The same article said that the preaching was so powerful "that people are shaken on the benches . . . and coming to the altar they fall prostrate under the power of God and often come out speaking in tongues."[13] The article told of "children from eight to twelve [who] stand up on the altar bench and testify of the baptism with the Holy Spirit and speak with tongues." Frequently people were taken upstairs to the room set aside for prayer for the sick; there was another upstairs room for those seeking the baptism of the Holy Spirit. Spontaneity was the norm and created great expectancy among the worshippers. There were no formal offerings taken in the services, though metal "mailboxes" were nailed to inside walls and by the door to place gifts with a sign: "settle with the Lord." Prayer for the sick was a regular part of the services and occasionally demons were cast out of people. Testimonies of miraculous healings abounded.

By summer the revival gained momentum and more and more people were attending the services, with as many as 350 worshippers crowded into the downstairs meeting room and sometimes double that. One September report said there were "twenty-five blacks and 300 whites" at the meeting.[14] Some said that a glow was visible from the building blocks away.[15]

Frank Bartleman said that there were no musical instruments in the meeting during the early period, though later on this changed. Bartleman also talked of the "gift of song" in the Azusa meetings.

It was indeed a "new song" in the Spirit. When I first heard it in the meetings a great hunger entered my soul to receive it. I felt it would exactly express my pent up feelings. I had not yet spoken in "tongues." But the "new song" captured me. It was a gift from God of high order, and appeared among us soon after the "Azusa" work began. No one preached it. The Lord sovereignly bestowed it. . . . It was exercised either in solo fashion, or by the company. It was sometimes without words, other times in "tongues". . . . It brought a heavenly atmosphere, as if the angels themselves were present and joining with us. And possibly they were.[16]

The crowds attending the mission's services were a multi-racial and socioeconomic mix for sure. Frank Bartleman wrote the statement now immortalized in Pentecostal history: "The 'color line' was washed away by the blood," referring to the integrated gatherings at the mission that defied segregation. Although led by a black man, Bartleman said there "were far more white people coming than colored coming."[17] At the mission, all races, poor, rich, men, women, young and old, worshipped alongside each other and Bartleman proclaimed, "All were equal."[18]

The Azusa meetings were filled with stories of tongue speech that were understood as actual human languages. Following faithfully the Pentecostal message he learned from Parham, Seymour taught that Spirit baptism was an experience that empowered the believer to be a more effective witness for the gospel, and like Parham, he believed that xenoglossalalic tongues enabled missionaries to proclaim the gospel in foreign languages never learned. As mentioned in the last chapter, this position was later modified as the sad reports came back from missionaries who tried the "shortcut" method and found it didn't work. At the time, however, the mission asserted that the

> gift of languages is given with the commission, "Go ye into all the world and preach the Gospel to every creature." The Lord has given languages to the unlearned [:] Greek, Latin, Hebrew, French, German, Italian, Chinese, Japanese, Zulu, and languages of Africa, Hindu, and Bengali, and dialects of India, Chippewa and other languages of the Indians, Esquimaux, the deaf mute language, and in fact the Holy Spirit speaks the languages of the world through His children.[19]

Stories of skeptics and scoffers who visited the revival are so remarkable some think they are apocryphal. "Proud, well dressed preachers" who came to the meetings to "investigate" were said to have "their high looks . . . replaced with wonder, then conviction comes, and very often you will find them in a short time wallowing on the dirty floor, asking God to forgive them and make them as little children."[20] Frank Bartleman had it right when he wrote in August 1906 of the Azusa Street outpouring: "The revival will be a world-wide one, without doubt. Could he have imagined just how world-wide it would one day be?"[21]

THE LOS ANGELES REVIVAL

When Seymour arrived in Los Angeles in 1906 the city was in the midst of tremendous growth. With a population of over

230,000 it had nearly doubled since 1900. The immigrant population, many from the Midwest and South, looked to the church to help find stability and community in the midst of so much transition. Over a third of the area residents attended churches and these statistics did not include "the many who participated in the newer sectarian groups. Various holiness organizations as well as independent missions had successfully established themselves in the city."[22]

Many Christians in Los Angeles were hungering and praying for revival. For over a year reports of the 1904-05 revival in Wales had been circulating. Famed English expositor, G. Campbell Morgan, and others spoke in superlatives about the revival, encasing it in Pentecostal terminology. The Welch revival was, for many, "Pentecost continued." Led by a common coalminer, Evan Roberts, the revival emerged spontaneously following a season of extended prayer. The revival quickly spread throughout Wales with thousands of conversions. It was widely publicized and it provoked revivals around the world. Many radical Christian groups found new hope for revival in the United States, seeing the Welch awakening as a confirmation that God was again granting a mighty visitation. Scores of holiness newsletters and publications across America printed stories of the happenings in Wales.

Joseph Smale, the pastor of the Los Angeles First Baptist Church, was especially captivated by the reports of the Welch revival and he traveled there in 1905 to see for himself the spiritual awakening. When Smale returned to California he began prayer meetings in his church and started revival meetings as well. His fervor for renewal eventually forced him to leave his church. Smale rented a Burbank meeting hall and formed the New Testament Church.[23] The church was organized for "evangelical preaching and teaching and Pentecostal life and service."[24] Frank Bartleman was one of the revival enthusiasts at Smale's church and he corresponded with Evan Roberts. In March 1906, Bartleman wrote a tract entitled "The Last Call" that spoke of a final last-days revival before Christ's return. His tract ended with a prophetic statement: "Some tremendous event is about to transpire."[25] Bartleman's account of the Azusa revival illustrates how important the Welch revival was in inspiring prayer and expectation for a great Los Angeles revival.

When the revival broke out at the Apostolic Faith Mission it ignited the smoldering embers of revival expectation, and by the summer of 1906, the Azusa Street events had catalyzed the spread of revival throughout the area. Joseph Smale's church quickly embraced the Pentecostal message and small Pentecostal missions were springing up in the surrounding communities. In later years many churches in the Los Angeles area would owe their existence to the Apostolic Faith Mission.

CHARLES PARHAM VISITS THE REVIVAL

By September it was clear to everyone that something special was occurring. That month the mission began publishing a newspaper called *The Apostolic Faith*. The first issue reveals their self-understanding of the events with the headline "Pentecost Has Come: Los Angeles Being Visited By a Revival of

Bible Salvation as Recorded in the Book of Acts." The banner article continued, saying that "Pentecost had surely come" along with the "Bible evidences . . . speaking in tongues as they did on the day of Pentecost. The scenes that are daily enacted in the building on Azusa Street and at Missions and churches in other parts of the city are beyond description. . . ."[26]

Seymour faced the struggles that come when attempting to pastor a revival. He had written Parham several times since April both reporting on events and requesting that Parham visit as soon as possible to help "set things in order." The growing mission forced Seymour to organize and with this came criticisms. Bartleman, fiercely distrusting of religious institutions and denominations, left Azusa Street in August because of a decision to hang a sign with the mission's name on it. He thought it smacked of needless organization that would lead to institutionalization. Also in August, Seymour formed the "Board of Twelve" to help provide leadership and local control for the mission.

The mission was also experiencing opposition from mainstream churches. Particularly painful was the opposition from many of the holiness groups who rejected the idea of Spirit baptism being distinct from sanctification, and especially the contention that tongues was the evidence of the experience. Pheneas Bresee, founder of the Pentecostal Church of the Nazarene in 1895, actively opposed the Azusa Street revival from 1906 on (in 1919 they would drop "Pentecostal" from their name in order not to be confused with the Pentecostals). There were also signs of rivalry among the various missions in the city. Seymour wanted the counsel of the man he saw as his overseer.

Charles Parham planned to visit the mission in September but his trip to Zion, Illinois, delayed his arrival until October. The September issue of *The Apostolic Faith* called Parham "God's leader of the Apostolic Faith Movement" and provided a brief history of the Topeka outpouring. Without question Seymour saw himself representing Parham in Los Angeles and was eager to have him come. The newspaper carried a greeting from Parham that anticipated his trip. "I rejoice in God over you all, my children," he wrote and asked the group to "Keep together in unity until I come, then in a grand meeting let all prepare for the outside fields. . . ."[27]

Parham had not only heard the reports from Seymour that spoke in grand terms about the revival. He was also hearing reports of what he thought was excessive emotionalism and, still smarting from past criticisms of his own revival in Topeka, Parham arrived in Los Angeles ready to act decisively to bring things under control. When he attended the first meeting and observed what he thought were extreme behaviors of worshippers, he was aghast at what he was convinced was "animalism" and rebuked Seymour and the congregation saying "God is sick to His stomach" at their behavior.[28] Parham believed that mission workers were manipulating those that came to the altars seeking Spirit baptism. Further, he did not want his work ridiculed for the antics of fanatics, who were accepting as evidence of Spirit baptism "chattering, jabbering wind-sucking, and jerking fits."[29] In his mind the tongues he heard at Azusa

Street were not the real thing but the product of emotional hypnotism.

Parham was especially put off by the interracial mingling of blacks and whites. Several years later he told of his disgust as "Men and women, whites and blacks, knelt together or fell across one another; a white woman, perhaps of wealth and culture, could be seen thrown back in the arms of a big 'buck nigger,' and held tightly thus as she shivered and shook in freak imitation of Pentecost. Horrible, awful shame!"[30]

Parham's first reaction was to try and take over the work. To his credit, Seymour, supported by his leadership team, resisted Parham and rejected his leadership. They asked him to leave. Parham left in disgust and started his rival Los Angeles mission five blocks away at the Women's Christian Temperance Hall which by December claimed to have a following of 300. It would be a fair assessment to say that Parham lost his place of influence over the young emerging Pentecostal movement with his stance in the fall of 1906. From here on the focus was on the revival at the Apostolic Faith Mission on Azusa Street. Parham's competing work at Temperance Hall did not endure and closed in 1907 after the scandal emerged about Parham's alleged indiscretion.

After the Parham debacle in late October, Seymour and his leadership team established a new organization separate from Parham and the December issue of *The Apostolic Faith* stated clearly that Parham "is not the leader of this movement of Azusa Mission." The paper acknowledged that in the past they had said he was, but that was before "waiting on the Lord." They affirmed that their movement had no human founder or leader but that "The Lord is our founder and He is the Projector of this movement." The article called Seymour "simply the humble pastor of the flock."[31]

This became the standard interpretation of their origins among the early generations of Pentecostals. As mentioned in the previous chapter, they regularly affirmed that they were a movement without a founder. "The Holy Spirit is our Founder," was a common assertion by many in the movement. On the one hand this is simply not true. Parham and Seymour both have key roles in the formation of modern Pentecostalism. What is true is that Pentecostalism has never had one dominant founder/leader but has possessed multiple companies of creative, innovative, savvy leaders that have helped propel it into the force it is.

Seymour is an example of such a leader. Despite his lack of much formal education or theological training, he ably led the Azusa mission through its years of revival and was an adequate spokesman, if not a highly skilled one. He also brought his own unique vision to the young Pentecostal movement. Given Seymour's African-American heritage, he saw the world out of a unique cultural context that helped fix in him a hope in the biblical promise of love and unity among all Christians. He forged an egalitarian vision that is one of the most enduring pieces of the Pentecostal ethos.

Seymour saw in the promise of Joel—that Peter declared fulfilled on Pentecost—a liberating truth regarding Spirit fullness (2:28–32). This was a gift poured out "on all people," no matter their color (Acts 2:17–21). This was a gift given to all God's children . . . "for all whom God will call" (Acts 2:39).

As Seymour led the Apostolic Faith Mission, he consciously or not, embodied that vision.

Seymour put together a talented team of leaders that complemented his leadership abilities. In the early days of the revival the leadership team was interracial, reflecting the congregation's racial mix, but somewhat overlooked is its gender diversity, with women holding significant leadership positions. The Azusa Street leadership team helped in regular pastoral duties like evangelism and visitation and sometimes served in the public services at the mission. The small cadre of servant leaders worked together to administrate the revival. Seymour and the group gave oversight to a ministry that "commissioned missionaries and evangelists and ran a rescue mission."[32] The circulation of the mission's newspaper had as many as fifty thousand readers at its height. In just a few short months the Apostolic Faith Mission was a vital center of spiritual renewal.

Seymour faced several challenges to his leadership over the years, usually from white leaders. He watched the interracial character of the revival change as whites gradually left, returning to segregated churches and missions. These events led to an adjustment of his view on tongues as Bible evidence. He questioned whether tongues could be seen as the primary evidence of Spirit baptism if the fruit of the Spirit was not present as well.

Cecil M. Robeck has surmised that Parham's behavior and strident attacks against Seymour and the mission—that continued for years and grew in their racist tone—contributed significantly to this adjustment. Joined with his broader experience of bigotry and then observing tongue speaking believers abandon the mission, one can see why he would challenge Parham's initial evidence formula. Importantly, Seymour never rejected tongues but saw the baptism with the Holy Spirit as more fundamentally evidenced by love and unity. He still believed Spirit baptized people would speak with tongues and that it was a genuine and significant gift from God, but one that was *a sign* of the Spirit's empowering, not *the sign*.

In the light of these adjustments, Robeck points out that Seymour became a theological forerunner to the way charismatics later formulized Spirit baptism in contrast to classical Pentecostals and their notions of tongues as "initial evidence." Ironically, though an acknowledged father to their movement, Seymour's moderated position on the evidential value of tongues wouldn't allow him to hold ministerial credentials in many Pentecostal denominations today.

Whatever the case, Seymour believed that the baptism of the Holy Spirit should have an ethical impact on the lives of those who received it. In his mind those who persisted in racism or other sins were not necessarily Spirit filled just because they spoke with tongues.

THE REVIVAL SPREADS

In the months after Parham's departure in the fall of 1906, workers were sent out to spread the Pentecostal message. This, along with reports of the revival in the network of holiness publications, started a steady flow of "Azusa pilgrims" coming to Los Angeles to check out the revival. Across the South, the nineteenth century holiness movement and its radical expressions had birthed several new denominations. Many of their leaders made the trip west. Probably most important was G. B. Cashwell, from Dunn, North Carolina. Cashwell arrived in Los Angeles in November of 1906 and after "receiving his Pentecost," he returned to Dunn, which became a kind of "Azusa East" with a revival breaking out under his leadership. At Dunn, leaders were baptized in the Holy Spirit and brought their whole denomination into the Pentecostal movement.

C. H. Mason, the African-American co-founder of the Church of God in Christ went to Los Angeles in March 1907 for a five-week stay at Azusa Street. After he was baptized in the Holy Spirit and spoke with tongues, he went home and split his denomination when most of the movement followed Mason into the Pentecostal understanding of Spirit baptism. William Durham, a Chicago pastor, also visited Azusa Street in February, 1907, and "prayed through" to his Spirit baptism on March 2. After returning to Chicago, his church became an important Pentecostal center. Many of those who later became leaders in the Assemblies of God denomination experienced Spirit baptism through Durham's ministry. The list and testimonies of the Azusa pilgrims could go on and on as similar events were repeated time and again. By the summer of 1907, centers for the new Pentecostal movement developed in Portland, Chicago, New York, and at various sites throughout the South.

The Azusa Street revival itself continued strong for about three years, though the numbers rose and fell significantly as crowds were highly mobile and visitors far outnumbered members. The attendance dropped after 1909 and there was a resurgence in 1911. The core of the mission never was greater than "50 or 60 people."[33] As strong centers of Pentecostalism were established around the nation, the Azusa St. mission slowly faded in both importance and memory.

Notably the mission incessantly called for the missionizing of the world with an eschatological urgency that characterized the times. *The Apostolic Faith* regularly carried stories about missionary efforts. Although missionary enterprise was never systematically organized, it was a central passion that naturally followed their interpretation of the purpose of the baptism of the Holy Spirit. In a later chapter we will explore in more detail the story of Pentecostal missions.

THE REST OF THE STORY

Seymour married Jennie Evans Moore in May of 1908. She became his stalwart confidant and co-worker, usually leading the ministry in his absence. The couple lived in the upstairs quarters over the mission. Their marriage may have provoked an internal controversy when another female associate, Clara Lum, left soon after the marriage. Lum, who served as the editor for *The Apostolic Faith* newspaper, moved to Portland joining Florence Crawford, another former Azusa Street associate. Her departure, taking along the mailing lists for the newspaper, was a significant blow to Seymour's ability to give leadership to the emerging Pentecostal movement. Efforts to recover the mailing lists were to no avail and Seymour found himself cut off from a significant audience. Mystery still surrounds the details regarding the loss of the mailing lists but without question it signaled Seymour's fading influence on the movement he helped start.

After 1911 the mission was no longer a revival but just another small African-American congregation in an expanding urban environment. Though Seymour traveled occasionally, he was largely ignored and forgotten within Pentecostal circles. He faithfully pastored the Apostolic Faith mission until his death on September 28, 1922, at the age of 52, after suffering a heart attack. Though Seymour always urged his little church to "love our white brothers" there is no doubt of his disillusionment that his dream of racial harmony went unrealized. According to Cecil Robeck, Seymour saw "himself as someone who ultimately had been rejected by the people he had been called to serve, and feelings of inadequacy attended his later years."[34] His wife Jennie led the ministry until her health failed in 1929. The old building was torn down in 1931.

BROUGHT TO THIS MOMENT:

In Light of the Azusa Street Revival

In the book, *The Ten Greatest Revivals Ever* (Vine Books, 2000), Elmer Townes and Douglas Porter summarize a cluster of spiritual awakenings that occurred between 1900 and 1908. Each reflected a call upon the Holy Spirit, with a hunger and will to: (1) submit to His "bending" (Evan Roberts, Wales); pursue His power in prayer (R. A. Torrey, Keswick, et al.), and; yield to His manifest, supernatural presence (William Seymour, Azusa

Street). Of striking significance are the results Townes and Porter realized upon polling seventeen recognized evangelical leaders, asking them to rank the order in which they would place the ten epic seasons of revival discussed in the book in terms of their global impact. The season including Azusa Street headed their studied response (see their pgs. 18-21).

It is not a matter of Charismatic or Pentecostal opinion to note that it is beyond debate that this community's statistics of growth a century later, not to mention the 100 year evolution of changed attitudes and openness toward the Holy Spirit's person, works, gifts and fruit everywhere in the Church, indicate the Azusa Street revival as unquestionably the most globally impacting event since the birth of the Church. The simplest assessment of this fact is probably the most accurate: while Christ is the Builder of the Church, the Holy Spirit is the Expediter of the building project! To open to any moment, and thereby maximize the possibilities of God's hand of power penetrating and transforming individuals, churches, societies or nations, of foremost need is an openness to the Holy Spirit.

The Holy Spirit's selection of William Seymour as the primary leader in the setting that would eventuate in a worldwide spread of a Book of Acts dimension of evangelism, miracles and spiritual passion, is not difficult to assess with history's privilege of hindsight.

He proved to be a remarkably balanced person of deep, heart-yielding humility, without any quest to advance a private or personal agenda. He manifests an evenhanded way of leadership, though faced with the unique challenges of pastoring amid a swelling revival in his midst.

He was a notably intelligent leader, peculiarly blessed with a capable intellect and sensitive discernment, but untainted or tempted by the human vulnerability to intellectualism which sometimes attends those privileged to educational levels Seymour's socioeconomic status disallowed.

He was of an ethnic descent that profoundly qualified him to both demonstrate and, under the Holy Spirit's hand, lead with God's heart in a non-political, dramatically divine quest to erase the "color line" in the Church that Jesus birthed.

He was undeterred by neither the notoriety nor criticism of his role that this spiritual epicenter brought him. He was unapologetic of the supernatural, and notably welcoming of "speaking in tongues." And though at first holding to "tongues" as the initial evidence of one's being filled with the Holy Spirit, he later yielded that dogma while still holding to the deep dynamic and desirability of speaking with tongues as of spiritual benefit.

It can be said without exaggeration that William Seymour, however limited by his mere humanness (as anyone else would be), was a person who answered to his "moment." And he did so in a way that, in a very real sense, has led to our being faced with the same "moment" today, because the nature of the times, of prophetic Scripture and of the primary leadership in the Church almost uniformly say the same things. Around the world today, wherever the living Church exists, leaders agree: we are cresting toward the grandest revival in history, and simultaneously descending into the greatest maelstrom of social and economic problems in history as well.

The gripping words of Joel's prophecy—"In the last days, I will pour out My Spirit upon all flesh"—ignited a century long passion to reach every nation and tribe with the Gospel. The belief that the Holy Spirit's outpouring was for that purpose, not merely personal blessing, fired hearts then and stirs expectancy today. But our answering to "this moment," not simply "expecting" it, will call us to demonstrate the same grace in response that Seymour did.

- This moment calls for balance, humility and a surrender of private agendas and "personal kingdoms." Any quest to flow with the river of the Spirit in the stream of grace prophesied for the end times begins at God's Throne (see Ezekiel 47:1-12). It is to that place the Holy Spirit seeks to bring each of us—that in surrender to God, and a will to move into the stream of His Spirit's moving, His life, love and power may extend to ever-deepening dimensions and ever-distant reaches of His power to the nations.

- This moment calls to a surrender of our minds—to God's Spirit of Truth and Wisdom, while refusing the folly of either fanaticism or intellectualism. This does not call the intellectually gifted away from their brilliance, but summons that all human glory be brought under the sway of the omniscience of the Holy Spirit. There is no more brilliant thinker than the one whose mind is yielded to the Maker who created us as physical-emotional-intellectual and spiritual beings. The maximizing of the first three features of our humanness is sparked to new heights when yielding to the fourth: our spirit yielded to His Spirit.

- This moment calls the entire Church to lead the way in overthrowing the global, human-race-wide bondage to ethnic separatism born of sinful pride, economic exploitation, historic hatreds and unforgiving retaliation. When asked what he saw as the world's great problem, Billy Graham immediately responded: "Racial prejudice." "The revelation of God's Word is that there is only one race— for He has made from one blood every nation of men to dwell on all the face of the earth" (Acts 17:26). The divisions and strife that exist among various tribes, tongues and nations (Greek, *ethnos*) began with one brother killing another shortly after human sin separated humankind from God, His love and His law. The Church—emissaries of a transcendent Kingdom—must manifest the Holy Spirit's love in ways that reveal God's newer, better, living way of relationships.

- Finally, this moment calls for a dual commitment—(1) to lay ourselves bare, to be delivered from the fear that so seeks to "control" the Holy Spirit as to restrict His supernatural manifestations; and, (2) to lay aside the legalism that either inclines to trivialize or tends to mandate "speaking with tongues." The inescapable value of this powerful, private means for prayer, worship and intercession is unquestionably the reason God's Spirit lavished this grace upon all who were present at the Church's birth. The apostolic instructions as to their exercise were never to inhibit, but to release their orderly function. Paul sets the tone for their appreciation: "I thank God I speak with tongues more than all of you." (1 Cor. 14:18). There was a reason—and it's still as reasonable and vital today.

William Seymour was a man with a broken spirit before God, and stands as a practical model before us as candidates to answer to our "moment." Since his time, times have obviously changed: 100 years have transpired. Technology alters the landscape, and global politics seem more complex—wars and social strife have escalated, and it seems a short fuse is burning down toward this planet's center. But the call of God calls us to the last of "the last days"—to answer the "moment" to which we've been brought.

Key stepping-stones are noted. One man walked that path a hundred years ago, having no idea the impact that the services he led in one small chapel on a side street in Los Angeles would have on the world. The same Holy Spirit broods over the Church today . . . and wants to come to the street where you live. And not one of us has any idea what impact His grace upon us may be . . . if we will answer to our "moment" on His terms.

The Pentecostal Explosion

The September 1906 issue of the Azusa Street publication *The Apostolic Faith* carried a story about A. G. Garr and his wife and their call to be missionaries in India. The article said that through the gift of tongues "Garr was able to pray a native of India 'through' in his own language."[1] This incident convinced Garr and his wife that they were called to the Far East and that God had supernaturally given them the Bengali and Chinese languages through their tongue speech. In spring of 1906, Garr, pastoring the Burning Bush Mission in Los Angeles, heard of the Azusa Street revival and attended meetings there. He was baptized in the Spirit in June, becoming the first white minister to speak with tongues. Garr's wife was soon Spirit baptized also and testified to speaking Chinese.

Garr shared his experience and call to India with his church but the board rejected his newfound Pentecostal way and Garr quickly resigned. When he told his story at the Azusa mission the response was much different. Excited with the news, the Apostolic Faith Mission congregation gave the Garrs several hundred dollars for their travels. Since William Seymour was teaching the same message Charles Parham had given him, namely that tongue speech was xenoglossa and that through this gift God was going to speed the evangelization of the heathen in the last days, the testimony of the Garrs was a confirmation to Seymour. A prophecy given in 1906 at the mission reflects their missional mindset at the time: "The time is short, and I am going to send out a large number in the Spirit of God to preach the full Gospel in the power of God."[2]

The Garrs, like other early Pentecostals, were certain that there was no time to spare for the hard work of language study. Christ was returning at any time and they needed to hurry to the mission field. By the beginning of 1907 they were already in Calcutta to start their ministry. The Garrs were among the most well-known of the early group of Azusa Street missionaries.

Another missionary warned Garr that the language he spoke with in tongues was not Bengali but Garr was convinced otherwise testifying that two Indian boys had confirmed that he was speaking Bengali.[3] After arriving in India, Garr soon realized that the Bengalis did not understand him when he tried to communicate by speaking in tongues. Still, he preached the Pentecostal message, declaring that Spirit baptism came with the "Bible evidence" of tongues speech. A small revival broke out in Calcutta under his preaching. People were deeply convicted of sin and fell to the floor, "howling, shrieking, groaning . . . sobbing, writhing, shaking. . . ."[4] Like Azusa Street, the Calcutta revival saw people singing together in tongues or making melody in "wordless song" in harmony that was "awe-inspiring." There were reports of "holy laughter" and a supernatural wind blowing through the meetings.

A. G. Garr Sr. went on to minister for nearly a decade in the Far East before returning to the U.S. in 1916. One of his most significant contributions to early Pentecostalism was the way in which he redefined the "Bible evidence" doctrine. Facing his disappointment that the Indians did not understand his tongue speech, he grappled with the doctrine. Garr still maintained that tongues were the evidence of the baptism with the Holy Spirit, but he no longer believed the gift was intended to speed world evangelization. Instead, speaking with tongues was a gift for "spiritual empowerment." Speaking in tongues enhanced the realization of God's presence and the supernatural character of the Christian life as "those foreign words flow from the Spirit of God through the soul and then are given back to Him in praise, in prophecy, or in worship."[5] Pentecostal historian Gary McGee believes Garr's reformulation later became the standard interpretation of glossalalia among most classical Pentecostals.

PENTECOSTAL MISSIONS

Garr's story serves as a marvelous entry point into the history of the expansion of the modern Pentecostal movement at the beginning to the twentieth century. He is but one of the small army that demonstrated radical Christian commitment to fulfill Christ's Great Commission to reach a lost world. As we have seen in chapter two, the Holy Spirit was active throughout the Christian centuries and renewal has always been a feature of the life of the church. Nevertheless, there is no doubt the twentieth century—the Charismatic century as we are calling it—has been an unprecedented period of Christian renewal and expansion. At the center has been the activity of Pentecostal/Charismatic missionaries and workers.

Garr's story also brings us back to the discussion on Pentecostal origins and the significance of the Azusa Street revival. Was it the starting point of the worldwide modern Pentecostal movement? Or did the renewal have multiple starting points? If so, where does that put the Apostolic Faith Mission's place in the Pentecostal story?

While the revival in Calcutta associated with Garr was clearly linked to Los Angeles, another larger Pentecostal-like revival was already under way in South India before he and his wife arrived. This revival was associated with Pandita Ramabai. A remarkably gifted woman, Ramabai was converted and became a social activist in India, championing the cause of poor women and children. She established the Mukti Mission near Khedgaon for women and children and provided homes for prostitutes and orphanages in several villages. In the summer of 1905, a revival broke out under her leadership that emphasized Spirit baptism. The revival was characterized with supernatural manifestations and deep transformation in those touched by the Holy Spirit.

The first night of the revival a young woman, sleeping in a

Mukti Mission dorm room, woke up to see what she thought was fire coming down on her. The dorm matron saw the fire too and ran to get a pail of water before realizing it was a manifestation of the Holy Spirit. Soon other women "were on their knees, weeping, praying, and confessing their sins."[6] The newly Spirit baptized women began exhorting the other women to repentance.

At first, tongues were not a part of this awakening until 1906 when many people who were baptized in the Spirit did speak with tongues, including Minnie Abrams and several other Western missionaries at Mukti. The revival was centered in prayer for conversion and Spirit baptism. Reflecting on the revival, Ramabai said that "the Mukti girls prayed for more than twenty-nine thousand individuals by name daily."[7] The revival continued into 1907, and since it preceded Azusa Street, it was not influenced by the idea of tongues as evidence of Spirit baptism nor did the Ramabai revival see tongue speech as xenoglossa. Further, they allowed for Spirit baptism without the necessity of tongues.

The Pentecostal revival in the nation of Chile was also independent of Azusa Street but was influenced by the Ramabai revival. Minnie Abrams had originally gone to India to work with the Methodist Episcopal Church but decided to work with Ramabai instead. After the 1906 revival broke out she wrote a book titled *The Baptism of the Holy Spirit and Fire*. Later Abrams learned that fellow Methodist Episcopal Church missionary Willis Hoover, serving in Chile, was increasingly frustrated with the Church's work in the South American nation and she sent Hoover a copy of her book. In Gary

McGee's words, the book "added the tinder that sparked the large Pentecostal movement . . . " when in 1909 Hoover experienced the baptism of the Spirit and spoke with tongues, the Chilean Pentecostal revival was conceived.[8] Eventually Hoover was forced out of the Methodist Church and established a network of distinctly Pentecostal churches. Although clearly having roots in the Wesleyan/holiness movement in North America, the Chilean Pentecostal churches were not a by-product of the Los Angeles revival.

A series of revivals broke out in Korea from 1903 through 1907 that gained even more momentum with news of the revival in Wales. The Korean revivals emphasized the importance of the Holy Spirit's empowering presence. Though there is little mention of tongues in the Korean revivals, there were numerous miracles, healings, and exorcisms. Meetings at the time drew hundreds filling up meeting halls with large numbers converting to Christianity. Throughout that time people spoke of receiving the baptism of the Holy Spirit. When classical Pentecostals finally entered Korea in 1928 through American Pentecostal missionary Mary Rumsey, the Korean Peninsula was already prepared to receive the Pentecostal message.

Again, important to remember, is the influence the Welsh revival had on the Azusa Street. As mentioned already, the widespread news of the awakening in Wales created an expectation for revival motivating many Christians to prayer. Revival historian J. Edwin Orr has argued that Wales provoked a whole series of revivals around the world.[9] It is true that the events both in Topeka and Los Angeles should be kept in perspective and it must be acknowledged that all Pentecostal awakenings at the beginning of the twentieth century cannot be traced back to either. It is also true that Pentecostal-like revivals preceded the twentieth century in many places, not the least of which was the 1831 revival in Scotland, associated with Presbyterian pastor Edward Irving.

Notwithstanding, it is impossible to conceive of the Pentecostal and Charismatic movements as we know them today without the Topeka and Los Angeles revivals. Particularly, Azusa Street became both a launching place and a symbol for the emerging Pentecostal movement. It deeply impacted a few key people who in turn impacted others both in the United States and internationally. For example, Gary McGee points out that the biggest impact of Azusa on world missions was not its direct influence but people it indirectly touched. Many people only heard stories of the revival in Los Angeles and yet it had profound influence on them. Norwegian Thomas Ball Barrett heard of the Azusa revival while staying in New York in 1906. He was baptized in the Holy Spirit and corresponded with Azusa Street leaders and after returning to Norway, Barrett spread Pentecostalism throughout Scandinavia and other parts of Europe.

Several of Barrett's converts to Pentecostalism would carry the message to other nations. Alexander Boddy, an Anglican pastor won to Pentecostalism by Barrett, became an influential Pentecostal leader in England. German holiness leader Jonathan Paul embraced the Pentecostal message through Barrett and brought Pentecostalism to his nation, although it faced many challenges in the first decades of the twentieth century.

Lewi Pethrus, a Baptist pastor in Sweden, became one of Barrett's most fruitful converts. Pethrus went on to lead a vital and growing church—for decades his church in Stockholm was the largest Pentecostal church in the world—that spurred a significant Pentecostal movement which became the largest Free Church in Sweden.

Although the Los Angeles Apostolic Faith Mission never formed any structured missions organization, its missional ethos sparked numerous other revivals around the nation that became sending centers for the fulfillment of the Great Commission. Small Pentecostal denominations formed and, along with other holiness denominations that came into the new movement, developed their own missions programs. Independent groups banned together to create small mission societies to send out missionaries. Much of this was an outflow of the excitement generated by the news of the Azusa Street revival.

One of the most unique stories of early Pentecostal missions involves two Swedes, Daniel Berg and Gunnar Vingren. The two immigrants were living in South Bend, Indiana, where both embraced Pentecostalism. After Vingren began pastoring a South Bend Swedish Baptist Church in 1910, he and Berg were captivated by a prophecy that repeated the word "para, para." An interpretation of the prophecy said that Berg and Vingren were to go to Para. With no idea where the place might be they visited the Chicago Public Library and after searching found a province in Brazil with that name.

Through the generosity of friends, the two men raised enough money to buy two one-way tickets to Brazil but on the way to New York to catch a ship they gave their money away to another missionary. Miraculously, as they walked the streets of Pittsburgh, an unknown woman approached Berg and Vingren and gave them the exact amount they needed for the voyage to Brazil.

These "missionaries of the one-way ticket," borrowing Vinson Synan's term for them, arrived in Brazil in the fall of 1910 and within a year they were planting Pentecostal churches. Years before the American Assemblies of God denomination was founded, the new movement in Brazil was organized and named *Assembléis de Deus* (Assemblies of God). Today the Pentecostal Church in Brazil numbers nearly 25 million members.[10] This is a remarkable tale of the supernatural direction of God and many other stories like this can be told.

The early mission efforts of the young Pentecostal movement were admittedly scattered but exemplified a zeal for world evangelization and signaled in their infancy the force they would become over the course of the twentieth century. Gradually Pentecostals, utilizing their pragmatic organizational skills, became more strategic and focused in fulfilling the Great Commission. Even after 100 years, the imminent return of Christ remains a motivating force for Pentecostals. In addition, Pentecostalism's unquestioned success in cross-cultural missions is tied to their unequivocal commitment to signs, wonders, and spiritual gifts as central to the proclamation of the gospel.

UNITED STATES PENTECOSTALISM

As missionaries took the Pentecostal "good news," or the "Full Gospel" as they regularly termed it, overseas, numerous workers took the message all over the United States. In the decade after 1906, Pentecostalism not only grew, it also fragmented. What started as a blend of many strands of radical Christianity quickly splintered into various and sundry expressions of Pentecostal faith. Again, the Azusa Street revival was the spark lighting the fire.

Mentioned briefly in the last chapter, the revival expanded into several centers in Los Angeles and around the region. By the end of 1906, churches in Pasadena, Glendale, Monrovia, San Pedro, Hermon, and other Los Angeles basin cities had accepted the Pentecostal message. Workers from the Apostolic Faith Mission spread out over California. Florence Crawford headed north to conduct meetings along the California coast, eventually arriving in Portland where she started a growing Pentecostal work. Crawford left Portland to tour east and into Canada, returning to Portland later in 1907, where she based her ministry. Although Frank Bartleman left Azusa Street in August 1906 to start his own Pentecostal mission, he toured much of the United States in 1907, spreading word of the revival in Los Angeles. Fed by testimonies in the holiness press and the Azusa workers, Pentecostalism began to take root in America.

William H. Durham

Sometimes pastors brought existing congregations into the movement. Sometimes new churches were started. One of the most important examples of the former is the case of William Durham. As mentioned in chapter four, while pastoring a small mission in Chicago, Durham heard of the Azusa Street revival and traveled to Los Angeles in 1907, where he prayed earnestly to be baptized in the Holy Spirit. On the evening of March 2, he spoke with tongues. William Seymour, who had left the room in which Durham was praying, felt led to return. "Seeing him 'slain in the Spirit' (falling down under the power of God) and speaking in tongues, Seymour raised his hands over Durham, prophesying that wherever this man would preach 'the Holy Spirit would fall on the people.' "[11]

Durham returned to his North Avenue Mission and by summer of 1907 it was the "Azusa Street of the Midwest."[12] During his stay in California, his wife Bessie led nightly prayer meetings that "primed" the little mission for Durham's wholehearted endorsement of Spirit baptism evidenced by tongues.[13] The new Pentecostal gospel message and Durham's gifted preaching style helped gain a large audience.

By summer the North Avenue Mission was a thriving center of Pentecostalism. Crowds of the curious along with sincere seekers packed the daily services. So powerful were the meetings that some testified to seeing "a thick haze—like blue smoke—resting over the assembled faithful, a reference to the palpable 'shekinah,' or 'glory,' that once filled the ancient Hebrew temple as a sign of God's presence."[14] Indeed many told of sensing the "very presence of God" in the revival services and like at Azusa Street, worshippers sang the "heavenly chorus" as one or two would sing out extemporaneously in tongues with others joining in. Sometimes this singing lasted more than an hour.[15] Meetings often lasted into the morning hours and people were heard speaking in tongues at all hours of the night.

As the mission grew, new building additions were needed to accommodate the crowds. Durham was industrious and savvy and soon established a ministry base with trained workers and a publishing arm to help spread the message. He also set up multiple meeting places in Chicago and by 1912 the North Avenue Mission had started thirteen other Chicago Pentecostal congregations.[16]

Durham's church carried the same passion for outreach and mission that characterized Azusa Street. Regularly, the mission's services were stirred by the testimonies of visiting missionaries and, early on in the Chicago revival, Durham nurtured relationships with Italian immigrants, who in turn traveled about and spread Pentecostalism nationwide, eventually reaching into Italy. Daniel Berg and Gunnar Vingren, the missionaries who went to Brazil, were once at the North Avenue Mission. Durham's ministry touched many of the urban ethnic communities in Chicago and the Italian scenario was often repeated. The mission ministered to Chicago's poor as well.

Thousands of pilgrims traveled to Chicago to witness the revival. This led to one the most significant contributions of Durham's ministry, the many future Pentecostal leaders he introduced to the Full Gospel. There are many examples. In 1909, Robert Semple, a young missionary preparing to go to China, came to Chicago with his wife, Aimee Semple. The couple stayed at the mission for a year during which Durham and Aimee Semple frequently formed a team, with Durham speaking in tongues and Aimee interpreting Durham's tongues speech. Aimee Semple, whose life is the focus of the next chapter, is better known as Aimee Semple McPherson, the well-known Pentecostal evangelist in the period between 1920 and World War II. Durham traveled with the couple to Canada for their China send-off.

E. N. Bell, who later became an important early leader of the Assemblies of God, took leave of the church he pastored in Texas, and stayed a year with Durham in Chicago. Pastor and evangelist A. H. Argue, a key leader in founding the Pentecostal Church of Canada went to Durham's Chicago ministry where he was baptized in the Holy Spirit. Oneness Pentecostal founder Howard Goss was also among the many leaders who traveled to Chicago. A number of leaders from John Alexander Dowie's nearby Zion, Illinois, community came under Durham's influence as well. His impact went far beyond just introducing people to Pentecostal Spirit baptism. He would also set in motion the first controversy of the young movement as we will later see.

G. B. Cashwell

As news of the Azusa Street revival spread in the holiness presses, it soon reached the regional stronghold of the American holiness movement, the South. In the last two decades of the nineteenth century the radical holiness fervor in the Southern states had birthed several small holiness denominations. These movements were the "second blessing" folk who believed that sanctification was a distinct, second work of grace, subsequent to salvation. Many in the South had heard of B. H. Irwin's "baptism with the Holy Spirit and fire" teaching in which Spirit baptism was distinct and subsequent to sanctification, adding a third stage to the salvation experience (see chapter 2).

When the holiness groups heard about tongues and other physical manifestations happening in Los Angeles, this was not entirely new to them. For over a decade there were reports of scattered instances of people speaking in tongues along with unusual behavior. What was different about the message coming out of Azusa Street was the teaching that tongues were the proof, or evidence, that one had received the baptism with the Holy Spirit. Vinson Synan has pointed out how significant this distinction was for the Southern holiness groups. "Many of the holiness people had felt that some physical evidence would often accompany sanctification to prove that one had 'prayed through.'" These proofs greatly varied. For some it was the "holy dance" or "hallelujah earthquakes"; for others it was "shouting in drunken ecstasy."[17] News that tongues were evidence of a third stage baptism of the Holy Spirit was something new, and given the strong emphasis on restoration of New Testament Christianity so prevalent at the time, the Azusa Street revival seemed to be just that: a restoration of apostolic experience. It could not get more biblical in the minds of those who were excited and expectant over the events in California. This was the book of Acts coming to life.

Gaston Barnabas Cashwell, of Dunn, North Carolina, was a preacher associated with A. B. Crumpler's Pentecostal Holiness Church (officially named The Holiness Church of North Carolina), a name reflecting its restorationist orientation, though "Pentecostal" was dropped in 1901. Crumpler, a former Methodist pastor, formed the new holiness denomination in

1900 because of the failure of Methodists to continue to emphasize the sanctification experience. Like many holiness groups at the time, the Pentecostal Holiness church preached the radical holiness gospel of Jesus as Savior and Sanctifier, and also taught divine healing, and the premillennial second-coming. The group was ripe for the Pentecostal message and G. B. Cashwell was so stirred by the news of the Azusa Street revival that he decided to go to California to see it for himself.

Like Crumpler, Cashwell left the Methodist Church to pursue a more "apostolic" Christian experience. After arriving in Los Angeles and going to the Apostolic Faith Mission, Cashwell's Southern racist roots almost made him leave. In the meeting he attended there were few whites present. He was forced to face down his own prejudices if he wanted to experience his "Pentecost." After attending several meetings, Cashwell humbled himself and requested that William Seymour pray for him to be baptized with the Holy Spirit. Seymour and a group of African-Americans gathered around Cashwell and he was Spirit baptized and spoke in tongues.[18]

Cashwell returned to Dunn, North Carolina, and immediately rented a building to hold revival meetings. He intended to make his meetings an Azusa Street East and that's what they became. With the first meeting on December 31, 1906, the Dunn revival meetings, while lasting only a few weeks, became the catalyst that swept most of the Southern holiness movements into Pentecostalism. G. F. Taylor, a young preacher in Crumpler's church, was so expectant when he attended the Dunn meetings that he was baptized in the Spirit within minutes of seeing Cashwell. Taylor, following the Dunn revival in

1907, wrote a book *The Spirit and the Bride* that proved an important defense of Pentecostalism in the South. People began streaming in from all over the Southeast to be a part of the revival and many of the ministers in both the Pentecostal Holiness Church and the Fire Baptized Holiness Church went to see Dunn, coming away convinced the revival was of God. Most were Spirit baptized.

Holiness Church leader A. B. Crumpler stayed away from the Dunn meetings, suspicious of Cashwell and opposed to the new doctrine. It was a decision that would later cost him control of his denomination. J. H. King, leader of the Fire Baptized Holiness association was also absent, somehow unaware of the Dunn meetings. King had initially been receptive to news of the Los Angeles revival and could agree with most everything Seymour taught except tongues as "Bible evidence." King tried to keep an open mind and he invited Cashwell to his Toccoa, Georgia, church in February 1907. There in the second meeting King was baptized in the Spirit and spoke in tongues. Over the next decade the Fire Baptized Holiness and The Holiness Church merged (Crumpler unable to accept the Pentecostal message resigned his leadership and Taylor succeeded him) and along with other mergers the Pentecostal Holiness Church was formed, today one of the largest classical Pentecostal denominations in the USA. J. H. King assumed leadership in 1917.

After the Dunn and Toccoa meetings, Cashwell traveled throughout the South spreading the Pentecostal message. Another newly formed holiness denomination based in Cleveland, Tennessee, was also influenced by Cashwell. A. J. Tomlinson, the leader of the young holiness group, the Church of God, invited Cashwell to Cleveland in January 1908 and during one of the meetings received his Pentecostal Spirit baptism. Tomlinson immediately brought the whole movement, many of its leaders already baptized with the Holy Spirit, into Pentecostalism. Today the Church of God (Cleveland) is the third largest classical Pentecostal church in America.

More than any other single leader, Cashwell, the "Pentecostal apostle of the South," introduced the radical holiness churches in Dixie to the Azusa Street revival and its message on Spirit fullness and speaking with tongues. The irony of this is that Cashwell himself left Pentecostalism. Disaffected because he could not control the movement he helped create, he returned to Methodism in 1909. Though he later regretted his involvement, it was too late to undo what had been done and for the last one hundred years the Southern states have been a Pentecostal stronghold.

THE FINISHED WORK CONTROVERSY

Since Parham's Topeka discovery of tongues as evidence of Spirit baptism, the early Pentecostal movement was almost exclusively dominated by a "three stage" perspective. First there was conversion, then crisis sanctification, followed by the baptism with the Holy Spirit, accompanied by tongues speech. Joined with the emphasis on divine healing and the imminent return of Jesus Christ, it has been called the "five-fold" gospel.[19] This formula is deeply influenced by the Wesleyan-holiness movements. It was William Durham who first challenged this view and ushered in the first serious dispute within nascent Pentecostalism.

In 1909 Durham continued as one of, if not the, most influential Pentecostal leader. He traveled widely as a frequent speaker at conferences and revivals, while maintaining the leadership of his Chicago revival center. In the summer of 1909 his wife died of complications from childbirth, followed by the death of his baby daughter just six months later. These events seemed to push Durham to an even greater commitment in giving himself to leadership of the Pentecostal movement.

In May of 1910 he announced his controversial teaching at a Pentecostal conference at Stone Church in Chicago. He titled his message "The Finished Work of Calvary" and challenged the idea of sanctification as a subsequent, second work of grace. Drawing on non-Wesleyan themes from his earlier ministry experience and from the Keswick "deeper life" teachings, Durham emphasized that sanctification was a matter of identification with Christ and that by faith in what was accomplished on the Cross, the Christian could live victoriously. As the believer identified in faith with Christ's death and resurrection, the sin nature was crucified and the resurrection power was made available. For Durham and others who adopted his views, sanctification was a progressive and ongoing transformation in contrast to an emphasis on a crisis experience.

This teaching was an open challenge to what most Pentecostals thought. Durham himself earlier affirmed sanctification as a second experience, followed by Spirit baptism. Now he was saying that since his Spirit baptism he had struggled with the sanctification teaching. Baptism with the Holy Spirit had opened his eyes to see that the whole Christian experience was centered in Christ and His finished work through the Cross. Instead of the three stage approach, he was proposing that it was just two stages: first conversion and then baptism in the Holy Spirit.

Durham later bluntly asserted the Bible did not teach a "second definite work of grace." He went on to say that "the second work theory is one of the weakest and most unscriptural doctrines that is being taught in the Pentecostal movement. . . ."[20] Durham maintained that no subsequent work of grace was needed because salvation was complete in Christ. At conversion the believer was sanctified "in Christ" and made a "new creature." His new teaching exalted Christ and His atoning work.

Using every speaking opportunity he had and utilizing his publication, the *Pentecostal Testimony*, Durham aggressively popularized the new insights he saw as the "most important teaching in the Bible."[21] The finished work teaching stirred great controversy, with leaders lining up on both sides.

Many immediately embraced the finished work teaching, especially those who were influenced by A. B. Simpson, Dowie or Keswick leaders. E. N. Bell and many other men who later formed the Assemblies of God denomination were clearly in Durham's "two-stage" camp as were a large number of Canadian Pentecostals.

Opposition came, however, when in February 1911, Durham traveled to California to spread his message there. He intended to speak at Elmer Fisher's Upper Room Mission, the largest

Pentecostal mission in Los Angeles but Fisher, committed to the sanctification message, refused him when he got wind of Durham's new doctrine. Instead Durham went to Azusa Street with his finished work ideas. William Seymour was on a ministry trip on the East Coast. The Azusa Mission's attendance had faded by 1911 and Durham's preaching soon brought new crowds. Frank Bartleman wrote that "the saints flocked back to the old place and filled it again with the high praises of God . . . It was called by some the second shower of the Latter Rain."[22] Within days the place was so full that hundreds were turned away. The meetings continued until Seymour returned in May. Seymour was deeply distressed by Durham's finished work teaching that so challenged his own holiness heritage and when Durham refused to stop teaching the doctrine, Seymour and his trustees locked him out of the mission.

Durham, with the help of Frank Bartleman, promptly found a temporary meeting place and eventually a larger hall to accommodate the growing attendance. He took with him over half of Seymour's workers. Bartleman reported that Durham's Sunday services were attended by a thousand people with 400 at the nightly meetings at his new site.[23] Bartleman wrote of Durham's Los Angeles mission:

Here the "cloud" rested and God's glory filled the place. "Azusa was deserted." The Lord was with Brother Durham in great power. God sets His seal especially on present truth to be established . . . He was used mightily to draw anew a clear line of demarcation between salvation by works, between law and grace. This had become very much needed, even among Pentecostal people.[24]

The Durham affair was another setback for Seymour and another confrontation with a white man who when leaving did not hesitate to take people with him. It is safe to say that the Apostolic Faith Mission never regained its former glory after Seymour took his stand against Durham.

Bartleman was right about lines being drawn through Durham's finished work teaching. Durham's opponents felt he was attacking the "doctrinal foundations of the movement" and no one attacked Durham more stridently than Charles Parham. Early in 1912, he said Durham had, by teaching such heresy, committed "the sin unto death" and prophesied that he would die within six months. Durham, unfazed, continued propagating his message throughout 1911 and into 1912, still based in Los Angeles but traveling extensively. Probably weakened by the stress of travel and family crises, Durham contracted tuberculosis and died rather suddenly at age 39 in Los Angeles on July 7, 1912. Parham saw Durham's death as vindication of the sanctification position and said, "How signally God has answered."[25]

If Durham's untimely death was God's judgment, it was hard to tell from the events that followed. If anything, the finished work teaching gained even more ground and eventually became the doctrinal position of the majority of Pentecostals in the world. His premature death did prevent him from penetrating the South with the new doctrine and for the most part the Pentecostal-holiness denominations were never seriously threatened by it. Without question the fabric of Pentecostalism was changed by the debate and any idealism about unity was dealt a severe blow. Even Durham's friends felt at times he was too forceful in asserting his finished work teaching. Some hoped that after his death a more conciliatory tone would be possible. This would not be the case.

THE "NEW ISSUE" CONTROVERSY AND THE ASSEMBLIES OF GOD

On the heels of the finished work controversy came a new one. Ironically, it emerged out of attempts to forge new bridges between the differing camps on either side of the recent debate over sanctification. Within weeks of Durham's death, a new revival broke out in Dallas, Texas, in late July, 1912. The revival was centered around the ministry of healing evangelist Maria Woodworth-Etter, who had only recently embraced Pentecostalism. As thousands flocked to evening revival meetings, excitement was again in the air. As with Azusa Street and Chicago, "pilgrims" came from around the nation to see what God was doing. In the midst of this, Woodworth-Etter, aware of the recent controversy, exhorted her hearers to center themselves in Jesus instead of fighting over theories. The meetings were filled with prophecies of Christ's imminent return. The meetings concluded at the end of the year, and as 1913 dawned, people expected God to do something new to restore His church in preparation for the second coming of Christ.

In follow-up to the Dallas meetings, a camp meeting was arranged for April/May 1913 at Arroyo Seco, California. While the meetings were a moderate success and drew people from across the country, they did not live up to the expectations coming out of the Dallas revival. Woodworth-Etter attended the meetings but was disappointed that her calls for unity centered in Jesus seemed unheeded. It was clear that the meetings were mostly for the "finished work" folk. William Seymour attended, coming up from Los Angeles, "but was not given the courtesy of sitting on the platform with the other ministers."[26]

Still, expectations for the "new thing" ran high and when R. E. McAlister, a Holiness pastor turned Pentecostal, spoke at a water baptismal service the "Oneness," or "new issue," controversy was born. Basically what McAlister did was bring attention to the baptismal formula of the New Testament. He pointed out that Jesus commanded in Matthew 28:19 to baptize in "the name" (singular) of the Father, and the Son, and the Holy Spirit, and that when the New Testament church baptized people in the book of Acts, it was in the name of Jesus Christ. Soon the buzz of the camp meeting was that McAlister's revelation was the "new thing" they were expecting. Some leaders were cautious and concerned while others felt it was of God. Frank Ewart, a former Baptist minister who helped organize the Arroyo Seco meetings, was particularly caught by McAlister's insight. Ewart had taken over Durham's Los Angeles church after his death. He became a major architect of the new doctrine and, along with other "Oneness" Pentecostals, openly challenged Trinitarian theology, calling it "Constantinianism." In this scheme there was only one person in the Godhead and the titles Father, Son, and Spirit referred to ways the one God manifested Himself at various times in redemptive history. The emphasis, however, for the Oneness movement was Jesus Christ and baptism in His name. Eventually, they called for all believers to be rebaptized according to the apostolic formula in the name of Jesus only. Given its "Jesus-centrism," a number of Pentecostal leaders heartily accepted the new teaching.

This new doctrinal skirmish took place during the same time that a number of white Pentecostal leaders were organizing a larger association of pastors and churches. While the majority of Pentecostals outside the South eschewed denominations, they occasionally banded together in small regional associations of ministers for mutual support and encouragement. In April 1914, with E. N. Bell as primary leader, a number of these regional groups came together in Hot Springs, Arkansas, to form the "General Council of the Assemblies of God," conceiving what would one day become the second largest classical Pentecostal denomination in the United States (the largest in the world counting global membership).[27] In their minds they were not forming a new denomination but simply banding together to foster consensus and cooperation. At these first meetings there was no hint of the brewing Oneness controversy. In fact, this early association, while clearly in Durham's finished work camp, was not hostile in tone toward the Wesleyan holiness Pentecostals.

Meanwhile, Oneness Pentecostalism was spreading. Evangelist Glen Cook, who now worked with Oneness advocates Frank Ewart and R. E. McAlister, went on a 1915 eastern-America preaching tour declaring the new doctrine and calling for rebaptism. In Indianapolis he won over G. T. Haywood. Haywood was one of the few African-American pastors in the new Assemblies of God association. Not long after this, E. N. Bell, so instrumental in starting the Assemblies of God, along with Howard Goss embraced the Oneness message much to the alarm of other leaders in the new association. As the General Council of the Assemblies of God met in 1915 and 1916 the controversy was the front and center issue as both sides were in attendance. It was an especially heated dispute.

Finally, in the Fourth General Council meeting at St. Louis in October 1916, led by the group's General Secretary, J. Roswell Flower, the issue was settled when the Trinitarian camp won out, clearly aided by E. N. Bell's return to the Trinitarian side. Preparing a doctrinal statement—contrary to their earlier promise to have no creed—that flatly rejected the Oneness position, the Pentecostal movement was divided yet again. In taking their stand, the Assemblies of God lost 156 of their 585 ministers and over one hundred churches.[28] The Oneness denominations, The Pentecostal Assemblies of the World and the United Pentecostal Church, were eventual by-products of the split.

Sadly, doctrinal division was only part of this story. Before the formation of the Assemblies of God, many Pentecostal pastors and evangelists held their ministerial credentials through C. H. Mason's Church of God in Christ, the primarily African-American Pentecostal denomination, already mentioned. Credentials were important to these leaders for more than just legitimizing their ministries; they secured railroad fare discounts and privileges for travel, so essential at the time. Increasingly, given the blatant racism of the period, many Pentecostal leaders, particularly those from the Southern states, were uncomfortable holding credentials with the Black organization.

Significantly, C. H. Mason was not formally invited to the first General Council of the Assemblies of God in 1914, though he and a few other blacks attended as observers. Nothing could have been more of an affront to the vision of William Seymour and the early days of Azusa Street, and for that matter, to the ethnic outreach vision of Durham in Chicago. For many white Pentecostals, race was unfortunately not a "theological issue."[29] One must wonder what the twentieth century would have looked like if more Christians had embraced what Seymour taught as central to Spirit fullness, Christian unity among all peoples.

Instead, as the new century's second decade drew to a close, Pentecostalism was fragmented in a profusion of groupings along regional, racial, and theological lines. Since 1906 there surely was a Pentecostal explosion, one that caused both growth and division. Oddly, its very fratricide likely contributed to its growth even during the difficulties of the First World War. Pentecostalism was changing and no one more exemplifies those changes between the World Wars than the story of Aimee Semple McPherson, the central focus of our next chapter.

BROUGHT TO THIS MOMENT:

In Light of the Spread of the "Spirit-filled" Experience

This chapter outlining the early, rapid and global spread of the Gospel via the passion awakened among the twentieth century's Pentecostal-Charismatics indicates the central focus of the movement: To touch all humankind with the love of God, preaching salvation through Jesus Christ and confirming that witness in the miracle working power of the Holy Spirit. This is the no-nonsense priority of all "Spirit-filled" believers. But there is a pivotal issue that travels alongside that priority: it is the important place of discipling converts by:

- calling them to be baptized in water (Matt. 28:19, Mark 16:15);
- leading them to an experience of receiving "the fullness of (or baptism in) the Holy Spirit" (John 1:29; Acts 1:8); and,
- growing them in the truth of God's Word through Bible teaching and preaching (Matt. 4:4, I Pet. 2:2).

The second of those three is distinguished by the expectation that this experience will generally include "receiving your prayer language"—that is, being enabled by the Holy Spirit to "speak in tongues."

There is no way to discount the place of "speaking with tongues" when we look at both the birth and the development of the Charismatic Century. It is a subject inescapably present with the birth of the Church, and manifestly renewed in dimensional participation by multitudes with the break-through that took place with the onset of the Holy Spirit's movements this past century. In that light, the Charismatic Century sooner or later brings those who examine it to their own "moment"—a moment of truth, asking: "What do you think about 'tongues'?" Or more specifically, "Would you be willing to discover how enriching this resource can be to your prayer life?" Let's look at questions commonly asked . . . or better, misconceptions often present for lack of biblical under-standing.

1. Q: What is "speaking with tongues"?
    A: Speaking in tongues is an enablement given freely by the Holy Spirit of God to any who welcome His fullness and overflow, its first expression usually being words unknown to the speaker but words of worship to God's praise (Acts 2:11). It is not the product of human understanding but it is at the choice or invitation of the human will. Since the speaker most commonly is worshipping in a language unknown to those hearing it, it will not be recognized—hence, the tendency of mockers to suggest it is "gibberish."

2. Q: Why is the experience called "the baptism in the Holy Spirit"?

A: Because Jesus' multi-faceted ministry distinctly references His role as the One who "Baptizes with the Holy Spirit" (John 1:33), and that this is revealed as a distinct and separate ministry from His role as "The Lamb of God who takes away the sin of the world" (John 1:29). Further, Jesus Himself used the term when He promised His disciples that "you shall be baptized with the Holy Spirit" (Acts 1:5).

3. Q: Doesn't I Corinthians 12:13 say we are baptized by the Holy Spirit when we receive Jesus as Savior?

A: Being filled with (or baptized in) the Holy Spirit is, as noted in #2, an action of Jesus as Baptizer. It is distinct and separate from a person's new birth, when the Holy Spirit "baptizes" (i.e. spiritually immerses) the individual into the body (family) of Christ. While one's new birth and baptism in the Holy Spirit may chronologically occur in immediate proximity, these experiences are neither simultaneous nor synonymous (Acts 9:17; 10:44-48).

4. Q: Why is experiencing the "baptism in the Holy Spirit" so important?

A: Being filled with or baptized in the Holy Spirit is important because Jesus commanded that His disciples expect and receive this experience. The "experience" is the entry point, but the continuing purpose of this baptism is to provide spiritual power for living, serving and bearing witness to

Christ. Further, this baptism is biblically accompanied by supernatural signs, indicating an entry into a lifestyle of faith and expectancy of the Holy Spirit's abiding fullness, enabling presence and powerful resourcing (Acts 10:46; 11:15-18; 2:4; I Corinthians 12:7-11).

    5. Q: Is speaking with tongues a onetime experience or continual?

A: It is clear from the apostle's teaching on this practice that it is ongoing, practical, beneficial and desirable. Indeed, since the NT text so commonly links believers speaking with tongues to their being "filled with" or "receiving" the Holy Spirit, there is every reason for each believer to expect this spiritual resource (a) as worthy expression of praise to God (Acts 2:11), (b) as fulfilling one of the signs Jesus said would characterize believers (Mark 16:15-19), (c) as timelessly available (Acts 2:4; 10:44-48; 19:1-6), and (d) as continually nurturing and practical (I Cor. 14:3; Jude 20).

These biblically-based answers make it clear why Pentecostal-Charismatics welcome this experience and urge every believer to receive the same, noting "the promise is unto you, and to your children, and to all who are afar off, as many as the Lord our God will call" (Acts 2:39). The blessing of speaking with tongues is meant for daily, private worship and prayer, benefiting and edifying the daily life of the believer. It is the "breath" of prayer that accompanies the "food" of daily Bible reading, enabling a fruitful life of service, as Jesus promised, with "rivers of living water" continually flowing forth from a life filled with, praying in, serving by and witnessing with supernatural ability (John 7:37-39).

Perhaps you, dear reader, have been "brought to this moment" and have either never received the fullness of the Holy Spirit, or possibly have neglected opening to the rich benefits of "spiritual language"—that is, "speaking with tongues." If your heart is open and desires to receive Jesus' promise, "Blessed are those who hunger and thirst after righteousness, for they shall be filled," then come to Him now. This helpful prayer may assist your coming to Him:

A Prayer for Inviting the Lord to Fill You with the Holy Spirit

Dear Lord Jesus,

I thank You and praise You for Your great love and faithfulness to me.

My heart is filled with joy whenever I think of the great gift of salvation You have so freely given to me,

And I humbly glorify You, Lord Jesus, for You have forgiven me all my sins and brought me to the Father.

Now I come in obedience to Your call.

I want to receive the fullness of the Holy Spirit.

I do not come because I am worthy myself, but because You have invited me to come.

Because You have washed me from my sins, I thank You that You have made the vessel of my life a worthy one to be filled with the Holy Spirit of God.

I want to be overflowed with Your life, Your love and Your power, Lord Jesus.

I want to show forth Your grace, Your words, Your goodness and Your gifts to everyone I can.

And so with simple, childlike faith, I ask You, Lord, fill me with the Holy Spirit. I open all of myself to You to receive all of Yourself in me.

I love You, Lord, and I lift my voice in praise to You.

I welcome Your might and Your miracles to be manifested in me for Your glory and unto Your praise.

I'm not asking you to say "amen" at the end of this prayer, because after inviting Jesus to fill you, it is good to begin to praise Him in faith. Praise and worship Jesus, simply allowing the Holy Spirit to help you do so. He will manifest Himself in a Christ-glorifying way, and you can ask Him to enrich this moment by causing you to know the presence and power of the Lord Jesus. Don't hesitate to expect the same things in your experience as occurred to people in the Bible. The spirit of praise is an appropriate way to express that expectation; and to make Jesus your focus, worship as you praise. Glorify Him and leave the rest to the Holy Spirit.

6

Aimee, America, and Pentecostalism

In the ten years following the Azusa Street revival the Pentecostal movement grew from a small revival in Los Angeles to a worldwide movement. In America it spread throughout several states and regional Pentecostal centers were established. It also gained its share of critics and outright opponents. America was changing and so was Pentecostalism, and for that matter, the entire Christian church. The nation encountered the First World War and its aftermath. Then there were the "roaring twenties" followed by the Great Depression. The uncertainties brought about from the gathering clouds foreshadowing another global conflict cast their shadow as well. The decades between the world wars were a turbulent time filled with a mix of euphoria and despair for Americans.

The Christian church in the U.S. faced these challenges along with its own. None was greater than the battle over modernism. Reaching back into the nineteenth century, the influence of the higher criticism of the Bible coming out of the German universities deeply impacted American theological education and captured many Christian leaders. Modernists questioned the authority of the Bible, questioned the historicity of the Gospels, including the virgin birth, miracles, and physical resurrection of Jesus Christ. The more conservative branches of the church, led most loudly by many of the radical groups that presaged Pentecostalism, vigorously opposed these "modern" ways.

This led to a great struggle for control of the seminaries and ministry training institutions of the church. The battle raged in the first three decades of the twentieth century and birthed the fundamentalist movement. The term "fundamentalism" came from a series of books that were published from 1910 through 1915 that defended traditional, conservative Christian beliefs. At the time fundamentalists did not always fit the intolerant, hyper-conservative stereotypical connotation so often applied to them today. Many of the early fundamentalists in the 1920s were simply defending historic Christian doctrine against an assault by the modernists. J. Gresham Machen, a Presbyterian seminary professor, disliked the term fundamentalist—as many did—yet led a vigorous life-consuming challenge to what he believed was a threat to the very heart of the Christian faith: the trustworthiness of the Bible. It proved to be a significant transitional time for the church in America.

During this time no person was more visible in American religion than the evangelist/pastor Aimee Semple McPherson and her life is a lens to observe the changes in the Pentecostal movement. She was without question the most well-known Christian leader in America during this time and arguably one of the most important of the century. Her story both foreshadows and illustrates Pentecostalism's struggle for acceptance while maintaining its distinctives. But before looking at Aimee we need to consider what Pentecostals were facing in the movement's second decade.

CRITICISM

The rich and varied seedbed from which Pentecostalism sprang was also fertile soil for its critics. The Keswick and Wesleyan holiness streams, streams that more than any other spawned Pentecostal ideology, also spawned many of its most passionate opponents. Though these radical evangelical groups agreed on so many points, the insistence by many Pentecostals on evidential tongues became the spark that lit the fires of controversy.[1]

The Keswick stream had emphasized Spirit baptism as empowerment for service, and evangelist D. L. Moody was its most notable spokesman in the U.S. R. A. Torrey, a longtime associate of Moody and pastor of Moody Memorial Church in Chicago, championed the importance of Spirit baptism. As with many others at the close of the nineteenth century, Torrey argued that the baptism with the Holy Spirit was separate and distinct from regeneration. In his words, "One can be regenerated and still not be baptized in the Holy Spirit."[2] He also believed one would know whether they had received the experience or not. In his view it was not primarily about holiness—and certainly not eradication of the sin nature—but about empowerment for witness and service. Still published today under the title of *The Baptism of the Holy Spirit*, Torrey's book, while not advocating tongues, utilized language that Pentecostals later adopted (the book is still used by many non-Wesleyan Pentecostals as an introduction to Spirit baptism).

This is somewhat ironic considering Torrey's rather vocal and vigorous opposition to Pentecostalism. For Torrey the notion of evidential tongues was offensive since he believed Spirit baptism could be manifested in different ways. Though Torrey was convinced that the movement was theologically flawed, he seemed more put off by reported cases of moral failure among Pentecostal leaders.

Torrey was not alone in his dislike of Pentecostalism. Evangelist and Bible teacher H. I. "Harry" Ironside, who pastored at Moody Memorial after Torrey, questioned Pentecostalism and rejected it, concerned over an emotionalism and enthusiasm he thought were driving some people mad.

British Bible teacher and longtime pastor of Westminster Chapel in London, G. Campbell Morgan, called the Pentecostal movement the "last vomit of Satan."[3] British leader Jesse Penn-Lewis called Pentecostalism a demonic attack on the church and harangued Pentecostals as the "poorer class."[4] There were scattered and occasional acts of vandalism to property and even fewer assaults on people, but for the most part the opposition was a spirited war of words. The unprecedented growth of Pentecostalism makes all the more strange the charge by some that Pentecostalism was just a passing fad.

Some of the strongest opposition came from the Wesleyan holiness camp. One of the early critics was Holiness pastor Alma White who took a direct swing at William Seymour. It seems that when Seymour left Texas for California early in 1906 to take his new assignment, he traveled through Denver, Colorado, and visited White's Pillar of Fire holiness church there. In extremely derogatory terms she lamented that Pentecostalism was started by a "black man"[5] and derided Seymour personally. Published in 1919, her booklet *Demon and Tongues* denounced the movement as a demonically inspired heresy.

A number of the small, newly formed holiness associations and denominations either opposed Pentecostalism or were split by it. Pheneas Bresee, as mentioned in chapter four, was a strong opponent of Pentecostalism in the Los Angeles area and his Pentecostal Church of the Nazarene denomination harshly criticized the young movement. Bresee believed the movement too small to be of consequence. Not wanting to be identified by the growing movement it felt was in error, the holiness denomination dropped "Pentecostal" from its name in 1919. The Salvation Army and several other smaller holiness groups distanced themselves from the Pentecostals as well.

A. B. Simpson, founder and leader of the Christian Missionary Alliance (CMA), struggled to fashion a response to a movement his ideology helped birth. Simpson had formulated what he called the "Fourfold Gospel" in which Jesus was Savior, Sanctifier, Healer, and Coming King. As a part of the Keswick "higher life" movement, Simpson was expecting a "latter rain" revival with a restoration of the gifts of the Spirit including tongues "as in Acts."[6] Typical of restorationists,

Simpson believed the book of Acts provided a normal pattern for the church. He was very much in the "two-stage" camp, advocating first regeneration followed by a subsequent Spirit baptism. Simpson's influence on the developing pneumatology (doctrine of the Holy Spirit) at the end of the nineteenth century was significant and by 1900 he had established a large following of leaders and churches.

When the Pentecostal movement erupted, many of the people associated with Simpson were understandably interested in the "latter rain" restoration of tongues popularized by the new movement. Simpson was initially open to the new message but after seeking the gift of tongues for himself to no avail, he became increasingly cautious and critical. By that time a considerable number of CMA folk were swept into Pentecostalism. At first Alliance leaders tried to accommodate Pentecostals because of the positive reports of healings and supernatural activities. Eventually, however, concerns about excessive emotionalism and overemphasis on tongues as initial evidence brought more direct confrontation with those who had embraced the Pentecostal message.

Simpson's major concern centered on the demand that speaking in tongues created an unnecessary "preoccupation with the spiritual manifestations rather than cultivating a devotion of God. . . ."[7] He also criticized the idea of tongues as xenoglossa (or missionary tongues). Simpson and other leaders within his movement were concerned about the division Pentecostals were causing in CMA churches. Nevertheless, Simpson and CMA leaders continued to maintain a distanced appreciation for the deepened spiritual passion evident in their members who were Spirit baptized and spoke with tongues. In 1914, CMA leadership took a position that acknowledged speaking with tongues as a gift that "in many cases" occurred in Acts when people were baptized with the Holy Spirit; but they rejected any notion that tongues were an essential sign to the experience.[8]

The net result was that many of those convinced of the initial evidence position left the CMA, and the denomination, without directly forcing anyone out, became less tolerant of Pentecostals in their midst. The CMA has become known for its position of "seek not, forbid not" as it relates to the gift of tongues, the practical result being that few in the CMA speak with tongues.

While most opposition to Pentecostalism was coming from the more radical evangelical groups, many conservative and mainline churches either ignored or were unaware of Pentecostals in the early years of the movement. Whatever the case, they were less vocal with their concerns. Many of these churches were too embroiled in the debate over modernism to be caught up in battling Pentecostalism. Most Americans were unaware of the movement or saw it as an odd religious aberration.

Still, criticism and disaffection against Pentecostals forced them to define themselves rather than leave it to their critics. The Pentecostal aversion to creeds gave way to pragmatism. They needed to more clearly articulate what they believed and they did so in more formal creedal statements. In many instances the debate also made Pentecostals even more partisan and defensive. They saw themselves as being persecuted for what they believed to be faithfulness to Scripture—of course the other side felt they were equally faithful.

More than ever Pentecostal rhetoric called for separation from the world. Critics were often accused of committing the unpardonable sin by resisting the Holy Spirit. Strident defenses were accompanied by calls to holy living that seemed to lead to legalism and self-righteousness. In 1917, Pentecostalism was widespread but small, and in North America, it was increasingly culturally isolated.

It is also important to remember the internal controversies we explored in our last chapter, namely the finished work struggle and Oneness controversy that had by 1916 divided Pentecostals into several camps. In addition, since the movement's conception was linked to Parham's Pentecostal formula— the idea that Spirit baptism is evidenced by tongues—there were those who challenged the formula. This issue created further strains as Pentecostals attempted to explain just who they were in the face of growing scrutiny. All through the Charismatic Century there would be continued debate about evidential tongues.

Pastor and evangelist F. F. Bosworth was a key figure in the debate in the Assemblies of God. Bosworth was baptized with the Spirit when Charles Parham first visited Dowie's Zion, Illinois, in 1906. Bosworth wènt on to plant a Pentecostal church in the Dallas, Texas, area. In 1912, he hosted Maria Woodworth-Etter's crusade that lasted for several months.

The revival brought Bosworth national recognition and in

1914 he was appointed to the executive presbytery of the newly formed Assemblies of God. Already somewhat controversial by his support of African-Americans and his racially integrated meetings, Bosworth became a major voice for those in the new denomination who valued tongues speech but believed it was only *one* of the signs of Spirit baptism. After realizing his position would not win out, he quietly and respectfully withdrew from the Assemblies of God in 1918. The challenge to the initial evidence doctrine tended to make the emerging classical Pentecostals even more strident in its defense, which added to their sectarian tendencies.

AIMEE SEMPLE McPHERSON

Pentecostal evangelist Aimee Semple McPherson launched out in ministry in the midst of this milieu of change and flux. Beginning in 1915 with small meetings, she inaugurated three decades of ministry that made her a celebrity and birthed a new Pentecostal denomination.[9] Her ministry was one of the first bridges connecting Pentecostalism to mainstream America and was a harbinger of the shape of post–World War II neo-Pentecostalism.

We first met Aimee at Durham's Chicago North Avenue Mission. She and her new husband Robert Semple spent a year at Durham's mission before going off to China to serve as missionaries. Arriving in Hong Kong in June of 1910, both Robert and Aimee contracted malaria after a trip into China and

Robert died in August. Aimee was only nineteen years old and eight months pregnant when Robert died. She was left alone to bear her daughter in Hong Kong in September.

Looking Back

Aimee Elizabeth Kennedy was born on October 9, 1890 on a farm near Ingersoll, Ontario, Canada. Her father was a Methodist but it was her mother Minnie's Salvation Army culture that was most impacting, leaving a deep impression on Aimee's emerging faith. The Army's uniforms, bands, and use of theatrics provided a colorful and creative backdrop for evangelism.

Aimee's quick wit and verbal skill were soon evident. Troubled by doubts after hearing teaching in high school on evolution, she decided to believe the Bible over evolution and became an able spokeswoman for the biblical creation story. Still, Aimee was caught between the more rigid faith demands of her mother's Salvation Army's holiness code and her desire to be involved in the social life of Ingersoll. Her attractive flair and youthful exuberance made for many friends. It was in the midst of this struggle in December 1907 that Aimee attended a Pentecostal revival meeting. There she was fascinated by the "Irish lilt" Pentecostal evangelist Robert Semple and his message about the baptism of the Holy Spirit and speaking with tongues. More than anything she came under conviction that she needed to fully surrender her life to Christ, even if it meant forsaking the social life she loved.

After several days of struggle Aimee yielded her life to God's call. Not long after her commitment she was Spirit baptized and spoke with tongues. Aimee came to believe God was calling her to be an evangelist and when Robert Semple proposed to her in 1908, she accepted. The two were married in August in a Salvation Army ceremony at her parent's home. After a short stay in Stratford, Ontario, they planted a church in London, Ontario, and by early 1909 they were in Chicago with Durham.

Early Years of Ministry

After Robert's death in Hong Kong, Aimee returned to New York City in the fall of 1910 with her infant daughter Roberta. Together with her mother she served in a Salvation Army rescue mission. While in New York City she met businessman Harold McPherson, and after moving to Chicago, Aimee and McPherson were married in October 1911. For the next three years Aimee was involved in raising her daughter Roberta and her new son Rolf Potter McPherson, born in March, 1913.

In the winter of 1913 Aimee had a serious illness and was hospitalized. In her struggle to recover she believed God was signaling to her that she had to recommit to an evangelistic call. In July 1915, when her husband Harold, though having earlier agreed to her evangelistic call, objected to her decision to reenter ministry, they separated briefly. Harold eventually joined Aimee and they ministered together for a season with her husband working in the background, helping organize his wife's gifted public ministry.

The ministry had begun. The McPhersons purchased a tent

and started off on the evangelistic circuit. They traveled about in the "Gospel Car" covered with various Bible verses and slogans. The family barely survived with the small offerings they received. The rigorous and demanding life of itinerant evangelism was hard on the marriage and Harold decided that it was not the life he wanted. The couple reached an agreement to part. Aimee, insistant of her call, was irrevocable and irresistible. Aimee hoped the two would one day reunite but Harold divorced Aimee in 1921. Neither ever spoke unkindly of the other throughout their lifetimes.

Expanding Ministry

From 1915 to 1921 Aimee crisscrossed the nation by car and rail, accompanied by her mother Minnie and often her two children. Slowly her evangelistic campaigns grew and by 1921 she was becoming a sensation everywhere. Along with good news of forgiveness of sins through a relationship with Jesus Christ, she preached the Pentecostal message of the baptism of the Holy Spirit and speaking with tongues. Although Aimee's "Foursquare Gospel" message of Jesus as Savior, baptizer in the Holy Spirit, Healer and Coming King would not be expressed as such until 1922, it was already forming. Healing became a central part of her meetings and by 1919 people were flocking to her meetings to be healed of their sicknesses and afflictions. Aimee steadfastly maintained she was not a healer, Jesus Christ was. Testimonies of healings and miracles became part and parcel to her crusades and she was soon filling the largest auditoriums in city after city. In 1917 she began publishing *The*

Bridal Call, a monthly publication that popularized her teachings and helped develop her support base.

Some of the healing stories were spectacular to say the least. Crippled people from birth walked; the deaf had their hearing restored. A 1920 healing of a boy in Washington, D. C., stands out as an example. The little boy was carried forward by his mother so the evangelist could pray for him. As the evangelist started to pray for the child:

She rubbed the twisted flesh of his knees and thighs . . . she took his wrists and his hands high over his head. Three men in black suits mumbled around him while Aimee held his wrists. Suddenly he felt pulled up from his knees, by a draft, toward the ceiling. He stood on straight legs, not legs that he could remember, and took firm steps toward his mother,

"My God! Look at my son! He walks…" The [mother's] lower lip trembled; she began crying; she picked her child up and held him in her arms, kissing him.

When she put him down, the boy started out into the aisle. He hesitated at first, then walked faster, and gradually began to run. . . .

"Look, mama, look," he cried out, "see how I can run! Oh, mama, see! You're crying . . . but look, mama, I can run and it doesn't hurt me either."[10]

Stories like this were not unusual as Aimee would often pray for hours over the sick until each one had received a personal touch, leaving her exhausted by the end of the service. Over a series of meetings she would literally pray for thousands. Always the proclamation of salvation in Jesus Christ was central with hundreds converted.

Los Angeles and Angelus Temple

After a very successful crusade in Los Angeles at the end of 1918, land and money were provided for a home that was built for her, Minnie, and the children, fulfilling an earlier vision Aimee had. A nanny was also provided so that Aimee and her mother could travel without always taking the children. Already attracted to the people and climate of Southern California, Aimee not only found a home for the family but a base for her ministry. As she later told it, God directed her to "build a house unto the Lord in Los Angeles." Weary from the road in the summer of 1920, Aimee was back in Southern California for some time of rest. While there she felt drawn to Echo Park in Los Angeles where she and her mother found a plot of land. She sketched rough plans for a church building on the site and later that year the land was purchased. In January 1921 *The Bridal Call* announced "Echo Park Revival Tabernacle to be Erected in Los Angeles."[11]

The original plan was to build a wooden structure seating twenty-five hundred people but the burgeoning ministry throughout 1921 soon forced revised plans of a marble structure seating over five thousand.[12] In September 1921 Aimee incorporated the Echo Park Evangelistic Association in Los Angeles to support her expanding operation. All the more remarkable when one considers that women could not even vote until 1922.

Aimee was known early on for her speaking ability. She was said to hold her audiences "spellbound" preaching for an hour or more. The increasing publicity by the press only increased the crowds at her meetings. Significantly, her ministry drew the support of many non-Pentecostal pastors and church leaders. Though ordained with the young Pentecostal denomination the Assemblies of God as an evangelist in 1919, she had strong support among Methodists and from many Baptists also.

At a time when Pentecostals were drawing fire from many quarters, McPherson escaped much of the scathing attack. Part of this was due to her call for unity around the essentials of the gospel. Another reason churches supported her ministry was that at her crusades, converts and others who responded to altar calls filled out cards and were then referred to existing local churches. She also sought to tone down in her services some of the hyper-emotionalism common in early Pentecostal meetings, occasionally stopping some outbursts. Further, over time, Aimee would challenge both the excesses of Pentecostalism and the cold spirituality of much of the mainstream church. Her message resonated with the grassroots believers. Many saw her as a restorer of the true gospel message as she proclaimed according to Hebrews 13:8, "Jesus the same yesterday, and today, and forever." She was preaching a gospel of hope and people responded.

Her moderated Pentecostal stance was not received well by

the Assemblies of God where she held ministerial credentials. At first, during the initial period of her return to ministry, the Assemblies' publication *Pentecostal Evangel* carried stories of Aimee's meetings; they were glad to call her their own. In 1920 she spoke at the Assemblies of God General Council. At the same time, Aimee was wrestling with just how to maintain a connection to churches outside the Pentecostal movement. Perhaps because of this concern she removed the word "Pentecostal" from the top banner of her publication.[13] This did not sit well with some Pentecostals.

Aimee's relationships with other churches, particularly her acceptance in 1920 of ministerial license credentials from the Methodist Church, brought increasing suspicion of her Pentecostal pedigree by a number of Pentecostal leaders and added to the criticisms, along with her decision to quiet some Pentecostal manifestations in her meetings. Disputes over property ownership at the construction of the Los Angeles building finally brought her to decide to conclude her denominational affiliation in January 1922.

Throughout that year, construction continued on the building and Aimee continued her evangelistic travels, including a trip to Australia. During a particularly successful crusade in Oakland, California, she preached on the text in Ezekiel 1:4-10 and declared the "Foursquare Gospel." As she talked of the four living creatures the prophet describes, she said the four faces of each creature, a man, a lion, an ox, and an eagle, typified the full orbed ministry of Jesus: respectively, Christ the Savior, Christ the Baptizer with the Spirit, Christ the Healer, and Christ the Coming King. In her parlance this "foursquare gospel" replaced "full gospel." This became her Pentecostal message.

On January 1, 1923, Angelus Temple, at a cost of $1,500,000, was dedicated with great fanfare. The cornerstone of the building carried the theme that caused McPherson added trouble with some Pentecostals. It read: "Dedicated unto the cause of interdenominational and World Wide Evangelism" (the problem word was interdenominational). Over the next many years Aimee would profoundly influence the Los Angeles area, and although traveling far less, her life and ministry would continue to capture national attention.

That same year she started a training institute—later called Lighthouse for International Foursquare Evangelism (LIFE)— based at the Temple for future evangelists, missionaries and pastors. In 1924, the ministry started a radio station, KFSG, to help spread the Foursquare message. The church also initiated international missions enterprise.

McPherson's ministry reached across the classes in the area. The rich, the middle class, the poor all helped fill Angelus Temple's meetings. People lined up hours ahead of scheduled services and it was not unusual for thousands to be turned away. Aimee's services were colorful, theatrical, and dynamic. The music was excellent and her sermons captivating. She regularly preached "illustrated" sermons where she employed dramatic props to clarify her message. In one of her most famous illustrated sermons, Aimee, dressed as a police officer, drove a motorcycle onto the stage, screeched to a halt, and jumped off the bike, blew a police whistle, and shouted, "Stop, you're going to hell."[14] The people loved it.

The church ran a commissary that provided food and clothing to the needy, endearing her to thousands during the Depression years. Reflecting the ethos of early Pentecostalism and William J. Seymour, the commissary gave to all regardless of race or creed. Aimee frequently championed the working class, calling for "higher wages and greater benefits for police and firefighters. . . . "[15] She "railed against organized crime" and her ministry often liberated women from prostitution.[16] Aimee argued for the role of women in ministry and was a strong voice for the disenfranchised. Her work drew admiration from all cultures and economic strata.

Her interdenominational cooperation continued and she sought to work with other churches and groups whenever possible. Her Angelus Temple meetings were attended by Methodists Baptists, Roman Catholics, Presbyterians and the like. In fact, her earliest vision for the Temple was that it would be a place for people from all churches to attend and then go back to their churches with the Foursquare Gospel. When she started the Bible institute at Angelus Temple she convinced Methodist Frank Thompson, author of the *Thompson Chain Reference Bible*, to help lead the school although he was not a Pentecostal.

She spoke into the Fundamentalist/modernist battle by publicly supporting William Jennings Bryan in the 1925 Scopes trail. Bryan showed his gratitude by contributing to McPherson's *Bridal Call*.[17] In sermons Aimee decried the Christians who attacked the authority of Scripture through biblical criticism. The Angelus Temple ministry, by taking a stand against modernism, maintained a cooperative relationship with the fundamentalist Bible Institute of Los Angeles (BIOLA), despite obvious theological differences. McPherson was not the cloistered Pentecostal characteristic of her day.

While still working with different denominations, McPherson realized she had created a huge following that needed to be organized. By the time she formally incorporated the International Church of the Foursquare Gospel in December 1927, it was already a substantial movement. Thousands attended Angelus Temple as their home church and there were numerous branch churches associated with her ministry. Often in her evangelistic travels, despite encouraging converts to attend existing local churches, small mission churches formed, attracted to the uniqueness of her Pentecostal message.

Difficulties

During the 1920s Aimee Semple McPherson was as much a celebrity in Los Angeles as anyone in Hollywood. She was constantly in the news and at the peak of her popularity. "Sister" as she was called by her followers, became the subject of even greater national attention when she suddenly disappeared on May 19, 1926, while swimming at a Southern California beach. Her mother and many close associates were convinced she had drowned, although her body had not been found. Nearly a month later an elaborate memorial service was held for Aimee, where thousands came to pay her tribute. Three days later, she wandered in from the desert, reporting to the Douglas, Arizona, police that she had been kidnapped and held for ransom in Mexico since her abduction. She had escaped her captors who fled before any could be found.

When she returned by rail to Los Angeles on June 26, a crowd of over fifty thousand gathered at the train station, with another 100 thousand lining the route to Angelus Temple. Her supporters were thrilled to have her back. Sensationalized speculation by the press rumored of a possible affair. Once she reappeared the accusations only grew worse in the press. A grand jury investigation found nothing to charge McPherson with but a zealous district attorney, insistent Aimee was not being truthful, brought perjury and obstruction of justice charges against her. These were later dropped for lack of any evidence. The publicity and ridicule still shadows her memory today even though her accusers were discredited, her account was never disproved, and her case was dismissed.

Despite all the press coverage the crowds continued to flock to the Temple services and Aimee was still trusted by most of her supporters. She continued to preach as many as twenty times a week, while maintaining a grueling schedule in writing, organizing, radio broadcasting, and traveling. The wear and tear by 1930 led to a nervous breakdown that sidelined her for a season. In 1931, both her children married. Tired and lonely, Aimee married David Sutton, a misguided relationship that ended in divorce in just two and a half years. Still, Angelus Temple was a beacon of hope during the 1930s. The commissary, despite financial strains created by the masses it served, was a lifesaver to thousands suffering with the rest of America during the dark Depression days.

Aimee proved ever resilient. Although criticized by secular and religious sources, her ministry continued notwithstanding periodic health problems the last fifteen years of her life. After a 1936 trip around the world Aimee came home to America expressing deep concern over the rising fascism in Europe and the threat it brought to world peace. When WWII broke out Aimee championed the purchase of war bonds, especially honored armed service personnel who attended services at the Temple, and continued to preach the Gospel of the saving, healing, empowering, soon-returning savior, Jesus Christ. This message of hope resonated with the masses. She did lose the support of some non-Pentecostal leaders because of her difficulties, but people from all denominations came to her meetings, read her books, and listened to her on the radio.

On a September 1944 trip back to Oakland, the city where Aimee first framed publicly her Foursquare message in 1922, she told an audience of ten thousand about the origins of her message years earlier there in Oakland. The crowd was moved and her ministry seemed on a new upsurge. To the shock of many, the next day, on September 27, Aimee's weakened body succumbed to an apparent accidental overdose of her regular prescription medication. Thousands attended her memorial services as multitudes across the nation mourned her passing.

PERSPECTIVES

Whatever one's assessment of the life of Aimee Semple McPherson, she left an imprint. She was more than a religious celebrity. McPherson proved herself a most capable female leader in a world dominated by men. In many ways, whether consciously or not, she continued the vision of her Los Angeles fellow, William J. Seymour. Aimee's Angelus Temple ministry embodied in substantial ways the ethos of Azusa Street with its emphasis on ministry to all people, especially the marginalized. Her ecumenical work, while hindered in later years by adverse publicity, aimed at what Seymour called for: all Christians united in the Holy Spirit.

The irony of her ecumenical work was clear when the National Association of Evangelicals (NAE) formed in 1943. The association of some forty conservative Christian denominations formed in part because of the unhappiness of some over the hyper-separatism of Fundamentalists, who were increasingly divisive and harsh in tone during the 1930s in their battle against modernism and liberal theology. Preferring the term evangelicals, the NAE, still committed to biblical authority and historic Christian doctrine, wanted to present a more moderate and conciliatory tone. In order to create a more united front for a common voice, the group hoped that peripheral theological issues could be set aside. Among the founding denominations were Pentecostals who once objected to McPherson's cooperation with non-Pentecostal groups, and when McPherson's Foursquare Church applied for acceptance in the NAE, the group delayed the decision so long that Foursquare leaders withdrew the application in frustration. The Foursquare Church did reapply in 1952 and was accepted long after McPherson's passing.

At the very least, McPherson set a trajectory of cooperation and unity years earlier, that other Pentecostals now followed. Maturity brought a new appreciation for the breadth of the body of Christ and the need for unity. Aimee also demonstrated that Pentecostals could function in the mainstream and be accepted. In many ways she was a kind of proto-charismatic. Whatever the case, by 1945, Pentecostalism was evolving in new ways. At the same time it was changing, voices were calling for new dimensions of renewal. This we will explore in our next chapter.

BROUGHT TO THIS MOMENT:

In Light of the Increased Place Given Women In Ministry

No one person more characterized "Holy Spirit-filled ministry" during the 1920-1930 decade than Aimee Semple McPherson. She not only stood head and shoulders above any other woman of her time in renown, but her leadership as a woman in a male dominated world placed her apart—as a mouthpiece for moral values, as an instrument of social action and as a preacher and healing evangelist of amazing impact.

But the phenomenon of Aimee Semple McPherson's ministry as it is remembered today is not usually related to the almost incredible flow of miracles that attended her healing ministry, or in the multitudes that came to Christ through her preaching ministry, or in the "ahead of her time" creativity in communications that is common today but brought her criticism as being unduly "novel" or "flamboyant." Rather, it is phenomenal that the record of her life and leadership is clouded by a fog of misinformation that recycles and perpetuates itself to this day.

This pattern began in her lifetime, finding its place in society at large in an era when "yellow journalism" was more common than today. Today, newspapers are held to a greater social accountability for accurate reporting than during the "Roaring 20s" when daily papers more characterized the contrived and superficial traits of today's tabloids.

While admired by hosts of the general public, she nonetheless bore the brunt of prejudicial comment by reason of the facts:

1. she was a *woman* evangelist [and thereby frowned on by much of the ecclesiastical community of her time]; and,
2. she was a *Pentecostal* [with a miracle-filled, charismatic ministry [at a time when traditional evangelicalism raised its most vigorous assaults upon those "tongue speaking holy rollers"].

Today it is still true—so much of the Church still lives in the ensconced prejudice against women in pulpit ministry. It's another issue that must be "brought to a moment" of confrontation with the balance that God's Word presents on the subject. The breakthrough of the Holy Spirit that has extended great grace through the last 100 years brought with it a new place for the possibilities of women in leading Church roles.

The voice of women allowed in the Pentecostal church resulted from more than merely the success of the women's suffrage movement, just as the place of women in today's charismatic community is not the fruit of the feminist movement. Rather, across and throughout the century, more and more women were released to public ministry as the Holy Spirit unchained whole sectors of the Church from biblical blindness on the subject.

For example, the two oldest arguments *against* women teaching or speaking in church have been I Corinthians 14:34 and I Timothy 2:11, 12:

- "Let your women keep silent in the churches, for they are not permitted to speak, but they are to be submissive, as the law says."
- "Let a woman learn in silence with all submission. And I do not permit a woman to teach or to have authority over a man."

Objectivity with honesty is opening the door to women as an unprejudiced, forthright look at the whole passage increasingly takes effect. The timeless fact is that the context clearly indicates that the male-female *domestic* relationship is being referenced. Both of these passages are relating to married couples! First Corinthians 14:35 and First Timothy 2:13-15, respectively, reference (a) husband and wife speaking at home [I Cor. 14:35], while (b) it is consistent with the I Tim. 2:11-15 passage to see it as a continuum, describing a married couple. [Those familiar with the Greek *aner* are aware it may be translated "husband" as well as "man," and since Adam and Eve are used to illustrate the point, it requires prejudice to insist this passage is socially generic rather than domestically specific.] Note: This also makes clear why v. 15 changes from singular ("she") to the plural ("they"). The *married couple* is addressed throughout the passage.

Not only do these texts, so commonly quoted, *not* subordinate women to men (i.e., the female of the species to all male counterparts) neither do they provide grounds for silencing a woman's preaching-teaching gift when males are present. However, beyond the immediate subject, it *is* important to note that each passage *does* contain guidelines that establish issues of *order* and *leadership* within biblically-based marriage relationships—focusing the husband's duty to lead in a servant spirit, and for the wife to partner with his leadership in a quiet-spirited way.

All this provides a biblical basis for "ongoing reformation" in regard to the Church's view of women in ministry. The Charismatic Century, among other things, has demonstrated a new stance in the matter—brought beyond the historic male chauvinism so common in the Church. And it has not been either the result of a casual attitude toward the Scripture, nor in a reduction of continuing careful regard for biblical revelation concerning God's divine order for the husband-wife relationship.

The above, elaborated by means of a close look at the Greek text, was not what occasioned the earliest breakout of a more biblical attitude—one permitting women ministerial license as

pastors, evangelists and teachers. It was merely a case of yielding to the unavoidable simplicity found in the Word of God,
which declares in His "last days" outpouring of the Holy Spirit
would release a new place for women, as well as men. This
"release" is directly hinged to the era of the Holy Spirit's ministry, when God would *"pour out of My Spirit on all flesh; your
sons and your <u>daughters</u> shall prophesy, your young men shall see
visions, your old men shall dream dreams, and on My menservants
and <u>maidservants</u> I will pour out My Spirit in those days; and they
shall prophesy"* (Acts 2:17, 18; Joel 2:28, 29—emphasis added).

While an even broader body of Bible-based evidence might
be marshaled on the subject—evidence verifying God *never*
intended to reduce the potential of a woman's leadership
capacities—that is not the subject of this book. But what *is*
before us is the fact that the Charismatic Century has brought
the global Church to "a moment" regarding its willingness to
rethink its attitude toward women and church ministry. Honesty with the truth of God's readiness to deploy women as well
as men in the ministry of His Word, and to enable them for
ministry in the power of the Holy Spirit, is *not* a surrender
to the politicizing or animosities of militant feminism in our
culture.

Indeed, women in the Body of Christ should *never* be put at
a disadvantage or repressed by prejudice. Sadly, such behavior
on occasion seems to drive women toward a worldly, revulsive
or unladylike, reactive pushiness. But we have been brought to
this moment, and the twenty-first century *needs*—indeed, *cries
out* for churchmen to give place to churchwomen! The harvest

is too great, and the need for the versatility and variety of ministries too opportune, to overlook the great resources and gifts that the Creator has placed in *both* genders. And while integrity with God's Word does not require a 50-50 distribution of genders in the pulpits of the Church, it does call for a 100 percent readiness to permit the rise of each *called* and *gifted* woman . . . in our time.

We've been brought to this moment!

Oral Roberts and a
New Wave of Renewal

When William Seymour died on September 28, 1922, few outside his small church took notice. Forgotten by most Pentecostals, Seymour's desire to see the integration of the races through biblical church unity was a fading and unrealized vision in most of Pentecostalism.[1] In 1924 the Oneness denomination, the Pentecostal Assemblies of the World, the last remaining organized interracial fellowship of churches, split along racial lines. Pentecostalism now fully reflected the endemic segregation of American society and there would be very few exceptions over the next five decades.[2]

From the 1920s until after the Second World War, Pentecostals in America were in a time of transition and consolidation. It was a time of self-definition and yearning for broader acceptance. Like other radical Christian groups of the eighteenth and nineteenth centuries, Pentecostals were beginning the gradual journey toward moderation so characteristic of groups whose origins are on the fringes of society. It was not an easy trek.

The early enthusiasm of the revival bred fanaticism and self-righteousness in more than a few. Pentecostalism's rejection of the "world" helped add to their isolation, fostering rejection from those they rejected. The often hostile denouncements of Catholics and other "liberal" Christians created little sympathy for their cause. News of "snake-handling"—always an extremely rare practice—reinforced the stereotype many had of Pentecostals. Leaders like Aimee Semple McPherson, seeking to cast the full gospel message in a more inclusive light, were exceptions during the decades between the world wars.

The critical rhetoric of many Pentecostals was answered by harsh criticism as well. As already mentioned, many radical evangelicals who shared similar convictions with Pentecostals—minus evidential tongues and enthusiastic worship—were sharply critical. Some called speaking in tongues an outright demonic exercise and the movement itself a sign of apostasy. Others said tongues speech was the product of psychologically unstable people. Many fundamentalists openly called Pentecostalism "fanatical and unscriptural." It was an ironic criticism since Pentecostals supported the fundamentalist cause.

The period was also filled with many splits and divisions among Pentecostal churches. The tension between the Church's charismatic character and its institutional features was always present. Fellowships of churches would form only to have congregations break off with accusations of denominationalism. Relatively minor doctrinal differences would birth whole new movements. The Church of God split in a power struggle between the movement's leader A. J. Tomlinson and other leaders in the denomination. The resulting group, the "Tomlinson Church of God" was itself divided several times over the coming decades. Other groups divided over issues as trivial as whether it was worldly to wear neckties. Some divisions were more substantive and theological in nature. Arguments over whether divine healing was provided in the Atonement split Pentecostal groups. Disagreements over church government led to the creation of whole new movements. It was a far cry from the Azusa Street vision of a united church.

Nevertheless, Pentecostalism as a movement continued to grow if not spectacularly, then steadily. Still on the margins of American society, the hope-filled Pentecostal message evoked response particularly among working class and poor folk. Troubled times in the 1930s made for a ready audience. Pentecostals were most effective in reaching urban environments with their storefront churches and missions. Though the majority of Pentecostals were still drawn from the lower social classes of the economic ladder they were beginning their ascent into the middle class. As the Great Depression slowly gave way to FDR's New Deal and the mobilization for World War II, Pentecostals increasingly prospered. Pentecostals were square in the middle of the postwar boom that brought even greater prosperity.

By 1940 the harsh tone of criticism faded among some Pentecostal groups who recognized the need to be joined to the broader, Bible believing Christian community. As we saw in our last chapter, many Fundamentalists alienated themselves by condemning all who disagreed with their doctrinal litmus test. The 1943 formation of the National Association of Evangelicals (NAE) included several Pentecostal denominations, helping bring a new respectability in the eyes of many Christians.

Another important event that helped counter the earlier disunity among Pentecostal groups was the creation in 1948 of the Pentecostal Fellowship of North America (PFNA). Founding groups included the Assemblies of God, The Church of God, the Pentecostal Holiness Church, Open Bible Standard Church (all founding groups in the NAE), and the International Church of the Foursquare Gospel. Uniting around a common statement of faith the PFNA gave a new ecumenical shape to Pentecostalism. It was a significant step in overcoming the extreme sectarianism that characterized early Pentecostals. Still, it was only a step in the right direction. Absent from the PFNA were African-American Pentecostals and Oneness Pentecostals.

The tumultuous times of transition from 1906 to post–World War II America had changed the nation and it changed Pentecostalism. In the struggle to define themselves and organize their expanding movements, Pentecostals increasingly were forced to institutionalize, bringing both needed stability and the ire of some who remained deeply suspicious of denominations. Their internal strife and splits were painful to many in the movement. Accusations of emotionalism and fanaticism caused a quieting of emphasis on exuberant worship and the exercise of spiritual gifts in some Pentecostal circles.

The new economic prosperity became evident as Pentecostal churches built new buildings in nicer parts of town and their members gained a higher standing on the social ladder. For some it was a mark of success. For others it was a sign that the revival fires that birthed the movement were being extinguished by accommodation to the world. What is certain is that a large number of second and third generation Pentecostals were not as passionate about their faith as were the founders of the movement. Among many in the Pentecostal grassroots, however, there was a longing for a fresh wave of revival. Raised on stories of the Azusa Street revival, a new generation of Pentecostals was expecting a new outpouring of the Spirit. It was indeed on the way.

ORAL ROBERTS AND THE HEALING REVIVAL

Few individuals better illustrate the changing shape of Pentecostalism than the healing evangelist Oral Granville Roberts. Roberts' life and ministry symbolized the move of Pentecostals from the margins to the mainstream. Picking up where Aimee Semple McPherson left off, Roberts' emergence and growing popularity in post–World War II America signaled a radical rearrangement of the Christian landscape. He made it apparent that the message of the gospel was fully dimensioned, proclaiming the saving power and healing grace of Jesus Christ. This was not a gospel just for those disenfranchised from society, it was a message for all people everywhere.

While he was only one of a cadre of healing revivalists,

Roberts, more than any other, struck a resonant chord drawing all social classes to its sound and awakened a new groundswell of revival. His ministry also helped prepare the way for the Charismatic Renewal that later penetrated the Roman Catholic Church and the mainline Protestant denominations. His is a classic story of how God uses ordinary people in extraordinary ways.[3]

Born in 1918, Roberts, the son of a dirt poor Pentecostal Holiness preacher, was raised in the midst of hard times, facing the Depression in dustbowl Oklahoma. He contracted tuberculosis and was bedridden for months, deeply depressed by the ordeal. Roberts was miraculously healed in 1935 of both his tuberculosis and a stuttering condition that had long embarrassed him. He would go on to tell the story of this healing countless times in churches and crusades. Under the ministry of an itinerant Pentecostal evangelist, Roberts was not only healed but also sensed a call to ministry. He soon joined his father in ministry and Oral started a steady ascent in the Pentecostal Holiness denomination. Initially, he traveled as an evangelist and then pastored one of the largest churches in his denomination.

In 1947, after marrying Evelyn Lutman, Roberts left his Enid, Oklahoma, pastorate to take to the evangelistic circuit again, this time with greater emphasis on divine healing. He began his ministry just as William Branham was gaining national prominence as a healing evangelist. Together Branham and Roberts led another wave of Pentecostal revival that gained national attention.

WILLIAM BRANHAM

William Marrion Branham was an even more unlikely candidate for national ministry than Oral Roberts. Born in 1909 in a crude log cabin in the mountains of Kentucky, Branham's family moved to Indiana where he was raised in abject poverty.[4] He had several unusual spiritual experiences as a child, believing that God had spoken to him. The things he heard always came true and these encounters contributed to a sense that his life had a special destiny. His father was an alcoholic and his family was never active in church. Being the "poorest of the poor," Branham saw his childhood years as "terrible." Still, he sought to live a pure life as a young boy, believing God had told him to neither drink nor smoke. His uprightness and mysticism brought painful ridicule during his teen years.

Branham sought escape from his life of poverty and went west to Arizona at age nineteen, where he worked on a ranch and even boxed professionally for a time. Feeling he was resisting God, he went back to Indiana in search of a relationship with God. Interestingly, even though he encountered God's audible voice as a child, he was convinced he still did not know Christ. After a season of earnest pursuit, he was converted in a shed behind his house. In a small Baptist church that prayed for the sick, Branham received a remarkable physical healing of a lingering injury, suffered earlier from an accident. Six months later Branham was baptized in the Spirit and sensed a call to preach. He was ordained as an independent

Baptist minister and in 1933 Branham launched out with a tent crusade in Jeffersonville, Indiana, that immediately drew interest. From his tent meetings the Branham Tabernacle church was planted, which he pastored for over a decade. His mystical ways were not a good fit for Baptist associates but his church accepted the enigmatic Branham and he continued ministry at the church, struggling through the Depression often without compensation.

Branham was introduced during this season to Oneness Pentecostals and was invited by them to conduct revival meetings. Suspicious of Pentecostal fanaticism, he declined their invitations and later believed God withdrew His anointing for several years as a result. Branham lost his wife and daughter in an Ohio river flood in 1937 and feared it was a part of missing God's will in refusing the invitation to minister to the Pentecostal folk. In order to support himself he took on various jobs, still pastoring the church.

Through his years pastoring the Jeffersonville church, he had visions and heard God speak to him. While working as an Indiana game warden he had an angelic vision that launched his healing ministry. In May of 1946 an angel appeared to Branham and told him that he was called by God "to take the gift of healing to the people of the world." The angel said that if Branham remained sincere nothing would withstand his prayers, "not even cancer."[5] Branham later said he initially argued with the angel feeling completely inadequate for his commission but the angel assured him that God would be with him and he would be given two signs. First, when Branham prayed for people holding their right hand with his left, a "physical effect" would happen to his hand. When he prayed for the person and the "physical effect" in his hand went away, then they were healed of their disease or affliction. The second sign was that he would be given help to get the attention of people who were not receiving his message. For them he would be given the ability to "know the very secret of their heart. . . . This they will hear."[6] The angel also told Branham that his ministry was a sign of the imminent return of the Lord. He returned to his congregation within weeks, and in a Sunday evening service announced to the church the angelic visit and divine call. During that very service he received a telegram from a minister friend in St. Louis asking him to come and pray for his sick daughter. The congregation raised the money for the trip and sent Branham off. His friend's daughter recovered.[7]

Branham was then invited to hold a revival at his friend's St. Louis church. Reports of his ministry got around and he was invited to hold meetings at a United Pentecostal Church in Jonesboro, Arkansas, which drew thousands from "twenty-eight states and Mexico."[8] The response was great in part, because the difficulties of the Depression and war years had dimmed the fires of healing that flamed in the 1920s with the ministries of McPherson, F. F. Bosworth, John G. Lake, and others. Adding to this were the conflicts and consolidation in the Pentecostal movement which had taken the focus off the supernatural. Branham was tapping into a hunger among many Pentecostals for a fresh outpouring of Holy Spirit power. Testifying of his angelic encounter and calling, people started streaming to his meetings thrilled by his story and the reports of miraculous healings, even that a dead man was raised to life. Branham quickly became a sensation.

Since Branham had little business savvy and was not a skilled organizer, he needed to recruit a team of co-workers to help him manage his ministry. Several skilled leaders joined with him and by 1947 he was traveling the nation conducting crusades entirely in Oneness Pentecostal circles. While on the West coast, one of Branham's key team members, Jack Moore, introduced Branham to Gordon Lindsey, an Assemblies of God evangelist. Although Jack Moore was a Oneness Pentecostal and Lindsey was Trinitarian, their friendship bridged their differences, helping Branham's ministry spread to the entire Pentecostal community and beyond. Lindsey was deeply impressed by Branham's humility and obvious call from God despite his Baptist roots and Oneness association. Lindsey offered to introduce Branham to the Trinitarian Pentecostals through a series of meetings in the Pacific Northwest in the fall of 1947. The services drew tens of thousands including both Oneness and Trinitarian Pentecostals in a rare show of unity.

Healings were frequent and spectacular. In Branham's theology, demons were the root problem of sin and sickness and deliverance was necessary for healings to occur. Branham said that he was dependent on the presence of an angel to help him see what the core issues were for the person needing prayer who would then guide him in how to minister to the person. He only prayed for the sick when he sensed the presence of the angel and the anointing of the Holy Spirit. Despite the stunningly supernatural dimensions of his ministry, Branham was never "showy" or flamboyant. He was simple, quiet, and matter of fact as he ministered.

In the 1950s people flocked to Branham's meetings to see his legendary exercise of the "Word of Knowledge," which was the fulfillment of the second sign the angel had told him about. Branham often called out a person's name (someone he had never met) and invited them to the platform where he would describe details of their life and sickness that were revealed to him supernaturally. The person receiving the ministry was astonished. This display of God's direct presence utterly amazed the crowds. Still, Branham maintained a humility through it all that associates saw as remarkable. When information he received was of a highly personal nature, he stepped away from the microphone and talked to the individual quietly sometimes about specific sins that were preventing a healing.

Throughout 1947 an estimated thirty-five thousand people were healed in Branham's meetings. Lindsey and Moore spread the news of this visitation of healing grace, beginning publication of the *Voice of Healing* as a way to introduce the "Pentecostal masses" to Branham's remarkable ministry.[9] Branham was riding a wave of renewal that promised only to swell and other healing evangelists were beginning to ride in his wake. Yet, just as the *Voice of Healing* magazine launched its first issue, Branham, worn out by the wear and tear of ministry—he often prayed for the sick for hours—announced in the spring of 1948 that he was sick and needed to halt his ministry, perhaps permanently. His associates were stunned but had to accept his decision. Branham took five months off before returning in October of 1948. After Branham resumed his ministry he picked up where he left off and for the next few years he was the preeminent healing evangelist in the revival.

HEALING WATERS

The postwar euphoria helped fuel an emergence of moderate evangelical Christianity, signaled by the founding of Fuller Theological Seminary in Pasadena, California, in 1947. The school was an expression of evangelicals who were committed to biblical inerrancy, yet uncomfortable with fundamentalism's harsh, often condemning tone. There was no greater example of this new evangelicalism than the ministry of Billy Graham, who burst into the spotlight through his 1949 Los Angeles crusade, widely publicized by William Randolph Hearst and his newspaper chain. The healing revival, receiving considerably less national press coverage, began to erupt during this same period.

Oral Roberts was just one of many healing evangelists coming onto the scene in 1947, all in the shadow cast by Branham's mushrooming ministry. Names like A. A. Allen, Jack Coe, T. L. Osborn, Morris Cerrillo, and O. L. Jaggers, to name just a few, became rising lights in the healing revival. Nevertheless, it was Roberts who soon rivaled Branham as the most best known healing evangelist.

Both men respected each other's ministry. When Branham had to stop ministry because of his health, Oral Roberts called for prayer that "he may be restored to strength for the mighty work that still awaits his labors."[10] In 1949 Branham said "that

Roberts' 'commanding power over demons, over disease and over sin' was the most amazing thing he had ever seen in the work of God."[11] Branham and Roberts were the "two giants" of the healing revival that emerged in 1947.[12]

They were an unlikely pair in many ways. Branham was short and middle aged; Roberts was tall and young. Branham's roots were Baptist; Roberts was a pedigreed Pentecostal. Branham's preaching told primarily of his angelic visits; Roberts taught more directly from the Bible. Branham was naïve in many ways; Roberts was a man of "immense common sense."[13] Branham was reclusive; Roberts was outgoing. Branham shunned wealth; Roberts was comfortable with prosperity. On the other hand, they were very similar at the core: both shared a simple faith and a genuine humility. Both were committed to evangelism and the priority of the salvation message. And both saw amazing healings in their ministries. Whatever their similarities and dissimilarities they stood at the forefront of a revival that fanned to flame Pentecostal passions.

While Branham was resting in 1948, Oral Roberts' tent crusades boomed. After resigning from his pastorate in 1947, he moved to Tulsa, Oklahoma, and established a ministry base that continues to this day. In November 1947, while in the beginning of his crusade ministry he began publishing *Healing Waters* magazine as the primary mouthpiece for his ministry. He wrote his first book on healing, announcing it in the magazine's first issue and he asked for both financial and volunteer support. Roberts' organizational skills were quickly apparent. He proved adept at building a team of co-workers who complimented his abilities. Importantly, he took advice from key associates who helped him wisely manage his growing enterprise.

In January 1948, Roberts borrowed $15 thousand to buy a tent for his healing crusades. Seating two thousand, it would be the first of several tents which kept getting larger, with his last tent able to accommodate twelve thousand. Crowds filled the tents. In 1952, in just eleven tent crusades, 1.5 million people attended and over thirty-eight thousand were converted to Christ while sixty-six thousand people were prayed for in the healing lines.[14]

People were drawn to the meetings for many reasons. Roberts' preaching was particularly powerful. He would pace the stage, microphone in hand, moving the audience. But this was not an act of oratory but a display of Pentecostal passion for the lost to forsake their sin and turn to Christ. Roberts proclaimed healing and deliverance in Christ. After his message, Roberts "removed his coat and rolled up his shirt sleeves" to begin prayer for those in the healing line.[15] He sat on the platform just above the ramp that brought seekers up to stand in front of him. He would lay his hands on the person and pray a brief but authoritative prayer. Sometimes Roberts was gentle and compassionate. Other times he became irritable, frustrated at demonic captivity and human unbelief. He often commanded demons to leave and people would shake and cry out as they left.

Oral involved the audience in the healing line prayer. He occasionally stopped and reminded them that Christ was the healer, not him. Other times he would ask them: Who is the healer? He always knew what their response would be. He frequently asked them to join with him to pray for people. The prayer times were deeply moving and held the audience spellbound as God's power was displayed. Thousands passed by and Roberts prayed for most of them quickly with just a touch. A few received his special attention. He later reflected: "I've probably had more people in our meetings for prayer in front of me than most doctors have in their whole life."[16]

There were always skeptics. Some critics complained that Roberts screened the prayer lines and kept the most severe cases off in the "invalid" tent. The truth was that many people were just too sick to be in the healing lines or too demonized to be allowed in the lines. Not everyone knew that Roberts always visited those in greatest need of healing in the crusade tents or in the rooms off the main auditoriums in which he held meetings. He admitted to being overwhelmed by the enormity of human suffering. While some healing evangelists avoided the severely ill, his biographer, David E. Harrell, said Roberts' regular visits to the sickest of all at his crusades were "grim test[s] of his own integrity."[17]

Roberts helped to facilitate an atmosphere of expectant faith in his meetings. He was also careful to maintain order which allowed the Holy Spirit to work while restraining emotional excess. He was keenly aware of the fanatical outbursts that had given rise to Pentecostal stereotypes. He wanted to appeal to the masses outside Pentecostalism and he called for a reverential restraint in his crusades.

Oral Roberts proved himself a shrewd innovator in the use of media. Early in his ministry he started radio broadcasts and was on over 300 stations by 1952. His most strategic move was beginning a television outreach in January 1954, broadcasting on nine stations. By 1958 he was on more than 130 stations. Significantly, television created an audience far broader than the Pentecostal grassroots who were Roberts' most enthusiastic supporters in the early years.

Oral Roberts recognized his ministry needed the financial support of Christian businessmen and he held luncheons during some crusades. Demos Sharkarian was a good friend and supporter of Roberts and Shakarian founded the Full Gospel Business Men's Fellowship (FGBMFI)—an "International" designation was added later—at least in part at Roberts' urging. Roberts was the organization's first speaker and he maintained close ties with FGBMFI throughout the 1950s and 1960s. FGBMFI was catalytic in the emergence of the Charismatic Renewal. The "fellowship" was just that. It was a group of lay people meeting over a meal to promote personal relationships to Christ and the fullness of the Holy Spirit through the testimonies of participants. The group was interdenominational and without classical Pentecostal partisanship. It became a great venue for introducing non-Pentecostals to Spirit baptism as local FGBMFI "chapters" multiplied across America and around the world. Holding meetings in local restaurants, hotels, and convention centers, the FGBMFI took the message of Spirit out of churches and into the mainstream of life. Over the two decades following its 1951 founding, the organization grew to over 300 thousand members with chapters in eighty-seven countries.[18]

By the late 1950s, whether through favor or scorn, Oral Roberts was a familiar name to many Americans. Through print, radio, television, and crusades he became a major player on the religious landscape. When the healing revival began to fade, Roberts' ministry continued to expand.

THE HEALING REVIVAL FADES

After Branham returned to ministry in the fall of 1948, his crusades continued to be well attended into the 1950s and he was the unquestioned patriarch among the healing evangelists. The healing revival peaked in the early 1950s. Gordon Lindsey, who managed Branham's ministry for four years, stepped down to invest more time promoting the vast number of evangelists that had burst onto the scene. His magazine, the *Voice of Healing,* carried stories and testimonials from the meetings around the country. He worked hard at building bridges between the healing evangelists and Pentecostal churches. Many pastors felt threatened by the success of the healing revival and were concerned that the movement might form into a denomination. Lindsey sought to create an association of evangelists and give assurances that there was no intention to form a new denomination or compete with local churches. In essence, the *Voice of Healing* was a rallying point that united many of the healing evangelists. Lindsey did his best to call for financial and personal integrity in the revival. Unfortunately, many evangelists strayed from that path.

While Branham, Roberts, and a number of other evangelists worked to maintain integrity, others let ambition, pride, and greed get the best of them. By the mid-fifties a number of scandals were well publicized and there were others on the horizon. Many evangelists made fantastic claims of healings that didn't stand up to scrutiny. Extravagant claims of attendance at crusades fueled arguments over who had the "biggest tent." This brought scorn and opposition particularly from conservative evangelical churches. Many evangelists fought back with their own inflammatory rhetoric. The medical community objected to some clearly false claims of healing that kept the sick from getting the health care they needed, often making their conditions worse.

The debate made clear a tension that had existed for a long time. Many Pentecostals, though not all, were deeply opposed to medical care, feeling it showed a lack of faith. Some evangelists even said that to pursue help from a doctor meant one would take "the mark of the beast."[19] Doctors and medical practitioners were presented as enemies of divine healing. It was Oral Roberts who most clearly articulated a stance that saw medicine as part of God's way to bring healing to humanity. Roberts and other moderate evangelists saw physicians and evangelists as working together in confronting the true enemy, sickness.

But most destructive of all were the recurring ethical problems of many evangelists. The press seized upon discovered indiscretions which caused all evangelists to be viewed with greater suspicion. An overemphasis on fundraising created an image that all evangelists were abusing the trust of those who gave. All this increasingly drew the ire of classical Pentecostal church leaders. The Assemblies of God began to emphasize the priority of the local church and the availability of healing there, seeking to counter the influence of some evangelists. Respected British Pentecostal leader Donald Gee tried to mediate the growing tension between churches and evangelists. Gee challenged the unethical behavior, while acknowledging the legitimacy of itinerant evangelism.

The strife and tensions contributed to decreasing attendance at meetings and crusades. William Branham got caught up in the Oneness versus Trinity debate and his gatherings shrunk from thousands to hundreds in the late 1950s. His naïveté in finance got the best of him as was evident when an IRS investigation found him owing the government $40 thousand dollars. The problem was not as much with Branham as with those who managed his organization. Yet financial strains hindered his effectiveness in the later years of his ministry. Feeling rejected and isolated, Branham increasingly turned the ministry inward, trusting only a few associates for advice, who didn't seem to be able to give the kind of perspective he needed. He had long avoided doctrinal controversy by pushing differences into the background. As the 1960s began he grew more strident in his preaching, openly declaring his Oneness views and decrying denominations as evil. His Calvinist roots showed up as he emphasized predestination. More and more he declared himself to be God's singular end-time prophet.

Branham died tragically in a car accident in December of 1965. Some of his supporters believed he would be raised from the dead and his body was not interred for several months. His messages were preserved and viewed with an authority that rivaled Scripture for his most zealous followers. A personality cult developed around his legend. These events were painful to many Pentecostal leaders who believed Branham had been a humble servant whom God had used powerfully, until he isolated himself and lost his way in later years.

Oral Roberts was one of the few who survived the decline of the healing movement. Although he was also the subject of ridicule and scorn in much of the press, particularly in the 1950s, he tried to stay out of the fray as much as possible. When viciously attacked he defended himself only on occasion. In the midst of it all, Roberts himself called for ethical integrity and financial responsibility among evangelists. A trip to Australia proved especially difficult when attacks from the press and the church caused him to cancel the crusade and return to America. Roberts weathered the storm and learned from the criticisms thrown his way. Nevertheless he grew mistrusting and wary of the press.

Initially, Roberts had the support of many Pentecostal leaders and his pastoral experience helped him understand local church pastors. He often held meetings for local leaders before his crusades. Over the decade of the fifties his ministry was increasingly ecumenical and his crusades were attended by many non-Pentecostals. His evangelistic emphasis and more moderate style helped draw support from the broader Christian community as well. By the early 1960s, while not backing off from the full gospel message, his emphasis had clearly shifted from divine healing to evangelization. His public ministry moderated even more.

His moderation created tensions with some classical Pentecostals but Roberts was astutely reading the times. More than any of the healing evangelists, he discerned the emerging Charismatic movement as the Holy Spirit was poured out on the non-Pentecostal denominations. Roberts wanted to move on with what he believed God was doing. His relationship with his own Pentecostal Holiness denomination became strained as he identified publicly with traditional churches. Many Pentecostals found it hard to believe that Episcopalians, Presbyterians, Methodists, and the like could be baptized with the Holy Spirit and remain in their churches (a story we will explore more fully in our next chapter). They were puzzled that anyone would want to stay in "dead" churches. They expected these people to join their "Spirit-filled" churches. But God was up to something new and Roberts saw it.

Part of the "something new" for Roberts' ministry was the establishment of a Christian university that would "raise up students to hear [God's] voice."[20] Over a meal with televangelist Pat Robertson in 1960, Roberts heard God speak those words. In a leap of faith he obeyed the voice he believed to be God's, and in November 1962 Oral Roberts University was established to perpetuate and multiply his ministry "thousands of times."[21] It was a bold venture that he was incapable of seeing completed without God's help. Roberts prayed and wisely recruited co-workers who understood higher education. He cast the vision and raised millions of dollars from faithful supporters and saw his dream realized as Billy Graham spoke at the dedication of Oral Roberts University (ORU) in April 1967.

As an ordained Pentecostal Holiness minister, building an interdenominational university severely taxed Roberts' already struggling relationship with his denomination. He did not want the university to travel down the "denominational trail."[22] The straw that broke the camel's back was Roberts' decision to join a large Methodist church in Tulsa. The pedigreed Pentecostal was now a full-fledged Charismatic. Many of Roberts' Pentecostal associates felt betrayed. In his mind it was about obedience to God's call. He saw the river of renewal widening and did not want to be limited by the sometimes narrow views of his classical Pentecostal heritage. Roberts had moved with the Holy Spirit into the mainstream. It wasn't that God gave up on classical Pentecostals; rather He had invited many others into the river.

Oral Roberts saw to it that the university, initially derided by many, became a first rate, accredited institution that won respect and recognition in the academic world. He remained an innovator and became more reflective in his older years. He readily admitted his mistakes. The expansion of the school to graduate education was most noted when ORU started its medical school and functioning hospital in 1981. He came under scorn again in 1987 when he stated publicly that God would "take him home" if he failed to raise enough money to keep the medical school and hospital open. Further ridicule followed when the medical school closed in 1989. Resilient as ever, Roberts survived the difficult season and continued his ministry at a reduced pace.

Oral Roberts' life wonderfully demonstrates the transition Pentecostals experienced midway through the Charismatic

Century, and through his media ministry, he helped catalyze the broadening reach of spiritual renewal into the historic denominations. Few have recognized how significant his leadership was in helping reshape the Christian church in the twentieth century. In 1985, David Harrell, author of a careful, objective biography, observed that Roberts was the most widely known Christian leader in America, except for Billy Graham, and yet has received little positive notice. Why? Harrell's comments are noteworthy.

Two reasons for this neglect seem apparent. The first has to do with the pervasive condescension of academics and intellectuals. It is hard to entertain the thought that an "Okie Holy Roller" should be taken so seriously. Furthermore, in spite of his astonishing success, Roberts remained outside the pale of respectability, an artifact from the dusty past of brush arbors and camp meetings. God still talked to him; he had personally beheld Jesus, and he believed in miracles. To some he seemed dangerous, to others absurd, or comical. Even if he were all of those, his omission from history is inexcusable.[23]

Harrell went on to say that he found Roberts "to be a sincere and honorable man" and his "faults, if faults they be, are not rooted in chicanery but in calling; he is motivated not by greed but by God, as he hears Him."[24] This assessment echoes the simplicity of devotion so central to Pentecostal's early days and yet so hard to maintain.

A FINAL NOTE

Before moving on, there is a piece of the story that deserves brief mention. The healing revival was only one of two distinct but similar spiritual stirrings after World War II. The "Latter Rain" movement was born in North Battlefield, Saskatchewan, Canada, in 1947 at a small Bible institute. A small group of students, leaders, and supporters experienced a revival that emphasized the "laying on of hands" to impart spiritual gifts and a particular emphasis on the spiritual gift of prophecy. Two brothers, Ern and George Hawtin, were early leaders of the revival that quickly spread among Pentecostals in Canada and the US.

The movement featured strong worship with a recovery of spiritual song with singing in tongues in mass, often a part of the early Pentecostal revival. The Latter Rain movement also taught that God was restoring all five ministry offices of Ephesians 4:11, including the neglected offices in the contemporary church of apostles and prophets. As with other revivals a few were given to extremes which helped discredit it in the eyes of many Pentecostal denominational leaders. Despite the extremes, the Latter Rain movement left a lasting impact in several sectors of the Pentecostal movement. Elim Bible Institute in New York embraced the revival as did leaders in several significant churches. City Bible Church in Portland, Oregon, pastored by Frank Damazio, serves as a respected model of the imprint of the Latter Rain movement.

BROUGHT TO THIS MOMENT:

In Light of Remarkable Healing Ministries

History distills one conclusion on the subject of the healing ministry of Christ: Satan hates it, and steadfastly works to succeed in stopping it, criticizing it or distorting it. He also clearly delights in stirring controversy around any ministry Christ raises up in His Church to do the works which He did.

It is a peculiar fact that even Jesus Himself was faulted for healing the sick, in the same way He was accused of functioning by the devil's power when He cast out demons. I have repeatedly witnessed this through the years of my own ministry; often being grieved by the sad readiness of those who, just as the Pharisees in Jesus' time, seem unduly ready to criticize healing evangelists, and rarely willing to affirm the fact that verifiable healings and deliverances do occur.

I was living through my teenage years when the sweeping spread of healing revivalists occurred in the 1950s. By reason of this, I both read of and observed how the Holy Spirit was glorifying Christ by manifesting unusual signs and wonders through ministries open to His works. At the same time, of course, I learned early of the existence of charlatans, fakes and pretenders of "power" who contrived deceptions. And while decrying those phonies, rather than bothering to note the difference between the real healing ministries and the counterfeits, many commentators used the deceivers to legitimize their suspicion and to sustain their scorn toward faithful servants with valid, Christ-exalting healing ministries.

The unfolding works of the Holy Spirit as we advance into the twenty-first century call us to expect increased operations of His power. At such an hour we are wise to caution ourselves against any temptation to yield to unbelief or scorn. In balance, we assure biblical wisdom by recognizing that caution has its place, but does not require a surrender to gullibility. Spiritual discernment is essential, but may be ours attended by a biblical expectancy and prayer for Christ-glorifying "signs, wonders, healings and miracles"—they're the kind of thing Jesus did . . . and still does!!

It is in pursuit of sustaining that passion that I offer this statement—one I have held before my own congregation throughout my years of pastoral leadership. Seeking and praising God, not only finding but living in the midst of a flow of regular signs of God-grace healings and deliverances, I wrote regarding our seeking "A climate of love, in which we constantly extend God's graciousness—a beauty characterized in Jesus' ministry of divine healing and spiritual deliverance."

My article read:

It's not a matter of choice. The ministry of healing in the local church is a primary leadership responsibility for those of us who pastor.

The climate for healing is developed and sustained where the love of God is pronouncedly declared and demonstrated. It rises with solid teaching and is released when we recognize that it's only our call to extend the grace of God and the truth of His Word regarding the ministry of healing. We aren't called to defend the Word, but to declare it. Unbelief feeds on defensiveness—that sense of needing to protect God from "failing" someone's expectations. Once I submit to that burden, I will cease to foster boldness among the congregation in praying for the sick, and I will be inclined toward withdrawal myself.

At our church, the time and place for healing is provided through a Personal Ministry Room. It's open following every service and staffed by people prepared to counsel and to pray about problems, healing, deliverance or the fullness of the Spirit.

To encourage this posture, I have also utilized the following declaration. I offer it for the use of any who would embrace their church's twenty-first century ministry in light of the way the Charismatic Century has brought us to a "moment" when Jesus' healing ministry is needed so badly—and when the Holy Spirit has made clear it is so abundantly available.

I Believe in God's Will to Heal

I believe in God's will to heal and deliver the sick and the tormented, and that He has revealed the fullness of His healing purpose in His Son, Jesus Christ. I believe it is in God's nature to work redemptively to heal by every possible means, inasmuch as His mercy and loving-kindness are ever open to provide grace for the relief of human need, pain, misery and sin.

185

Because I believe this, I offer praise to the Creator who has made all things well, affirming that all sickness and pain is adverse to His will and desire for mankind, and has only come upon the race because of mankind's fallen state. I declare thanksgiving to Him for the fact that—notwithstanding every effort of hell to steal, kill and destroy all of mankind, compounded by human weakness and vulnerability to pain, sickness, disease, deformity and tragedy—the Father has appointed multiple havens of refuge from sickness and pain: through natural recuperative processes; through climate and diet; through the charitable efforts of mankind; through hospitals, doctors and medicine; and through the divine means of healing gifts distributed by the Holy Spirit and ministered in the name of Jesus.

I believe in the power of Jesus Christ to heal the sick and afflicted, and to break any bondage of satanic sort when His name is invoked in any circumstance. I believe His power is as consistently available today as it was during His own earthly ministry and that through His cross He has provided the grounds for us to expect and receive healing and deliverance as surely as we may receive forgiveness and sanctification.

Because I believe this, I accept the ministry of healing as a part of the Lord Jesus Christ's commission that the Church go to the whole world with the gospel. I proclaim God's will and power to heal; and in Jesus' name, I instruct that the prayer of faith be offfered, that confession of sins be made unto deliverance, that elders anoint with oil and that hands be laid on the sick that they might recover.

I believe in the power of God's Word and Spirit to sustain and supply health when believers walk simply and humbly before Him in faith. I believe the fruit of such faith will be manifest in love and patience, and so I correspondingly reject any system that begets lovelessness or induces guilt when a believer in Jesus does not seem to be able to receive physical healing or personal deliverance from sickness or any other torment.

Because I believe this, I withstand every evidence of pain, suffering, sickness, disease, bondage or torment, convinced that the good fight of faith will prevail unto health. I am equally convinced that in any case where victory is not evidenced, that a victory of another order is being realized by the divine grace of Almighty God.

With faith such as this, I move in the ministry of prayer faith and healing, so that Jesus Christ is glorified and, in all circumstances, His Church is edified.

Indeed, "with such faith" Jesus and the Church will be "built up"—built up in physical, mental and emotional health; built up in spiritual wholeness and more effective ministry, and built up through the effective demonstration of the living Christ in a way that achieves added evangelistic impact.

This is a fundamental objective of all spiritual gifts and ministries—"Let all things be done for edification" (I Corinthians 14:26). Thus, the continuation of Jesus' healing ministry through His Church is an essential component of that full-spectrum ministry into which the Savior discipled His immediate disciples, and into which He directed them to relay to those they discipled.

Now, we are at a moment when more human brokenness—spirit, mind, emotions and body—are present on Earth than at any time. It's a moment to which we've been brought—a moment when Christ's healing ministry is needed . . . profoundly. And we have been accompanied to this moment by an awakening of faith for healing and miracles that is stirred by irrevocable evidences of the Holy Spirit's readiness to demonstrate His power for the glory of Jesus.

Let's embrace the moment! There are millions that need us to do so.

Dennis Bennett and
the Charismatic Renewal

THE CHARISMATIC MOVEMENT IS BORN

It was Palm Sunday, April 3, 1960, and Episcopal priest Dennis Bennett stood before his Van Nuys, California, congregation in the first of three morning services. St. Mark's Episcopal Church was a fashionable congregation in the San Fernando valley north of Los Angeles; a church with significant growth under Bennett's leadership over recent years. Over fourteen hundred people attended the Sunday services and twenty-six hundred were members of the parish. That morning Bennett didn't preach; he just gave his testimony about his life changing experience of being baptized in the Holy Spirit and speaking with tongues. Spirit baptism was far from the normal experience for a dignified and reserved Episcopalian priest.

Rumors had spread through the church and Bennett knew he had to address them.

Things went well in the first service of the morning but in the second service the climate abruptly changed. One of the associate ministers in the church "snatched off his vestments, threw them on the altar, and stalked out of the church crying: 'I can no longer work with this man.' "[1] Things became worse as the service concluded. Pandemonium broke out between the services as a small number of angry members did their best to rally others to resist the invasion of so-called fanatics. "One man stood on a chair shouting: 'Throw the damn tongue-speakers out.' "[2] Despite the "fury" of the opposition, church members who had experienced Spirit baptism stood by and testified of the wonderful blessing that tongues speech was in their lives.

Bennett was completely shocked by the strength of the reaction. He had expected some concern, but not this. One of his church board members bluntly told him before the third morning service, "You should resign."[3] Aware that those opposing him were entrenched and would not give up their fight, and not wanting to split the church, Bennett announced his resignation in the 11 a.m. service. At the time he didn't feel he was informed enough about Spirit baptism to adequately defend his position. In the days that immediately followed the chaotic weekend, Bennett could hardly have known that these events would one day be called the popular birth of the Charismatic movement.

It all started months before when Frank McGuire, a fellow Episcopalian pastor in the Los Angeles area, came to Bennett in wonderment over the transformation of a young couple in his parish. John and Joan Baker were baptized with the Holy Spirit in a Pentecostal church but felt directed by God to continue attending their Episcopal church. McGuire was shocked when the couple, long nominal church members—attending only Easter and Christmas services—started showing up every Sunday for church; they were joyful and volunteered to serve in many areas. He was especially surprised that they started tithing (giving ten percent of their income to the church).

When the curious McGuire asked the Bakers what had happened to bring the change, they told him they had been baptized with the Holy Spirit and had spoken with tongues. McGuire, like many in mainstream churches, had heard stories of wildly fanatical Pentecostals but was not able dismiss the couple as unstable people. He told Dennis Bennett:

> You see, they don't *act* peculiar. They don't shout, or jump, or do anything wild. On the contrary, when you're with them, you just can't deny the fact that they've *got* something. They—they glow, like little light bulbs! And they are so loving and ready to help. . . . [4]

McGuire asked Bennett if he wanted to meet them and after initially declining—put off at the notion of speaking in tongues—curiosity brought him to the Baker's small Monterrey Park home in August 1959. They enthusiastically explained how they had been Spirit baptized. Bennett was moved by their testimony but made no response at the time. He knew he needed what this young couple had but was uncertain how to respond.

It would indeed be a stretch for this well-educated, socially sophisticated Episcopal priest to embrace a "Pentecostal" experience of tongues speech and the like. Bennett was the son of a Congregational Church minister. Born in London, his family moved to the United States when he was nine, settling in the San Jose, California, area. He was converted personally to Christ in a youth meeting at his church. Years later Bennett sensed a call to vocational ministry and at age 26, quit his job and went back to college. He attended a seminary that was quite liberal theologically but Bennett survived with his faith intact though spiritual passion faded as the ministry became a job. After graduating in 1951, he decided to leave the Congregational Church and become an Episcopalian and was ordained as a priest in 1952. He went to St. Mark's in 1953 and became instrumental in its growth. He was by every means a successful, comfortable pastor with a wonderful wife and children.

Still, after listening to the Bakers he realized they had something he didn't. Bennett was spiritually frustrated. He realized few in his church were really changed by the Gospel and despite his outward achievement, he was dry on the inside. The Bakers talked so intimately about the Holy Spirit, yet to Bennett the Spirit was "a vague, 'theoretical' Being to me."[5] He started studying what the Bible had to say about the Spirit and found 240 references in the New Testament. He also realized that the book of Acts clearly referenced the association of speaking in tongues to being baptized in the Holy Spirit. Even the act of Confirmation in his church referenced the "strengthening gifts of the Holy Spirit."[6] There seemed to be something to this thing!

Nevertheless, it was hard to overcome his bias. While drawn to the obvious joy and "Presence of God" he saw in the Bakers—he kept on visiting them—he struggled with their ordinariness. They were "after all, 'mere laymen,' who had a very simplistic and narrow-minded idea of the Bible. Why, they were practically *fundamentalists*, taking the Bible at face value."[7] In the end, his spiritual hunger won out, and fueled by recognition that baptism in the Holy Spirit was taught in Scripture, Bennett told the Bakers he was ready and met with them in November to pray with him to be Spirit baptized. John and Joan gave him some instruction in how to pray and then John laid hands on Bennett and gently prayed, asking Jesus to baptize him in the Spirit. As Bennett told it in his book *Nine O'Clock in the Morning*:

I began to pray, as [John] told me, and I prayed very quietly, too. I was not about to get even a little bit excited! I was simply following instructions. I suppose I must have prayed out loud for just about twenty minutes—at least it seemed to be a long time—and was just about to give up when a very strange thing happened. My tongue tripped, just as it might when you are trying to recite a tongue twister, and I began to speak in a new language![8]

Bennett marveled at the experience. He didn't lose control! He could start or stop speaking in tongues as he wanted. Having had language training he recognized this was clearly not gibberish he was making up. What he spoke "had grammar and syntax; it had inflection and expression—and it was rather beautiful!"[9]

Over the coming weeks Bennett continued to visit with the Bakers and began to better understand his experience. Almost immediately, the Scriptures seemed to come alive in a new way. He realized, contrary to popular notion, speaking with tongues was something he could do at anytime. The Spirit didn't "take over." This wasn't some spiritual ecstatic experience where the will was passive. Frequently, in the past he had stopped praying because he ran out of words to say. Now he "could pray beyond the limitation of [his] intellect."[10] He had a choice. More and more he was filled with a sense of joy and peace. When he spoke in tongues he was speaking to God.

Slowly over the next few months Bennett introduced people in his congregation to Spirit baptism, often sending them to a prayer meeting that the Bakers were now leading. He said nothing publicly but people inquired and he answered them with his testimony. He found out there were a few other Episcopalian priests who shared his new experience and his friend and fellow priest, Frank McGuire, who introduced Bennett to the Bakers, was also baptized in the Holy Spirit. Importantly, Bennett's wife soon spoke with tongues.

The small meeting held in the Baker's home centered in prayer and worship. They sang choruses and joyfully praised God. One by one nominal Episcopalians were filled with the Holy Spirit and before long St. Mark's had at least sixty members who were Spirit baptized, many of whom were key leaders. Bennett figured out that this small group of sixty was now giving ten percent of the church budget. Bennett had three other associate pastors serving with him at St. Mark's. They still didn't know about his experience. As the news got around that people at the church were speaking in tongues Bennett had to answer their questions and it became quite clear that his most senior associate opposed the whole idea of speaking with tongues.

Bennett was unsure what to do. He had put off saying anything to the church for fear of the reaction. When a group of young people in the church were baptized in the Holy Spirit and spoke in tongues he knew it was time to tell the church and so the announcement that Father Bennett was a closet "glossolalic" was made. There was vocal and spirited opposition that would have clearly split the church if he stayed. Resignation was his only course.

It had been just over seven months since Frank McGuire had gone over to Bennett's house to talk about the "strange" behavior of the Bakers. Now Dennis Bennett was without a parish to pastor and under ridicule as a Pentecostal crank. How quickly things change.

A NEW PLACE, A NEW SEASON

In Bennett's formal letter to his St. Mark's congregation that followed the Passion Sunday uproar, he made it clear that he was remaining in the Episcopal Church. He also urged members "not to leave the parish or cancel their pledge[s]." He asked church members to support the interim pastor.[11] No doubt Bennett's gracious and conciliatory exit helped make possible his continued ministry within his denomination.

Uncertain what to do after resigning, Bennett sought the perspective of some friends in the Episcopal Church and visited both Seattle and Portland Dioceses in June 1960, where there was interest in offering him a pastorate, despite his Pentecostal experience. He and his wife decided to accept the appointment of a small, dying mission church, in the Seattle suburb of Ballard that was about to close. Bennett preached his first message there on July 15, 1960.

Meanwhile back at St. Mark's in Van Nuys, Bishop Francis Bloy of the Los Angeles Episcopal Diocese appointed a temporary priest with an order that there would be no more speaking in tongues at the church.[12] All this began to catch the attention of the press. Here was a tongues talking Episcopal priest who had created a furor in a respectable upper middle-class church. Before long Dennis Bennett and his baptism with the Holy Spirit was news in both *Time* and *Newsweek*.[13] Despite his departure the seeds of renewal were planted. Jean Stone, one of the members of St. Mark's that had been Spirit baptized, started publishing a quarterly magazine, *Trinity*, which spread news of events related to the emerging Charismatic movement around the world.

The presiding Bishop of Olympia, William Fisher Lewis, told Bennett to bring the fire with him because it would not be an easy task turning the nearly bankrupt church around. With little to lose now, Bennett decided to move forward unapologetically affirming his Spirit baptism. A core group of the committed few greeted Bennett soon after his arrival and because of the national attention asked him to tell them the whole story. They accepted his testimony as a needed message of hope and renewal and this little group began to meet every Friday to pray. Not many weeks later most were baptized in the Holy Spirit when a young Charismatic priest from Chicago visited their Friday prayer meeting. The fire had indeed moved north.

This group became the foundation of a Charismatic center that developed in Seattle. Within a year at least eighty-five members of the church were Spirit baptized. St. Luke's Episcopal Church was no longer dying. It would grow to be one of the strongest Episcopal parishes in the Northwest with a weekly attendance of two thousand. Over the next twenty years, "an average of twenty persons" were Spirit baptized every week.[14] Fortunately for Bennett, the bishop was open to Charismatics and he was given freedom to lead as he felt the Lord direct.

Bennett was determined from the outset to build a congregation that was not overly dependent on his constant presence. His vision was to see the people of St. Luke's "equipped to help each other, and those around them, too."[15] Before long Bennett was traveling nationally and internationally, sharing the news of his baptism with the Holy Spirit with Episcopalians, Lutherans, Presbyterians, and other mainline Protestants.

The attention given to Bennett by the press and his significant influence in the rapid growth of the Renewal into the broader church, has led many to date the beginning of the Charismatic movement to the events at St. Mark's in Van Nuys. Without question, Bennett is a true patriarch of neo-Pentecostalism. Nevertheless, the origins of the Charismatic go much farther back.

ECHOES OF AZUSA STREET

Our last chapter mentioned the importance of Oral Roberts and the Full Gospel Business Men's Fellowship International (FGBMFI) in helping establish a pathway for Pentecostalism to penetrate the broader Christian church. It is hard to imagine the emergence of the Charismatic Renewal without FGBMFI and the Pentecostal ecumenist, David du Plessis, whom we shall soon meet.

Full Gospel Business Men's Fellowship International

FGBMFI was founded by Demos Shakarian, whose grandfather pastored a small Los Angeles church that became fully Pentecostal after his grandfather visited the Azusa Street revival. Born in 1913 Shakarian was raised in that church, becoming a Christian early in his youth. He was Spirit baptized in 1926 and at the same time he was healed of a hearing problem. Shakarian joined in the family's prosperous dairy and meat packing businesses and became wealthy. Nevertheless, prosperity failed to satisfy deep spiritual longings in his life. What mattered most to Shakarian were his church and God's work. In 1937 several prophecies saying he would speak around the world brought new expectation to Shakarian and his wife. In 1941, a dramatic healing of Shakarian's sister through the ministry of evangelist Charles S. Price left a lasting impact on Shakarian. His sister's hip was shattered in a car accident and

Price laid hands on her for healing. As the Holy Spirit touched her, she shook violently for twenty minutes and her hip was healed completely. X-rays the next day confirmed the healing.

Shakarian was one of a new generation of Pentecostal businessmen. Prospering after the war years, he used his money and influence to promote Pentecostalism through youth rallies in Southern California. He garnered public attention with a 1948 rally that overflowed the Hollywood Bowl when twenty-one thousand people attended. Many senior leaders of the larger Pentecostal denominations were on the platform, including the late Aimee Semple McPherson's son, and new president of the Foursquare Church, Rolf McPherson. The event gave Shakarian a growing voice among Pentecostals. His involvement was not limited to the Pentecostal world. He actively supported the enormously successful Billy Graham Los Angeles crusade in 1949 and was a supporter of the lay led evangelical Christian Business Men's Committee (CBMC). All the while, Shakarian continued to work closely with Pentecostal evangelists. He was particularly impressed with Oral Roberts whom he believed to be "the world's most powerful preacher."[16]

Shakarian learned much about organizing meetings for businessmen through his participation in CBMC but longed for an environment that welcomed the Holy Spirit's dynamic activity. In 1951, at a Roberts' crusade in Los Angeles, Shakarian approached Roberts with the idea of a "Full Gospel" businessmen's organization. His vision was for men to tell other men about Christ and the Spirit-filled life. "Something clicked" in Roberts as Shakarian talked. Roberts suggested that Shakarian start the group right then and hold the first meeting the following Saturday while he was still conducting the crusade. He would be the group's first speaker. The event was announced before twelve thousand people at Roberts' crusade.

Shakarian, his wife Rose and Oral Roberts were surprised when only eighteen men showed up for the meeting at Clifton's Cafeteria in downtown Los Angeles. Shakarian was obviously disappointed but Roberts seemed unfazed by the size of the group and he even thanked God for the small turnout. Roberts spoke for about twenty minutes and then prayed for the newly formed organization,

> Let this Fellowship grow in Your strength alone. Send it marching across the nation. Across the world. We give You thanks right now, Lord Jesus, that we see a little group in a cafeteria, but You see a thousand chapters.

Roberts' prayer defied smallness and cast a vision for God's preferred future. It woke the group up and the men starting singing "Onward Christian Soldiers" and marching in place. While driving home from the meeting, Shakarian remarked, "within a year we're going to see amazing things."

The FGBMFI began having breakfast meetings regularly on Saturday mornings but the gatherings didn't take off the way Shakarian expected. For over a year after Roberts' prayer, the organization struggled to get going and Shakarian was deeply discouraged. While there was some moderate success in other cities where Roberts held crusades and personally invited men to attend a onetime event, things weren't going well for the only organized regular chapter. Shakarian desperately wanted direction from God and on a Friday night in December 1952 while talking with his house guest, Pentecostal evangelist Tommy Hicks, he told Hicks that if God didn't speak to him that night, the next morning's meeting would be the group's last. As Shakarian prayed that evening he had a vision in which God took him around the world showing him lifeless people that came alive through the Holy Spirit.[17]

The next day the atmosphere at the men's breakfast was different. One man was awakened the night before by the Lord and told to give one thousand dollars. Another, who ran a printing business 400 miles to the north in Watsonville, California, drove all night compelled by God to be at the meeting in a show of support. He believed he was to offer to help print a magazine for the group (the FGBMFI publication *Voice* grew to be one the most influential magazines of the Charismatic Renewal). Perhaps the greatest confirmation for Shakarian was that both men, unaware of his vision the night before, said they believed that FGBMFI "must go around the world."[18]

Within a year, eight more chapters opened up across the nation and FGBMFI held its first annual convention, attended by three thousand. The conference speakers were primarily the healing evangelists, including Oral Roberts, Jack Coe, Gordon Lindsey, and several others. The annual conventions became a major platform for emerging Charismatic speakers and teachers. FGBMFI's magazine *Voice* had a circulation of over 250 thousand in the early 1970s. The organization mushroomed in the coming years with more than three thousand chapters in eighty-seven countries by 1988.[19] FGBMFI had gone "around the world."

The chapter meetings for the FGBMFI at first were more centered on men's testimonies of how God baptized them with the Spirit, helped their business or brought physical healings. Meetings were held in restaurants or hotel ballrooms and speakers were not always professional ministers. Personal prayer and ministry usually followed the testimony time and "many were saved, healed, and filled with the Holy Spirit in the services."[20] The group always made it clear that they were not churches yet many pastors felt threatened by FGBMFI.

The interdenominational character of the meetings and the neutrality of the meeting places tapped into the spiritual hunger of many in traditional churches. FGBMFI gatherings were a venue that introduced tens of thousands of non-Pentecostals to the baptism of the Holy Spirit. The increasingly educated FGBMFI constituents helped the group move its emphasis from testimony—though never fully eclipsed—to Bible teaching. Large chapters, some attended weekly by hundreds, developed in many cities and created a "charismatic circuit" giving opportunity for various teachers to gain a following. Bible teachers like Bob Mumford, Derek Prince, and Kenneth Copeland built large support bases, at least in part, by traveling city to city, speaking at FGBMFI chapters.

Given the significant growth of FGBMFI, its founder and leader, Demos Shakarian, was enormously influential as the Charismatic movement blossomed in the 1960s and 1970s. Shakarian was a key player in fostering unity among Charismatics as well as dealing with disputes that threatened the movement's cohesion.

DAVID DU PLESSIS

Pentecostal historian Vinson Synan has said South African David du Plessis is the "one person, above all others, who served as catalyst and spokesman" for neo-Pentecostals.[21] His story is remarkable. He was sitting in his office early one morning in 1936. Evangelist Smith Wrigglesworth, who was staying with him, suddenly burst into the office and ordered the young du Plessis out from behind his desk. Wrigglesworth laid his hands on du Plessis and began to prophesy over him.

> You have been in "Jerusalem" long enough. . . . I will send you to the uttermost parts of the earth. . . . You will bring the message of Pentecost to all churches. . . . You will travel more than most evangelists do. . . . God is going to revive the churches in the last days and through them turn the world upside down. . . . [22]

Du Plessis was dumbfounded as Wrigglesworth went on to tell him more of what God showed him about du Plessis' future. It seemed impossible. What made it so hard to believe was partly because du Plessis, so much a classical Pentecostal who saw other churches as cold and complacent, couldn't fathom how dead churches could become a part of God's work in the last days. Like many Pentecostals of his day he was certain God would surely not revive Roman Catholics.

David du Plessis was an unlikely candidate for a worldwide

traveling ministry. Born in 1905, his parents became Pentecostals through the missionary work of John G. Lake, who brought stories of Azusa Street to South Africa. Converted to Christ in 1916, du Plessis served in the Apostolic Faith Mission, a Pentecostal denomination, from which many asssociated with the Church of God (Cleveland, Tennessee). When Wrigglesworth gave the prophecy, du Plessis, already the secretary of his denomination and editor of the organization's primary publication, seemed destined to continue to take an expanding place of leadership in the movement. Du Plessis did nothing to try and fulfill the prophecy on his own but just waited and continued to work as he had before.

In 1947 he went to Zurich to be a part of the first Pentecostal World Conference (PWF), an attempt to unite Pentecostals around the globe. Following the conference he resigned from his Apostolic Faith Mission roles and over the next decade was a key organizer and leader for the PWF. Initially, du Plessis moved with his wife and children to Switzerland. In 1948, du Plessis left his family behind and went to the United States, working to bring Pentecostals together and helping organize the Pentecostal Fellowship of North America (PFNA).

For much of 1948 du Plessis toured the United States, meeting with Pentecostal leaders to promote unity. Traveling in Tennessee with a Church of God colleague, their vehicle collided in the fog with a train and both men were injured, du Plessis more severely. Because of his long recuperation he missed the first PFNA conference he helped organize. Du Plessis then managed to raise enough money to bring his family to America. The whole ordeal was life transforming. During his recovery there was much time for prayer and reflection. One day while quietly praying in tongues, du Plessis heard God speak to him. "The time for the fulfillment of the prophecy Smith Wrigglesworth gave you has arrived. It is time to begin. I want you to go to the leaders of the churches." He argued with God. "Lord, what can I say to those dead churches?" And he heard back, "I can raise the dead."[23] He continued to argue but he knew he was being called to love those he felt would likely reject his message, yet he realized he must obey the call.

During his slow journey back to full health, du Plessis continued with the PWC, teaching at the Church of God's institution, Lee College in Cleveland, Tennessee. After graciously declining the invitation to formally join the Church of God, he moved in 1952 to Samford, Connecticut. Since God had told him it was time to reach out to the mainline churches, he sought direction for how to begin. Du Plessis felt a need to be near the headquarters of these denominations and importantly, the key ecumenical centers that served them. Now with the move the opportunity was at hand to start. The offices of the World Council of Churches were nearby in New York City. While living in Connecticut, du Plessis served as an interim pastor of an Assemblies of God (AG) church and, while not surrendering his South African Apostolic Faith Mission credentials, he affiliated with the AG and was ordained as a minister.

Sometime after moving to Connecticut, du Plessis read a report about Princeton Theological Seminary president John A. Mackay that stated what a great blessing Pentecostals were to Christianity in the twentieth century. Du Plessis was surprised because Mackay, a respected Presbyterian educator and ecumenist, earlier said that Pentecostalism was "the fly in the ointment in Protestantism." Du Plessis decided to call Mackay and ask about it. Reaching him on the phone, du Plessis asked if he had changed his mind. "Without hesitation, he heartily replied: 'I certainly did.' [Mackay] candidly stated that he had been wrong before, primarily through ignorance and misunderstanding." On the phone the two men began a significant and strategic friendship—Mackay was active in the World Council of Churches (WCC).[24]

Shortly after the call with Dr. Mackay, du Plessis felt the Lord tell him it was time to go to the WCC. He had no appointment and as odd as it felt, he took the train into New York City to the Fifth Avenue offices of the ecumenical organization. Arriving at the WCC and unsure of how he would be received, du Plessis awkwardly introduced himself as the secretary of the World Pentecostal Fellowship. He found himself warmly welcomed. Being a Pentecostal, du Plessis was a curiosity to them and he ended up staying and talking for the whole day. His audacious obedience established a beachhead that started a whole new season in his life.

John Mackay soon invited du Plessis to attend the 1952 International Missionary Council meeting in West Germany, a group that helped spawn the WCC. Many participants met and conversed with du Plessis and were impressed, having never met a "rational Pentecostal." It was at this conference that he became known as "Mr. Pentecost," a title he wore proudly as he established bridges into many mainline churches.[25]

Du Plessis was then invited to attend the 1954 World Council Assembly that met in Evanston, Illinois. It was evidence of his expanding acceptance in the ecumenical world. Over the next few years he continued to work with the WCC, and lecture at elite theological schools such as Princeton Theological Seminary, Yale Divinity School, Union Theological Seminary, and many others. The National Council of Churches (NCC) openly embraced du Plessis as had the WCC. He didn't limit his communication to Protestants either; he established conversation with Roman Catholics and by 1959 was received by three popes.

When Dennis Bennett spoke with tongues in 1960 and the Charismatic movement burst onto the scene, no one was more pleased than du Plessis who blessed this new wave of renewal. At the same time, Classical Pentecostals were struggling to understand how the Holy Spirit could be poured out on cigarette smoking, wine drinking Protestants and Catholics. After all the Holy Spirit and glossalalia was their own claim to fame.

Du Plessis' work with these "liberals" didn't sit well with many of his Pentecostal colleagues, who saw it as compromise. Of course, many years earlier du Plessis would have agreed. Now it was a part of his mission to work with groups he once saw as "dead." In addition, many viewed him as a maverick since he had no official denominational position that authorized him to speak for Pentecostals. Slowly he was cut off by the Pentecostals he had walked with for so many years. The AG asked du Plessis to cease his ecumenical work or resign from the denomination. When du Plessis would do neither, the AG revoked his credentials. He retained, however, his membership in the First Assembly of God of Oakland, California, (du Plessis and his family moved to the city in 1974).

Classical Pentecostals were in a difficult place. In the 1940s and 1950s they found increasing acceptance, as we have seen, among conservative evangelicals partly because they so heartily embraced the fundamental tenets of conservatives in the battle with modernists earlier in the twentieth century. Many Pentecostals were now aligned with the National Association of Evangelicals (NAE) and AG General Superintendent Thomas Zimmerman was elected president of the NAE in 1959. When a 1961 NAE editorial protested du Plessis' "coziness" with the WCC and ACC, the AG was put in an awkward position with their senior leader serving as president, while one of their members was getting national press coverage for his unauthorized ecumenical work. It was clearly an embarrassment that led to du Plessis' defrocking.

Du Plessis and his wife were hurt by the denomination's decision. Nevertheless, the day after he received the letter informing him of the decision, a Southern Baptist colleague shared a vision he had that promised God's continued blessing on du Plessis' life. Buoyed with new hope, he moved forward with an unrelenting determination to obey his call to be a "Pentecostal ambassador-at-large."[26] He continued his work with the WCC and NCC and as an invited guest for a session of the historic Vatican II. He was instrumental in establishing the Roman Catholic-Pentecostal Dialogue, which followed to a greater openness that grew out of Vatican II.

As the Charismatic Renewal spread through the historic

churches, du Plessis became more involved in working to unite the various expressions.

Some Pentecostal denominations not only opposed the ecumenical work of du Plessis but one went so far as to issue a position paper against it—though they later realized their opposition was a mistake. As the Charismatic movement grew by leaps and bounds and Classical Pentecostals gradually accepted it, du Plessis came back into favor. In 1980 the AG reinstated du Plessis as an ordained minister.

David du Plessis was instrumental in the climate of openness and dialogue with mainline churches that provided ready ground from which the Charismatic movement grew. Du Plessis' longtime friend, Vanguard University Provost, Russell Spittler, founder of the David du Plessis Center for Christian Spirituality at Fuller Theological Seminary, has given helpful perspective on du Plessis' life and work. "No one in the twentieth century so effectively linked three of the major movements of our time—the pentecostal movement, the ecumenical movement, and the charismatic movement."[27] Roman Catholic scholar Kilian McDonnell called du Plessis a "national treasure."[28]

Both David du Plessis and Demos Shakarian were Azusa Street descendants who paved the way for the most significant and far-reaching wave of renewal since the Los Angeles revival. And while Dennis Bennett is certainly the most notable figure in the public birth of the Charismatic Renewal, du Plessis and Shakarian (through FGBMFI), along with Oral Roberts, were without doubt essential "bridges" linking early Pentecostalism with the Charismatic movement.

OTHER STIRRINGS

Dennis Bennett drew national attention with his April 1960 announcement that he had spoken with tongues and was staying in the Episcopal Church but he wasn't the first mainline Protestant to do so. A few led the way before him. As we mentioned in the first chapter, most people in traditional Christian churches left to join Pentecostal congregations after being Spirit baptized. In the late 1940s and throughout the 1950s this slowly began to change.

In 1946 Lutheran minister Harald Bredesen was baptized in the Holy Spirit. He offered to resign as Lutheran minister but his resignation was refused by church leadership. Continuing to serve in the mainline Protestant world, Bredesen embarked on a remarkable journey leading others into Spirit baptism accompanied with tongues. During the 1950s he drew encouragement from David du Plessis and FGBMFI as he ministered among mainline Protestants.

Bredesen "had a gift for reaching key people."[29] Notably in 1957, then pastoring Mount Vernon Reformed Church in New York City, he introduced Christian Broadcasting Network founder Marion Gordon ("Pat") Robertson to the experience. Bredesen gained national attention when he helped spark a Pentecostal outbreak of Spirit baptism at Yale University in 1963 when a number of students, Episcopalians, Lutherans, and Presbyterians all spoke with tongues.

Additionally, he helped spread the renewal indirectly by introducing freelance writer John Sherrill to a young Assemblies of God pastor, David Wilkerson. Sherrill co-wrote Wilkerson's book *The Cross and the Switchblade*, which told the story of Teen Challenge, a most effective ministry to teen drug addicts and gang members that Wilkerson started in New York City in the 1950s. The book, along with Sherrill's book *They Spoke with Other Tongues*, was instrumental in popularizing neo-Pentecostalism.[30]

In 1959 Bredesen received a prophecy to not "hold anything back" regarding the Spirit baptism, a word which he obeyed. When St. Mark's Episcopal Church member Jean Stone established the Blessed Trinity Society in 1960—publisher of *Trinity*—in the wake of Dennis Bennett's departure to Seattle, Bredesen joined with Stone in popularizing Spirit baptism. Many thousands were led into the experience through his ministry over the next four decades.[31]

Bredesen was one of the early leaders who were baptized in the Spirit and showed that it was possible to be a renewing force bringing new life to churches many had given up for dead. Along with Jean Stone of *Trinity*, Bredesen popularized the term "charismatic renewal" rather than the more obtuse term neo-Pentecostalism, that most were using in reference to the emerging movement among mainline Protestants.[32]

Dennis Bennett's Pentecostal experience was the catalyst that caused the Charismatic explosion in the 1960s. The movement significantly reshaped the landscape of the church at large and slowed the liberalization of the historic denominations. By 1970, an estimated ten percent of the clergy and one million lay people were Spirit baptized but stayed in mainline churches.[33] Pentecostalism was clearly no longer on the margins. It was now in the center of North American Christianity. Smith Wrigglesworth's prophecy to David du Plessis was being fulfilled. God was reviving His Church.

We have yet to look at one other essential piece of the Charismatic explosion in the late 1960s and the early 1970s, the amazing story of the Roman Catholic Charismatic Renewal. That belongs to the next chapter.

BROUGHT TO THIS MOMENT:

When We Can't See "What's Next?"

The Charismatic Renewal of the 1960s and 1970s caught the whole Church by surprise. The Holy Spirit's sovereign workings among mainline Protestant churches and Catholics, which thereby leaped over the walls erected between Pentecostals and all other Christian churches, was an unpredictable breakthrough. As a Classic Pentecostal pastor, entering the 1960s as a youth pastor with only four years experience in pastoral leadership, I well remember the combined amazement and delight I felt upon hearing the ever broadening receptivity that first thousands, and then millions were showing toward the very experience with gifts from God that I and a host of Christians before me shared in common. The stunning thing was that now we were hearing reports of, and actually meeting people who were rejoicing in the very things for which they earlier either criticized or demonized us!

However, not all Pentecostals were happy about this, and—

of course—not all people in the same ranks as those protestant "Pentecostals" were happy either. And the change of terminology—referencing this awakening as "charismatic," not "Pentecostal"—was a God-given strategy that neutralized what would have been a sectarian term and opened the door to multitudes by providing a more biblical and scholarly term. It is not only interesting, but again underscores Oral Roberts' influence in the last half of the twentieth century, that he is the person who coined the term—taken from the Greek *charismata*, the word used for the gifts of the Holy Spirit.

As the "new movement" rapidly spread under the title "charismatic," it soon became a suspect "revival" among many Pentecostals—one primary reason being the irritation (or perhaps feelings of "rejection") felt. Many seasoned, oft-assailed-for-their-stance Pentecostals saw these "newcomers," who now freely opened to the things of the Spirit, as avoiding the onus of being "Pentecostal," and reacted by standing themselves against the "charismatics." It was a classic case of the attitude shown by the brother of the prodigal son, who refused to participate in his brother's party, essentially saying, "They haven't been as faithful to these matters as we've been all these years we've been persecuted, why should we be happy with them?" That seems a rather blunt assessment, but it was, in fact, the reality in many quarters at the time. The Assemblies of God issued a formal "white paper" (an authoritative report) against the charismatic movement in 1969, reflecting the feelings of many other Pentecostal groups as well. But it is to their credit that not long afterward they withdrew the statement and embraced the revival—as did the majority of Pentecostals.

The point in this review is not to stand in judgment on the mistake made by many Pentecostals in their first reaction to what the Holy Spirit brought to the Church at that time, because there were many Pentecostals who welcomed, tutored and graciously entered into embracing fellowship with their "charismatic" counterparts in other denominations. But there is a historic tendency that is observable throughout Church history, how a slowness to receive or a suspicion toward a "new wave" of the Spirit of God is generally shown by those already established in the Church. As David du Plessis put it—"It seems our response is like the ocean's tide: the thing that most resists the wave that is presently come in upon the shore is the backwash of the wave that came just before it."

And that brings us to our moment—to confront the issues that we will inevitably face as the twenty-first century continues to unfold. What will our response be as the Holy Spirit moves in ways that surprise or possibly upset us? Who can make that judgment? Who can say with certainty what those "movings" may be? Are they in motion already? Have we been resistant and not sensitive enough to diagnose or admit it?

Since the Charismatic Renewal, a "third wave" was identified, yet others who favorably acknowledged it saw it as only an expansion of the earlier movement. The unwillingness of some to accept as "charismatic" anyone who does not affirm "tongues as the initial physical evidence" became deepened in some quarters at that time. Was that wisdom or resistance? Opinions differ, but the question lingers: "How open—on either side of such issues within Christ's body—are God's people toward each other?" Because while, in the last analysis, the measure of His love will reflect the true depth of our openness to the Holy Spirit's works in our time, there are nay-sayers who cry out when they feel "love" has succumbed to a confusion that is irresponsible regarding "truth."

Further, revivals are never "neat." Outbreaks of the Spirit find imperfect vessels through which to begin, for there is no other kind anywhere among us humans, however well intended or spiritually mature. The fresh discoveries made when "truth" moves from the realm of precisely postured theology into the arena of dynamically and pragmatically applied and experienced vitality seldom seems to satisfy the "experts." It is too often true that battle lines are drawn before relational quests are pursued, and leaders align themselves against each other, standing themselves firmly at their "positions" rather than seeking one another humbly as "persons." Reactionary attitudes go both ways: the "renewed" party often is impertinent— heady with their taste of "new wine;" while the "more seasoned" party, feeling cautioned by aforementioned "imperfections," often manifests impatience if not impudence—certain the excitement is nothing more than shallowness at best and dangerous at worst.

It may be a hope beyond practical reason, but it isn't one beyond finding worthy expression here—and even more worthy, finding acceptance by all who seek God's Spirit as He continues "speaking to the Churches" today: May God make us gracious, humbly and gently available to "submit to one another!" Such "submission" would not involve abandonment of our good sense, discernment or of the Scriptures. But it does require:

1. A will to cast away the notion that any of us "have a corner on God's works and wisdom";
2. A heart to open to one another, hearing what we each say rather than what others say about us; and,
3. A readiness to open God's Word with each other without the presumption we are there to correct or enlighten the other, but that we are there to acknowledge that "His ways are not always ours," and that He—the Holy Spirit, who "wrote the Book"—intended us to see more than we have seen there to date.

This moment is being defined even as we speak. The River of God continues to flow in power—flow from heaven to earth—and only those who "hunger and thirst after righteousness shall be filled." That fullness is never static: as Ephesians 5:18 commands, "Keep on being filled with the Holy Spirit!"

The "next wave" may be rising now. The call to "catch it" is not a summons of God's Spirit to a surfer's ride for the fun of it, but to His surging tide for His purposes now. I must ask myself—and that you, as well, face the question.

Being brought to this moment, how will I respond to the Holy Spirit's surprises in my time?

9

Catholic Charismatics and the Three Rivers of Renewal

THE DUQUESNE WEEKEND

The assignment for the retreat was simple: they were to read David Wilkerson's book *The Cross and the Switchblade* because of its emphasis on the importance of the Spirit baptism. They were also to read the first four chapters of the Acts of the Apostles in the New Testament. With that about twenty-five Catholic students, a priest, and two faculty members from Duquesne University gathered for the weekend retreat. It was Friday, February 17, 1967, and the group traveled to the Ark and the Dove, a retreat grounds outside of Pittsburgh. History was in the making.

The retreat began in the evening with an uneventful short session. Saturday morning Ralph Keifer and Bill Storey, two professors from Duquesne who were baptized in the Spirit just a few weeks earlier, led the group in the ancient hymn, *Veni Creator Spiritus*, the same one Pope Leo XIII sang on January 1, 1901, as he dedicated the twentieth century to the Holy Spirit. Here now sixty-six years later, spiritually hungry Roman Catholics were asking to be filled and renewed by the Holy Spirit.

The retreat's focus was on prayer and discussion over the Acts passages they were reflecting on. After spending all day Saturday doing just that, the plan was for everyone to relax during the evening and celebrate the birthdays of three retreat attendees. One of the student couples at the retreat asked Ralph Keifer, who taught theology at Duquesne, if he would pray for them to be baptized with the Holy Spirit. The three quietly slipped out from the party which was meeting downstairs. Both husband and wife powerfully experienced Spirit baptism, speaking in tongues. While this was going on, another student, Patti Gallagher, left the birthday gathering just as it was starting and went upstairs to the chapel. She sensed an overwhelming presence of "the Spirit of Christ" and literally shook under God's power. Awed by it all, she went downstairs and invited others to come up to the chapel. As Catholic Charismatic leader Kevin Ranaghan later told it:

> By ones and twos the small group made their way to the chapel. And as they gathered together in prayer, the Holy Spirit poured himself out upon them.
>
> There was no urging, there was no direction as to what had to be done. The individuals simply encountered the person of the Holy Spirit as others had several weeks

before. Some praised God in new languages, others quietly wept for joy, others prayed and sang. They prayed from ten in the evening until five in the morning.[1]

The upstairs chapel became a holy place for the group. Patti Gallagher colorfully described what she witnessed that evening. She said that some students felt a "clicking in their throats or a tingling in their tongues"[2] but didn't know what it meant since it was something so new to them. "I suppose we could have spoken in tongues right away if we had understood how to yield to the gift." Some of the group "began to giggle and laugh" in the Spirit and some lay prostrate before the Lord. Gallagher said she heard one of the professors comment, "What is the bishop going to say when he finds out that all these kids have been baptized in the Holy Spirit?" One young man walked into the chapel and fell to the ground as he encountered the power of God.[3]

The two Duquesne professors went back and forth through the room laying hands on the students and praying for them. The group was filled with a sense of worship and praised God in emotionally expressive ways that as Catholics they were unaccustomed to. Another student rolled on the floor caught up in God's presence.[4]

Nevertheless, it was indeed a remarkable moment that Gallagher and the others never dreamed at the time would "impact the entire Church." Reflecting many years after that February evening in 1967, Gallagher said that the Spirit drew the group to the real birthday party which was in the "upper room." "Just as the Church was born at Pentecost in an upper room, the

Catholic Charismatic Renewal was born in an upper room too. God was moving sovereignly."[5]

Gallagher's words are not an overstatement. The "Duquesne weekend" as it is called, not only radically impacted the Roman Catholic Church, it made the Charismatic movement for the first time truly a pan-Christian phenomenon. Pentecostal stereotypes had already been challenged by the events of the 1950s and 1960s, and now it was impossible to view Pentecostalism as a movement on the fringes of the church. The Duquesne group was well educated and not at all anti-intellectual like many early Pentecostals. They were no less passionate about their experience but expressed it within their own heritage. It was an unlikely happening by any estimation.

EARLIER STIRRINGS

It all began in the fall of 1966 as Keifer, Storey, and two others on the faculty at Duquesne, concerned about the vitality of their Christian experience, decided to meet regularly for prayer and discussion. The small group wasn't sure just what the problem was but they began a journey of discovery. They were heartened by the transformation they saw in the book of Acts as the disciples were transformed on the day of Pentecost. Here were a group of people hiding in fear who were emboldened to witness after being filled with the Holy Spirit. Knowing they needed renewal, the group gradually came to expect that the Spirit would come upon them in much the same way.

Weeks earlier at the National Cursillo Convention they had

been introduced to David Wilkerson's book *The Cross and the Switchblade* by friends and lay Catholic leaders Steve Clark and Ralph Martin. Keifer, Storey and the others read the book and they were introduced to perspectives on the Holy Spirit they never understood before in Scripture. "It was like discovering Christianity for the first time."[6] Ralph Keifer also read John Sherrill's book, *They Speak With Other Tongues* that was convincingly straightforward about the importance of Spirit baptism and speaking with tongues.

The small prayer group became convinced they needed to meet someone who actually was baptized in the Spirit. These Catholics were apprehensive given the anti-Catholic sentiments of so many Pentecostals coupled with the stories of their wild worship. Pushing concerns aside, their quest brought them to a Charismatic prayer meeting on Friday, January 13, 1966, at the home of Florence (Flo) Dodge, a Presbyterian who was baptized with the Holy Spirit in 1962. Kiefer, Storey, and Patrick Bourgeois attended the meeting and were surprised by the intelligence and sensibility of the people. Flo Dodge remembers how much she was impressed with the sincerity and earnestness of the Duquesne group. Her guests were also impressed as they observed the way the prayer group prayed for each other and how they spoke in tongues "softly and unobtrusively."[7] These people were not mindless fanatics and seemed to have a sound Christ-centered theology and exercised their newfound charismatic experience with a joyful naturalness.

The next week only Keifer and Bourgeois were able to come back to Dodge's home. As with the first meeting they were struck by the sanity of it all and felt a great sense of openness that overcame theological differences. According to Keifer, "It was a strikingly nondenominational meeting."[8] Both men decided to ask the group to pray that they would be baptized with the Holy Spirit. Keifer recounted what happened:

> They simply asked me to make an act of faith for the power of the Spirit to work in me. I prayed in tongues rather quickly. It was not a particularly soaring or spectacular thing at all. I felt a certain peace—and at least a little prayerful—and truthfully rather curious as to where this would lead. . . . To me, praying in tongues was a rather minimal aspect, a purely concomitant phenomenon which seemed naturally to go along with this . . . because I knew historically that it had been a phenomenon which was widely accepted in the Church in its beginnings . . . [and] was not limited to the New Testament by any means.[9]

After Keifer's experience that Friday evening he began to lead others into the experience in the coming weeks. Each one felt a new sense of spiritual alertness that they had been yearning for and felt new grace to serve Christ in His church. The Bible opened to them in new ways as they studied and they were filled with new faith and peace. They discovered a new boldness to witness to friends. Significantly, they were changing and becoming better Christians from the inside out as the Spirit gave them desires. This new experience brought about the Duquesne weekend as the original four Duquesne faculty members, all now baptized with the Holy Spirit, decided to have the retreat for interested students to explore together their new experience.

No one was thinking of starting a renewal movement, but that is what came of the weekend retreat. For Charismatic Catholic Peter Hocken, the Duquesne weekend was the "beginning of a recognizable movement of charismatic renewal among Catholics."[10] These were committed Catholics who loved their church and wanted to be a force for revitalization. Although some Catholics were baptized in the Holy Spirit before, the events over the weekend of February 17-19, 1967, ushered in a spiritual renaissance for Roman Catholics and brought them to the forefront of the Charismatic movement. They were a part of a miracle that seemed impossible to many Classical Pentecostals. God was uniting His church in profound ways through the fullness of the Holy Spirit. Still it didn't happen in a vacuum.

Many things were happening in the Catholic Church that paved the way for the Duquesne weekend. As mentioned, the Charismatic century began with Pope Leo XIII's hymn of invocation to the Holy Spirit on January 1, 1901, as the twentieth century dawned. Just over three years earlier in 1897, Pope Leo XIII asked all Catholics to say a novena (nine days of consecutive prayer) to the Holy Spirit between the celebration of the Ascension and Pentecost. The inspiration for the Pope's call came from a young nun from Lucca, Italy, Elena Guerra, who had written the Pope several letters. Pope Leo XIII called Guerra "the Apostle of the Holy Spirit" because of her appeals that more focus be made on the Spirit. The Pope's encyclical meant that Catholics around the world gave new attention to the Holy Spirit.

In a culture given to cynicism, many may dismiss the power of prayer or the January 1 dedication of the twentieth century to the Holy Spirit as a mere religious exercise. But looking back from our present perspective, the events of the last 100 years show that God was moving in and among His people fashioning His design for the Charismatic century.

The Catholic Church changed throughout the twentieth century. More emphasis was placed on the role of the laity, which is especially significant when one considers that most of the leaders of the Catholic Charismatic Renewal were not ordained clergy. There was also a resurgence of biblical scholarship among Catholics after the Second World War, which was only heightened after the Charismatic movement hit the Church. In the milieu of the post–WWII flux, Catholics, long stanced that true salvation would only be found by Protestants returning to the Catholic fold, were showing a new openness to other Christians. Nowhere was this more fully expressed than in Vatican II.

In 1959 Pope John XXIII, at the "sudden inspiration" of the Holy Spirit, called for the first ecumenical council for the Roman Catholic Church, only the third council since the Reformation. Part of the purpose of the council was to foster Christian unity. Especially important was the prayer of Pope John XXIII that the council might be a "New Pentecost." Several themes emerged from the council's periodic meetings from 1961 to 1965 that helped create a favorable environment from which the Catholic Charismatic Renewal emerged. There was a particular emphasis on the importance of charismatic gifts in the church. A key leader to the discussion on the gifts of the Holy Spirit was

Belgium's Leon Joseph Cardinal Suenens, whose words helped foster an atmosphere friendly to the Renewal. Given the hierarchical nature of Catholic Church government, it is hard to imagine how the renewal could have happened without a prior openness and hunger of the Holy Spirit's gifts and graces.

In the desire to promote Christian unity, Protestants were declared to be "separated brethren" who are indeed part of the universal church. This new openness to non-Catholics was significant, as Vinson Synan said, because "before Vatican II, the [Charismatic Renewal] would probably have been viewed as a 'Protestant' phenomenon and therefore forbidden to Catholics."[11] The stage was set for meaningful dialogue that allowed Pentecostals "to contribute to the renewal of the Catholic Church."[12]

Setting the stage particularly for the Duquesne weekend was the Cursillo (little course) movement that started in Spain in 1949. The Cursillo weekend retreats, aimed at reinvigorating Catholics to practice their faith personally and in the faith community (in many instances it evangelized nominal Catholics), spread around the world. Both the Catholic lay leaders in Pittsburgh and others in Notre Dame and East Lansing, Michigan, were particularly influenced by their involvement in Cursillo events.

AFTER DUQUESNE

Even before the Duquesne weekend's Catholic "Pentecost," news was spreading about the baptism with the Holy Spirit. Duquesne graduate Bert Ghezzi, a doctoral student at Notre Dame, told Kevin and Dorothy Ranaghan and other Notre Dame graduates and students about Ralph Keifer's Spirit baptism. The Notre Dame group watched with great interest what was happening with their friends at Duquesne University. Keifer called the Ranaghans right after the February weekend and "urged" them to read the books by Wilkerson and Sherrill. In early March a group of nine young Catholics gathered at Ghezzi's apartment in South Bend to be baptized in the Spirit and while no spiritual gifts were manifested, they sensed something powerfully new had happened.

Just over a week later, Ranaghan, Ghezzi, and others who had prayed for Spirit baptism in the previous meeting (along with a few new seekers) decided to share their experience with Ray Bullard, the president of the South Bend chapter of FGBMFI. The group met in Bullard's basement with a small group of mostly Pentecostal pastors. It was a bit of a culture shock for the liturgically oriented Catholics to gather with the "anything goes" Pentecostals. As Ranaghan put it, their "differences were more than enough to keep us far apart from each other. Yet in spite of these personal differences, we were enabled to come together in common faith in Jesus, in the one experience of His Holy Spirit, to worship our Father together."[13] In Vinson Synan's book *In the Latter Days* Bert Ghezzi described what happened at Bullard's house:

[The Pentecostals] spent the evening attempting to persuade us that if you were baptized in the Spirit you had to be speaking in tongues, but we held fast to our conviction that we were already baptized in the Spirit because we could see it in our lives. The issue got resolved because we were willing to speak in tongues if it were not seen as a theological necessity to being baptized in the Holy Spirit. . . . Very late that evening, sometime after midnight, down in that basement room, the brothers lined us up on one side of the room, and they began to pray in tongues and to walk toward us with outstretched hands. Before they reached us, many of us began to pray and sing in tongues.[14]

Afterward the Pentecostals supposed the Catholics would now leave the Catholic Church like most had done before. The Catholics were shocked at this as they had no intention to leave. Bert Ghezzi later said, "Because we did not do that the Catholic charismatic renewal became possible."[15] This is what made the events of early 1967 so significant. This was a brand new distinctly Catholic expression of the Charismatic Renewal.

At the same time all this was going on at Notre Dame, Ralph Martin and Steve Clark, young lay Catholic leaders living at the time in East Lansing, Michigan, and working with the Cursillo movement, were Spirit baptized on a visit to Duquesne University. They wanted to join the Notre Dame group for an ad hoc prayer retreat in South Bend that had already been planned by Ranaghan's new Charismatic group. Some one hundred students, priests, and faculty from Notre Dame, Michigan State, Duquesne, and a few other schools gathered in a weekend that fully established the Charismatic Catholic Renewal as more than a passing fad or localized phenomenon.

The April retreat caught the attention of the Catholic and national press which catapulted the renewal into prominence. In just two months a movement was born.

Afterward the movement mushroomed and the Notre Dame Charismatic gathering of 1967 became an annual conference in 1968. The 1968 conference was attended by 150 Charismatics but by 1973, twenty thousand attended. The Charismatic Renewal at Notre Dame quickly gained the support of key professors like Edward O'Conner who became an important spokesman for the Renewal. At the beginning they were called "Catholic Pentecostals" but over time they adopted the term Charismatic to distinguish themselves from other Pentecostals.

The Charismatic Catholic Renewal structurally expressed itself quite differently than the Classical Pentecostal churches and was distinct as well from Protestant Charismatics. While it was more common with Protestants for whole congregations to become Charismatic, it was rare for an entire parish to do so. Rather, Charismatics usually functioned as a subgroup within local parishes. Spirit-filled Catholics met in weekly prayer groups for worship, prayer, Bible reading, and ministry. Though priests and nuns sometimes helped lead, more often lay leadership was the primary means of administrating the local prayer meetings within the Catholic Church.

Steve Clark and Ralph Martin moved from East Lansing to Ann Arbor, Michigan, in September, 1967 to serve in Catholic campus ministry at the University of Michigan. In Ann Arbor, Clark and Martin founded the Word of God community that grew to become the foundation for Charismatic renewal in the Catholic Church and a major center promoting ecumenism within the larger Charismatic movement.

At Notre Dame in 1971, Kevin and Dorothy Ranaghan along with Paul DeCelles founded the People of Praise community in South Bend. Both the Word of God community in Ann Arbor and the People of Praise were covenant communities where people lived together sharing resources, committing themselves to spiritual disciplines and submission to the communities' leaders. The communities were ecumenical in character but were primarily comprised of Catholics.

Although other Catholic communities developed around the nation, the Word of God and the People of Praise produced the most important leaders for the emerging Catholic Charismatic movement. Clark, Martin, and Ranaghan became strategic partners as the Charismatic Renewal burgeoned in the 1970s, working with other key leaders from Protestant Charismatic groups, Classical Pentecostals, and independent Charismatic leaders. The two communities started publishing the magazine *New Covenant* in 1971 which provided them with an expanding influence.

Given the academic orientation of the Catholics that helped birth the movement, almost immediately there was serious reflection given as to how to integrate the new Pentecostal experience into the Catholic tradition. The general consensus was that the experience of Spirit baptism was the "actualization" of the graces conferred through the Catholic rites of baptism (initiation) and confirmation. In other words, Roman Catholics believed that the Holy Spirit was already given to a baptized and confirmed Catholic but not fully experienced until the time when the individual became experientially aware of the Spirit's presence. Other Catholics tended to see Spirit baptism as the bestowal of something new to believers. All in all, given the desire to keep the movement within the Catholic Church, Charismatics continued to affirm the importance of active participation in the sacraments of the Church.

Consequently, though not entirely without opposition, Catholic bishops generally affirmed the movement that many saw as a direct answer to a hope for renewal that flowed out of Vatican II. Leaders like Cardinal Suenens of Belgium provided able and encouraging leadership as the movement grew. On Pentecost Sunday in 1975, twenty-five thousand Charismatic Catholics met at St. Peter's Square. Vinson Synan described the Rome gathering: "Near the end of the service, when the Pentecostals began to 'sing in the Spirit,' the organist and choir joined in an extemporaneous voicing of the 'eightfold Alleluia,' the international anthem of the movement."[16] By the mid-1970s, the Catholic Charismatic Renewal was the most vibrant distinct expression of the Charismatic movement.

THREE RIVERS OF RENEWAL

The Charismatic Catholics were interested in the history of the Pentecostalism that had clearly presaged their own Pentecostal experience and were particularly appreciative of Vinson Synan's 1971 book *The Holiness-Pentecostal Movement in the*

United States. Synan, a young Pentecostal Holiness pastor and educator, earned his Ph.D. in American History at the University of Georgia in 1967. In order to aid the publication of his dissertation, Synan added a section on Charismatic Pentecostals that helped the book catch the attention of the growing Catholic renewal movement.

In June, 1972, Synan was invited to the campus of Notre Dame to speak at the annual Charismatic conference. As a pedigreed Pentecostal, Synan was apprehensive about attending the event, long conditioned by the anti-Catholic rhetoric characteristic of most Pentecostals. But as he witnessed over eight thousand Roman Catholic Charismatics in a pre-conference session, singing in tongues with upraised hands in beautiful four-part harmony, he was both perplexed and awed. How could this be? After all, these were Catholics! He came to the conference not yet convinced that "Catholics could receive a full Pentecostal experience" equal to that in his own Pentecostal Holiness Church. Now, after seeing it with his own eyes, he could no longer question that Catholics indeed were experiencing the genuine Spirit baptism, the prized distinctive of Pentecostals.

Deeply moved, Synan got up from his seat and hurried off to a restroom in the basketball coliseum where the meeting was being held. In that campus restroom he heard God call him to contribute to the global awakening that was shaking the Catholic world and renewing the spiritual passions of so many other groups. He believed he was to be a bridge builder between classical Pentecostals and this growing move of God he was observing. At the time Synan could only imagine what lay ahead.[17]

After this, Vinson Synan was a regular at Catholic Charismatic conferences and became a leading player in one of the most unique features that characterized the Charismatic movement: its remarkable ecumenism. By 1970 there were three major groupings of Pentecostals. There were of course the Classical Pentecostals who were the direct descendents of the Topeka and Los Angeles outpourings. But there were two others: the Protestant denominational and independent Charismatics, and the new kids on the block, the Catholic Charismatics. Significantly, they were talking to each other!

By the 1970s there were organized Charismatic groups in most American denominations. There were Catholics, Episcopalians, Lutherans, Presbyterians, Methodists, Mennonites, Baptists, Orthodox, Wesleyan, Mennonite, and the list goes on. It was a turn of events which would have been hard to conceive of just a decade before. Charismatics were everywhere. They helped renew the church across America despite opposition from many denominational officials. Significantly, Classical Pentecostals, while at first unable to accept that God could pour His Spirit out on non-Pentecostals, were beginning to realize the Charismatic movement was, whether they liked it or not, a "God thing."

At a 1973 conference Synan talked with Ralph Martin about someday bringing these three rivers together in a public conference in demonstration of the unity of the Church of Jesus Christ through the Holy Spirit.[18] To Martin, Synan and many others, God was tearing down the walls that divided Christians thus fulfilling Jesus' high priestly prayer in John 17: 21-23. Catholic scholar Kilian McDonnell typifies the perspective of those in the Renewal, asserting that Spirit baptism was an "ecumenical grace," that created the active pursuit of visible Christian unity.[19]

In 1979 Michael Harper reflected back on what was distinct about the Renewal's ecumenism. Harper believed "Roman Catholics and Protestants found each other 'in the Holy Spirit' and 'in Jesus Christ.' "[20] It seems this made the Renewal's unity different from the more official and doctrinal efforts in the formalized ecumenical groups in the broader church. In the Charismatic Renewal, unity was centered in a shared experience of Spirit baptism, motivating efforts to establish authentic relationships among its leaders.

Dennis Bennett, the movement's signal patriarch, always maintained this was one of the chief reasons God brought the movement about and he echoes William Seymour's early cry for unity in a 1972 interview:

> It is nationwide, denominatiowide [sic], world-wide, and the focus is on people coming alive. There are healings, certainly, and these are important to the church's full life. The *dunamis*, the power of Christ, is coming through to His people, so that they are doing what Jesus did. I am not just talking about miracles. What is even more exciting is that the character of Jesus, the fruits of the Spirit, are being expressed in His people. . . . The charismatic movement is an answer to the divisiveness stemming from the pietist-activist differences between evangelical and mainline churches. After empowerment, people feel immediate concern for their fellow men. In some, it takes awhile

for action to result; but action does come. As the saying goes, "If you want the blessing of God . . . get out there and bless your fellow man . . ." If this isn't an answer to racism, I know of no better.[21]

These were not mere words. In October 1968 Bennett, and two other leaders initiated a morning prayer meeting to pray for the church in Seattle; the prayer group quickly grew as more area pastors attended. This led to a monthly brown bag lunch meeting for "a time of worship and sharing."[22] Eventually this meeting was attended regularly by as many as fifty Seattle pastors from "Catholic, Episcopalian, Lutheran, Presbyterian, Methodist, Baptist, Nazarene, Disciples of Christ, Mission Covenant, Christian Reformed, classic Pentecostal, and Jesus People" churches.[23] The group became known as the "Seattle Presbytery."

As the Charismatic movement grew, Bennett was one of the first to organize gatherings of key leaders in the movement. Early in 1971 he arranged a June meeting of Charismatic leaders that gathered in Seattle for a two-fold purpose: first "that we might have a greater understanding of what God is saying in regard to the renewal today," and second, that the renewal "might have a more unified expression of the will and purposes of God."[24]

Charismatic Catholic priest Francis MacNutt attended the first Charismatic leaders meeting and remembers that Bennett "conceived the idea and got everyone together," inviting many of the important "traveling ministries" within the Renewal.[25] Besides the above goals, Bennett wanted to discuss concerns about two issues in the Renewal. First, he and a number of other leaders, including Pentecostal ecumenist David du Plessis, were alarmed by the practice of public demonic deliverance sessions led by Charismatic Bible teachers Don Basham and Derek Prince. Second, Bennett, MacNutt, and Lutheran Larry Christenson were struggling with the practice of rebaptism. At many Charismatic meetings, speakers who taught the necessity of believer's baptism would call for their infant baptized attendees to be baptized again, often doing so in the swimming pools at the hotels hosting the events.[26] These issues were to be discussed in pursuit of mutual respect and understanding.

The event was held June 7-10 at Seattle Pacific College where the leaders were both housed and day sessions were held. In the evenings some spoke at various meeting locales in the Seattle area ministering to the congregations of pastors in the Seattle Presbytery. Disciples of Christ Charismatic, Don Basham, his deliverance ministry being part of the reason for the first meeting, said they were extremely guarded and cautious during the first day of the event. But slowly the men began to trust each other and open up and engage in meaningful dialogue. They didn't skirt issues of disagreement and at some sessions tempers flared during discussions. Basham writes that at one point David du Plessis approached him and pointedly stated:

"Don, your teaching on the baptism and the gifts of the Holy Spirit and your books have blessed many people," he said. "Now you are about to ruin your ministry with this demon business. Everywhere I go people come up to me complaining about your teaching."

I could only remind him how other critics were continually leveling the identical charge at him for promoting the baptism in the Holy Spirit and speaking with tongues. "But you give little weight to their accusations because you know the help your ministry brings to so many," I said. "I feel the same way about the deliverance ministry."[27]

The meetings, marked by the kind of conversation that Basham remembers, were not characterized by contentious attacks on each other but by honest attempts to achieve an understanding.[28] As the days advanced the leaders listened to concerns raised and sought to adjust where possible. All agreed to respect one another's position, and when there was a substantial concern or disagreement, to handle it biblically. Importantly, the group decided to meet again.

The 1971 Seattle gathering was the beginning of an annual leaders meeting that brought together the top leaders of the three rivers of renewal for nearly three decades.[29] Even its leadership reflected its truly ecumenical nature. Lutheran Larry Christenson, Catholic Kevin Ranaghan, and Classical Pentecostal Vinson Synan chaired the group at various times. Known later as the "Glencoe meetings," the leaders attempted to forge common ground between the various expressions of the Charismatic movement.[30] They admirably, but not always successfully, sought to adjudicate disputes that arose in the renewal in the 1970s and 1980s. Over the years many other groups organized under the banner of "Pentecostal and Charismatic unity" but none was as truly representative of the breadth of Renewal as the Glencoe group.

Perhaps the greatest contribution of this group was the formation of a committee to bring together the three streams of the Renewal in a conference in 1977. Because of the relationships developed at the Charismatic Leaders conferences, the committee planning the 1977 Kansas City conference had a solid foundation to build this "conference of conferences." Since so many of the various Charismatic groups in the denominations met for annual conferences, why not have them all meet together in one city and hold their own sessions during the daytime with joint sessions in the evening? Drawing on the trust and goodwill forged over the early annual leaders gatherings, the group stood together to hold a truly ecumenical and spectacular conference.[31] The Kansas City Conference on Charismatic Renewal was a great success. The joint evening sessions were held at Arrowhead stadium with over fifty thousand Charismatics in attendance, with Catholic attendance at twenty-five thousand. It was the high water mark of Charismatic ecumenism and possibly of the Charismatic Renewal. In the next twenty-five years, several other Charismatic conferences were held but none matched Kansas City in either sheer size or in broad participation.

CHARISMATIC CENTERS

The continued growth of the Charismatic movement among educated mainline Protestants and Roman Catholics created a hunger for Bible teaching. As a result more and more regional teaching conferences were held showcasing a growing number of gifted Charismatic Bible teachers. It was not unusual for Charismatics to travel several hundred miles to hear a favorite teacher.

There was also an increasing demand for printed teaching materials via magazines and books. One of the innovations of the movement was the use of cassette tapes featuring various teachers. In what was literally a "cassette tape explosion," new ministries started up across America, serving as "tape libraries" which distributed teaching tapes of Charismatic leaders. Millions of tapes were distributed in the 1970s and were an important avenue to spread the word of Spirit baptism. Small prayer groups multiplied where attendees listened to cassette tapes together, prayed, and exercised spiritual gifts.

While the majority of Charismatics were in denominational settings, there was an ever larger group of independent Charismatics not associated with any one particular church or organization. These were people who met in ad hoc prayer groups or those who simply attended teaching conferences. Even Charismatics in denominations were sometimes only loosely connected to their churches. For some Charismatics the excitement and euphoria over the Charismatic experience caused them to be extremely independent and wander from group to group in search of the newest teaching. One leader at the time called it "charismania."[32] Most Charismatics, however, were just looking for leadership to help them understand and express their renewed faith.

A number of Charismatic entrepreneurs came on to the scene to serve this expanding constituency. Pat Robertson, son of a former U.S. senator, a Yale Law School graduate, became one of the most influential Christian leaders in America. Baptized with the Holy Spirit in 1957, Robertson believed God wanted him to buy a television station in Portsmouth, Virginia. Knowing nothing about broadcasting and with little cash in hand, Robertson somehow managed to buy the station and began broadcasting three hours a day. He was the first to own a Christian television station and with a bold and expectant faith, he called the single station the Christian Broadcasting Network. From those humble beginnings, Robertson went on to build the network in Virginia Beach, Virginia, into a major center for the Charismatic Renewal. The talk show format program *700 Club* became extremely popular and was aired all over America by the mid-1970s.

Businessman Dan Malachuk founded a Charismatic publishing house, Logos International, in the 1960s that published many of the books which helped spread the Charismatic movement, most notably Dennis Bennett's testimonial *Nine O'Clock in the Morning*. Malachuk and his organization published the magazine *Logos Journal* which became one of the most popular magazines among Charismatics. Featuring articles on various Pentecostal and Charismatic themes, the magazine gave Malachuk a significant voice among Charismatic leaders and made his base in Plainfield, New Jersey, a center for the Renewal.

Also, in Ft. Lauderdale, Florida, Eldon Purvis, a Charismatic Episcopalian businessman, started the Holy Spirit Teaching Mission in 1965 to introduce people to Spirit baptism. One of the features of the Ft. Lauderdale group was their frequent teaching conferences held in Florida and around the nation. With the publication of the *New Wine Magazine* in 1969, he established a thriving center for the Charismatic movement by 1970. Significantly, Purvis gave voice to several popular Charismatic Bible teachers, including Bob Mumford and Derek Prince.

Another important center for the Charismatic movement was Melodyland Christian Center in Southern California. Pastored by Ralph Wilkerson, it was a rapidly growing independent Charismatic congregation, located next to Disneyland. The church regularly hosted Charismatic teaching conferences and opened its own seminary promoting Pentecostal/Charismatic themes. Founded by Presbyterian Charismatic theologian J. Rodman Williams, Melodyland School of Theology gave the church even more prominence.

Along with Dennis Bennett, St. Luke's Episcopal Church in Seattle and the Catholic Renewal groups in Ann Arbor and South Bend, there were several strategic centers for the movement which seemed poised for even greater growth and influence. Given its great diversity, it was uniquely cohesive. But bitter winds soon blew that forever damaged the ecumenical character of the Renewal.

CHARISMATIC CONTROVERSIES

Don Basham, Bob Mumford, Derek Prince, and Charles Simpson, four Bible teachers associated with *New Wine Magazine* in Ft. Lauderdale and themselves regular teachers on the Charismatic teaching circuit, were concerned about the hyper-independence of some Charismatic teachers. In 1970, after Eldon Purvis had personal problems that forced him to resign his leadership at the Holy Spirit Teaching Mission, the four men made mutual commitments to each other to be accountable in personal and ethical matters. Although each maintained their own independent ministries, they also decided to teach together more as a team.

Within a year the four were teaching regularly on the importance of discipleship and the need for submission to spiritual leadership. The teachings tapped into a vacuum. There were hundreds of prayer group leaders and independent Charismatic pastors who were looking for leadership. In addition, a large number of pastors, newly introduced to Spirit baptism, in many cases by Mumford and the other three men, saw them as their de facto spiritual leaders. When the four started teaching that every Christian, including leaders, needed to have a personal pastor, or "shepherd," using their term, they soon were faced with large numbers of people coming to submit to them, many of them young people in the Jesus movement.

The Jesus People movement was a generational revival that started in the late Sixties among countercultural youth who were increasingly disillusioned by the harsh realities flowing out from drug use and sexual experimentation practiced by many hippies. Popularized first in Southern California and the California Bay Area, the revival spread across America as young people by the thousands gave their lives to Christ. A sometimes ignored feature of the Jesus People movement is that it was significantly Charismatic and nondenominational.

A generation alienated from their parents was longing for someone to lead them and the Shepherding movement promised spiritual fathers.

The Shepherding movement was born in 1974 after two "Shepherds" conferences gave a higher profile to the teachings on submission and authority. Basham, Mumford, Prince, and Simpson, joined by Canadian Pentecostal Ern Baxter, were increasingly the center of controversy. By 1975 it became a raging debate as critics charged the men with seeking to take over the independent sector of the Charismatic movement and start a new denomination, a charge they adamantly denied. Complicating matters were allegations that some pastor/shepherds were abusing their spiritual authority and controlling the lives of followers.[33] The controversy was exacerbated by the fact that there was no Charismatic Leaders conference that year to help mediate the debate before it became so heated. When Pat Robertson said on the *700 Club* broadcast that the Shepherding teachings were heresy, it became a very public controversy.[34]

Several ad hoc leaders meetings in 1975 tried to resolve issues to no avail. There was some progress made at the 1976 Charismatic Leaders conference but strife remained. Notable leaders opposed to the Shepherding teachers were Pat Robertson, Demos Sharkarian, David du Plessis, and Dennis Bennett. While not necessarily endorsing everything the Shepherding leaders taught, they gained the support of Larry Christenson, Kevin Ranaghan, Steve Clark, and Ralph Martin. The controversy continued, though not as stridently, for over a decade until the Shepherding leaders dissolved their association in

1986. The strain caused by the debate bludgeoned the Charismatic movement's ecumenical idealism. Some leaders never participated again in the annual Charismatic Leaders conferences, preferring to start their own unity groups.

In the late 1970s and early 1980s there was another controversy that further eroded the unity of Charismatics. This time it centered in the teachings of Kenneth Hagan, Kenneth Copeland, and other so-called "faith teachers." Some critics charged that the "health and wealth gospel," was nothing more than a Christianizing of American "materialism."[35] Known by some as the "name it and claim it" group, those espousing the "word of faith" teaching taught that determined faith was necessary to receive God's promises. These teachings emphasized the importance of confessing Scripture promises and holding to that confession—hence the term positive confession—no matter what contrary evidence or circumstances one might face. Opponents felt that there was too much emphasis on the individual's faith which often produced a sense of condemnation in people who didn't receive what they believed had been promised by God.[36]

Despite the controversy over its teaching, the Faith movement grew during the 1980s and teachers like Kenneth Copeland were very successful in their use of media to popularize their teachings. Word of Faith patriarch Kenneth Hagan's Rhema Bible Institute in Broken Arrow, Oklahoma, was a training center for thousands of graduates who planted Faith churches and spread the Faith message. African-American Faith teacher Fred Price adeptly used television to introduce America to the Word of Faith beliefs. The controversy over their teachings tended to push the Faith movement inward into their own associations which didn't help Pentecostal/Charismatic unity.

By the late 1980s the Charismatic movement lost its cohesion and morphed into many different camps. The very public sex scandal associated with religious broadcaster Jim Bakker and his PTL network brought ridicule to Charismatics. This was followed in 1988 and 1989 by the downfall of Pentecostal evangelist Jimmy Swaggart with another sex scandal very much in the news that further damaged the image of Pentecostals and Charismatics in the public eye. More a question of poor judgment than personal morality, Oral Roberts' 1987 declaration that "God would take him home" if he didn't raise enough money to keep ORU's City of Faith open, became a joke to many—God was holding Roberts "hostage." Some wondered what had happened to the glorious Charismatic movement.

The Charismatic dream of unity made significant headway before human carnality got in its way. But just as William Seymour and his call for racial unity at Azusa Street went unrealized because of the blight of sin, the vision was put forth bidding others to follow in the quest. Love and unity are God's desire for His people. Ground was gained yet some was lost. The old Charismatic patriarchs were passing on. David du Plessis died in 1987; Dennis Bennett died in 1991. New leadership was already emerging and as always new waves of renewal were needed. America was radically changing and so must the church, because renewal is never a static deposit. It must always be lived.

BROUGHT TO THIS MOMENT:

When "Charismatic" Must Become More Than a Catchword

The twentieth century movement of the Holy Spirit that has spread the New Testament, apostolic era power, prayer and passion for ministry throughout every sector of the Church and in every nation of the world, was tabbed "charismatic" in the mid-1960s. Derived from the Apostle Paul's recurrent use of *charismata* in referencing the gifts of the Holy Spirit, a summary, non-sectarian, biblical word was adopted to describe the awakening—a renewal, involving for many a new discovery of spiritual resources that have been available since the birth of the Church.

Charisma-charismata (the singular and plural) is not a rarely used word in the Bible. It is used by both Paul and Peter seventeen times and occurring in seven epistles in the New Testament—with its root *charis* (grace or favor, underlining the generosity of God, the Giver of all good things) appearing about 150 times. If anything, the word is a beautiful one in meaning and significance, and its English form and usage carries a generally positive quality, describing a person blessed with winsomeness and a recognizable quality of distinct appeal.

For the first twelve to fifteen years of the "charismatic movement," the word was generally used to describe (1) believers in Jesus Christ who identified themselves as having been either renewed or born again into a lifestyle of (a) worship, (b) study of God's Word, and of (c) learning to exercise, or "move or function in the supernatural gifts of the Holy Spirit (I Corinthians 12-14). However, as with most languages, time and circumstance gradually affect both the meaning and the mood surrounding certain words: "charismatic," in the sense of its application to Christians is a significant case in point. It has become more of a catchword, bandied by advocates and opponents alike, notwithstanding the fact that the Bible word stands high above the melee. The word "charismatic" deserves to be recovered from sloganeering and from "pat" usage that either lauds or criticizes the disciple of Jesus so described.

For example, a comedian friend of mine whose audiences span everything from Hollywood studio crowd "warm-ups" to church banquets and conferences, plays off of the way the word has declined in its meaning. "I'm a Presbyterian," he says. "Most of us Presbyterians might be 'charismatics' except we're afraid that if we raised our hands God might call on us!" It's a funny line, and my reference to it is not to fault my friend's taste, but to note the reality it expresses—one which indicates the widespread "dumbing down" of the word, "charismatic." Instead of it describing people whose quest is to understand God's Word and His workings in and through believers by His Spirit's giftings, it reduces the word to a callisthenic. Further, however worthy the biblical expression of upraised hands in worship or praise is, for many today, the sum and lack of substance their perception or understanding brings to the word's definition.

I make the point not as a judgment upon those who "dumb down" the term, but as a critique of those of us called "charismatic"—that in many, many ways, we are as responsible for shallow views of others toward our testimony as they may be. It is true that some who fear or reject exposing themselves to the possibilities of a childlike (not childish) availability to the Holy Spirit's supernatural workings do speak condescendingly and trivially regarding charismatics. But it is equally true that sizable sectors of the "Spirit-filled" community provide ready caricatures of a lifestyle and ministry style that too often appears casual regarding the Bible's requirements for "order" in the manifestation of spiritual gifts, and seem mindless by failing to more faithfully maintain apostolically required "order" when the "uninformed" are present. [Some television broadcasting is notorious for this insensitivity. It is especially grievous, seeing that their heeding of the Word's directives in I Corinthians 14 would not require prohibiting manifestations, but requires instruction, interpretation and an administering of group and self-discipline.]

The problem is this: presuming the Holy Spirit is earnestly desirous of bringing the whole of Christ's living Church, it seems crucial that the biblical world at the core of His desire not become a caricature or a mere catchword. The word charismata—and all the wealth of meaning and promise it holds for every believer should not be subject to casual discard because of its misuse or inappropriate context. It is a word laden with spiritual significance, used and defined in holy, positive and power-filled ways in Scripture, and properly perceived, stands pure and noble, descriptive and dynamic, reminding us that God still freely offers the Holy Spirit's gifts to each of us. And His offer is not to provide a single experience or sporadic, widely spaced expression of His miracle graces through each of us, but to enfranchise each believer with the possibility of transcendent, spiritual resources for manifesting His love and power to the world through His Spirit's grace-gifts.

When "charismatic" was first employed it served as an embracing term. It moved beyond denominational designations to a dimensional description—the dimensions of (1) opening to the Holy Spirit in the same way first believers did at Pentecost and throughout the New Testament, (2) worshipping Jesus Christ with profound simplicity and unapologetic forthrightness, and (3) gaining teaching in the Word of God in a quest beyond accruing information to pursuing incarnation—that is, seeking to see Jesus' ministry being unleashed in and through the lives of multitudes.

It is in this "charismatic dimension" of living for Christ—within these core values and by their constant pursuit—that true "Spirit-filled" life is lived, irrespective of how people define their theology or describe their experience in the Spirit. The net result of all believers becoming "charismatic" is the total Church's movement beyond so many trapped by seeing themselves as "just a layman," to millions becoming "agents of the Kingdom of Love, Life and Light!" It's the pathway of that New Testament people Jesus had in mind when He announced His Church-growth-and-building-plan! He seeks the formation of a cadre of world-penetrating, love-the-lost, reach-and-care, "witnesses;" witnesses who are evidence for the case that Jesus is alive and at work through His Church! His plan calls for a people:

Taught and lead into God's overflowing promise of life in Christ, including His Spirit's fullness and answering the call to discipleship (Acts 2:1-40);

Trained in and shaped by God's Word unto ever-increasing faith and solid, practical day-to-day living in their home, workplace, family and private life (II Corinthians, chapters 3-4); and,

Targeted toward an accountable, balanced lifestyle nurtured in a well pastored community of believers (Acts 2:42-47).

This is what charismatic means—and it's what a century of an ongoing, internationally impacting revival was and is meant to bring about. And just as hundreds of millions have answered the call to their moment—and many continue with diligence in their pursuit of Christ's purpose today—we have been helped to this moment by their testimony and lives . . . to receive His power, touch the world He died to save . . . and to keep tuned to what the Holy Spirit is speaking to us.

10

John Wimber and the Third Wave(s)

Carol Wimber heard the screams outside and knew immediately it was her three-year-old son Sean. She ran from her house to a neighbor's backyard and found the little boy swatting frantically at the swarming bees. Joined by her husband John, Carol did her best to brush the bees off. After John ripped off Sean's shirt because the bees had gotten underneath, they picked up their child and ran back to the house. Sean's little torso was plastered with red bee stings and John Wimber instinctively prayed for his son. To the surprise of Carol he started praying loudly in tongues, interspersed with cries of "Jesus, heal him." As Wimber prayed he grew more confident that God was touching his young child. Carol kneeled with her husband and watched as at least fifty large welts began to disappear.[1] Sean went to sleep and when he woke up a few hours later he was fine except for one small red spot. God had healed him.[2]

This account may not seem unusual given the story we've been telling if it weren't that John Wimber was a recent convert to Christ unsure of what to believe about spiritual gifts. Wimber, who often described himself as a "third generation pagan," had never opened the Bible before his conversion but was fascinated by what he now read. Soon after becoming a Christian he asked naïvely at a church service, "When are we gonna do the stuff?" "What stuff?" came the reply. "You know the stuff in the book, the healings and the miracles, that stuff!" Wimber was told that "stuff" didn't happen anymore, that the gifts had ceased. He was warned to stay away from those "excesses." So, while they first marveled at Sean's recovery, before long John rationalized the whole thing, supposing Sean had somehow gotten better naturally. Besides, Carol Wimber questioned her husband's tongues experience thinking it might be satanic. This coupled with another bad experience at a Charismatic prayer meeting around the same time made them put the Charismatic movement on the shelf.

Just a year before the June 1964 healing of his son, Wimber was playing music in Las Vegas casinos. For a season in the early sixties he worked in the Los Angeles area arranging and playing music with the Righteous Brothers, recording several albums. Successful by the standard of many musicians—he was making a living of it—Wimber wasn't interested in spiritual things before his wife Carol decided to leave him, taking the children with her. The separation drove him to seek God—but as a thoroughgoing pagan he wasn't sure where to start. He bought a Bible and started reading it and after a call from

Carol, Wimber moved back to Los Angeles where he was converted at a Quaker Bible study.

Missouri-born in 1934, Wimber was raised by his mother in the home of her parents. The whole family moved to Yorba Linda in 1946. There was no Christian influence in Wimber's childhood and his only recollection of Jesus is that His name was used as a cuss word. As an only child he grew up alone and, encouraged by his mother, poured himself into music. After two years of college he pursued a career in music. Wimber was a gifted musician and planned to make it his life. He had no idea he would one day lead a movement of churches that would help catalyze new dimensions of the Holy Spirit's work. It would be an interesting journey.

Not long after becoming a Christian, Wimber ended his musical career and started working in a factory to make a living. He and his family got involved in the Yorba Linda Evangelical Friend's church and John found he was a gifted evangelist. From 1964 to 1970 he led hundreds to Christ and saw the church grow. In 1970 he joined the church staff as an associate pastor and his continued leadership helped the church become one of the largest in their Quaker denomination. In addition he helped plant several other churches.

Despite the success, Wimber wearied of his church work. One day, after chiding a young man for his lack of church attendance, Wimber heard God speak to his heart: "John would you go to this church if you weren't paid to?"[3] Wimber realized he had allowed church activity to replace his devotion to God. Broken and confused by this revelation he decided to resign the pastorate. He was uncertain what to do until he was offered a role helping establish and lead the Charles E. Fuller Institute for Evangelism and Church Growth. Given his ten years plus experience in evangelistic work and his obvious church growth skills, it seemed a good fit.

From 1974 to 1977 he crisscrossed the nation as a consultant for hundreds of churches in "dozens of denominations."4 Working with Fuller Seminary's C. Peter Wagner, a church growth specialist and missiologist, Wimber embarked on a season of fruitful ministry helping many churches experience marked growth. Also teaching as an adjunct professor at Fuller Seminary, Wimber began to be more open to the contemporary work of the Holy Spirit. Professors like Pentecostal, Russell Spittler, mission specialists Donald McGavran, Paul Hiebert, and anthropologist Charles Craft helped him see the viability of spiritual gifts as they relate to the evangelistic task in the developing world.

During this period Wimber read the writings of British Pentecostal Donald Gee on spiritual gifts, another step in opening up to the work of the Spirit. Perhaps most important for what lay ahead was the influence of Fuller Seminary professor G. Eldon Ladd and his teaching on the kingdom of God. More than ever before Wimber realized that God's Kingdom was more than a future hope, it was a present reality as well. In the ministry of Jesus, God displayed the "presence of the future" through healings and miracles. Ladd's emphasis on the Kingdom prepared Wimber to see the relationship of evangelism to signs and wonders.

In his new association with Peter Wagner, Wimber also

reckoned with the transformation he observed in his colleague and mentor at the Fuller Institute. Peter Wagner was a dispensational evangelical through and through who disavowed spiritual gifts as a died-in-the-wool cessationist. Wagner's experience on the mission field contributed to a radical reshaping of his perspective. While in Bolivia he attended a crusade meeting of E. Stanley Jones, Methodist missionary to India, which was a full-fledged healing service, and was healed of a persistent affliction. After returning to the States and pursuing studies at Fuller in world missions, Wagner was convinced that signs and wonders were an essential component to evangelization. Wagner's transition had profound influence on Wimber.[5] He wasn't yet ready to endorse contemporary signs and wonders, but he was on his way.

By 1977, Wimber himself was in a spiritual desert, again too busy for his own good. He was not praying much or reading his Bible, and like four years before he was at a point of crisis. About the same time his wife Carol had her own spiritual crisis and was filled with the Spirit, speaking with tongues. Deeply repentant that she had discouraged her husband years before from using tongues in prayer, she led many of her friends into the experience while husband John remained unconvinced. Carol ended up joining with others in a small prayer meeting, attended by as many as fifty people, though John had no interest in attending.

Within weeks of Carol's new experience, things came to a head for John. After despairing of his spiritual condition while on a plane ride to Detroit, Michigan, he went to his hotel room for the night and after agonizing in prayer over his physical and spiritual burnout, he finally heard God speak to him. "John, I've seen *your* ministry, and now I'm going to show you *mine*." In tears Wimber responded, "Oh God, that is all I've ever wanted."[6]

John attended Carol's prayer meeting and was initially put off by its marginally Charismatic orientation. In a conversation after the meeting, he was shocked to find out that his wife was speaking in tongues (she'd never told him), but he made an effort to stay open given his recent experiences. John could see that his wife was changing dramatically in the way she related to him and the children. John was dumbstruck by the change and knew God was at work. He finally cried out to God to change him the way Carol had changed. That evening lying on his bed, while Carol was at her meeting, the Holy Spirit fell on him and he wept and spoke in tongues for hours. Something changed that night within John Wimber; the winds of change were blowing.[7]

Over breakfast not long after this, Carol told John that she was open to their pastoring together again if God so led. Though John gave no response, he started attending her small group meetings regularly and it was soon evident that he was the group's leader. Over the next few weeks that followed, it became very clear that God was leading him to start a church. Nevertheless, Wimber was still unsure if the new church was to come out of this small group. He was stunned while traveling with Peter Wagner one day as he turned and said, "John, why don't you go home and start a church in Yorba Linda?" Just days later in New York City a Lutheran pastor somewhat sheepishly gave Wimber a note he believed contained a message from God. The note read, "Go Home."[8] He was now certain he was to plant a church in Yorba Linda. The issue now was just how he was to do it.

The small Charismatic prayer meeting the Wimbers were part of was made up mostly of members of the Yorba Linda Friends church he had co-pastored and of which they were still members. While the meetings were not overly charismatic, the hunger and passion people were feeling for God inevitably cultivated an environment for the exercise of spiritual gifts. Before long this "afterglow" meeting on Sunday evenings caught the attention of the church's leadership.

Wimber was called before regional denominational leadership and questioned about what was going on. He staunchly defended it as a genuine work of the Holy Spirit and the beginning of a revival. He asked the leaders to let the group become a church plant open to the gifts of the Spirit. At one point the superintendent asked Wimber if the group could "have the fire without the 'tongues'?" Wimber answered "no." "If this is God—and I believe it is—we are going to let Him do whatever He wants to do with us."[9] In light of this response, John Wimber was asked to resign his membership from the church he had served for nearly fourteen years. So the group of sixty launched out.

The group didn't want to be independent, so through the suggestion and recommendation of a friend, John Wimber and the people he now pastored associated with the Calvary Chapel association of churches. They planted Calvary Chapel of Yorba Linda, holding their first service on Mother's Day, May 10, 1977. Wimber started preaching a series on the Gospel of Luke that continued for ten months and from which came an emphasis on divine healing.

John Wimber was now well on the way to becoming the leader of the movement of churches popularly known as simply the "Vineyard" or the "signs and wonders" movement. What was unique about Wimber and the movement is they never called themselves either Pentecostal or Charismatic, but simply "empowered evangelicals."[10] No leader or group better illustrates what has been called the "third wave." Further, they demonstrate the expanding dimensions of the Holy Spirit's reshaping of the church in the 1980s and 1990s. But before telling the rest of the story we need to revisit the Jesus People movement.

CALVARY CHAPEL AND THE VINEYARD

In the previous chapter we briefly introduced the Jesus People movement. One of the most important expressions of that generational revival among hippies was Calvary Chapel of Costa Mesa, California, pastored by Chuck Smith. Smith, a onetime pastor in the Foursquare Church, left that Classical Pentecostal denomination, feeling he just didn't "fit."[11] After a successful independent pastorate in Corona, California, Smith became the pastor of a small church in Costa Mesa which quickly grew. Through his college age daughter, Smith was introduced to some young hippie converts in the Jesus movement and to the chagrin of some of his church members, he welcomed them into the church.

Smith was soon making room in his own home for these kids and creatively housing others through "Jesus houses" in communities around Costa Mesa that accommodated masses of young converts. Calvary Chapel soon outgrew its building and purchased a tent to facilitate the crowds of hippies that flocked to the church. Chuck Smith and his leadership team began weekly beach baptism services where thousands were baptized. By the early 1970s the church had a weekly attendance of over ten thousand.

Calvary Chapel became a recognized center of the Jesus Movement and soon spun off churches pastored by many of Smith's spiritual sons. It rapidly became a vital church movement. Importantly, while much of the Jesus Movement had a Charismatic orientation, Calvary Chapel and its derivative churches did not make room for spiritual gifts in its primary worship services. Rather, if exercised at all, it was in smaller home meetings. And while the Calvary Chapel church movement ostensibly acknowledges the Holy Spirit's charismatic work, the churches are best described not as charismatic but as more broadly evangelical. Although the association with Calvary Chapel initially worked well, the lack of charismatic emphasis later created tensions for John Wimber in his relationship with Calvary Chapel.

After the first meeting in May 1977, Calvary Chapel of Yorba Linda quickly grew and had to relocate twice in its first six months of existence, soon attended by over 300 people. In the midst of the growth, Wimber continued teaching through Luke's Gospel. As he taught, he became convinced that Jesus' message of the kingdom of God necessarily carried with it the promise of healing and deliverance. A turning point for Wimber came after inviting John Amstutz, a professor at the Foursquare Church's LIFE Bible College in Los Angeles, to speak at the new congregation's Wednesday evening meeting. As Amstutz taught on the spiritual gifts, Wimber realized he and the church couldn't just theorize about healing, they had to practice regular prayer for the sick. In other words, they had to start "doing the stuff."

And so they did. The problem was that despite constant prayer nobody was getting healed. Instead, the people who prayed for the sick caught the colds and flu of those they ministered to. But they persisted and some ten months later, a young woman was powerfully and instantaneously healed after Wimber prayed for her. Ironically, when called to the home by the young woman's husband, he fully expected she wouldn't be healed. Still he went and obediently prayed for the release of kingdom power.

He was so discouraged at the time, that after praying for her, he turned around to explain to her husband why everyone isn't always healed. As Wimber began to give his now memorized speech, he was surprised as the man smiled, gazing past Wimber to his wife. He turned back around to see her getting up out of bed completely well. Wimber was so thrilled that after he got out to his car to leave, he screamed out in joy, "We got one!"[12]

From that day on something changed and healing and deliverance began to flow. One of the unique features of Wimber's approach to healing and other spiritual gifts was its inclusive character. Healing wasn't to be administered by a select few but all believers were called to exercise any of the gifts of the Holy Spirit. These gifts, which include healings, were not possessed by the person who exercised them. Rather, they belonged to the Spirit who distributed them through available believers as God desired to meet the needs of people. Ministry in the spiritual gifts was the privilege of all Christians. In essence Wimber "democratized" the ministry in the Holy Spirit much in the way envisioned at Azusa Street some seventy years before.

To live out this vision, Wimber held training sessions, "clinics" as he called them, for members of his church. He demonstrated how to pray for people and then invited others to "practice" doing the "stuff" themselves. As Wimber often said, "everybody gets to play," referring to the call for the whole church to minister healing and other spiritual gifts. Perhaps nothing is more distinctive about the Vineyard movement than this participatory approach to ministry.

The church continued to grow and by 1980 over seven hundred were regularly attending. Although the church was practicing healing and exercising spiritual gifts it still was primarily evangelical in the character of its worship services. People were not generally speaking in tongues or prophesying in services. The time of song and praise to God was heartfelt but not overly exuberant. This soon changed.

In a May 1980, Sunday evening service, Wimber invited Jesus movement evangelist Lonnie Frisbee to give his testimony at the meeting. After Frisbee finished speaking he asked those present who were over twenty-five to bless those in the meeting who were under twenty-five (they numbered in the hundreds). As Frisbee continued to minister he invited the Holy Spirit to fall upon the congregation and as he did so, people began to fall, shake, sob, cry out, speak in tongues, and pandemonium broke out as literally hundreds were Spirit baptized.[13] It was so wild that some people walked out in disgust while others stayed caught up in the wonder of it all. Carol Wimber told of one young man

> who fell face down, pulling the microphone down under him, and if we had ever entertained the thought of keeping any kind of reputation of respectability, it went up to the ceiling along with [the young man's] voice—as he shouted uncontrollably in tongues with the volume turned up all the way because someone had crashed into the soundboard.[14]

Wimber was dumbfounded by it all, unsure what to do and was extremely uncomfortable with the whole thing. Somehow in the midst of it all, and though not endorsing everything as a manifestation of the Holy Spirit, he sensed God was at work. After the meeting Wimber couldn't sleep, wondering if he had allowed something to happen that would ruin his church. About five the next morning a fellow Calvary Chapel pastor in Denver, unaware of the events the night before, woke up and felt compelled to call Wimber and simply tell him that whatever was happening there in Yorba Linda was of God. It was an important encouragement. Later that morning in a "defining moment" for the Vineyard, Wimber told his church staff, "If ever there is a choice between the smart thing to do and the move of the Holy Spirit, I will always land on the side of the Holy Spirit."[15]

Wimber was not enfranchising fanaticism by what he said but acknowledging that when the Holy Spirit is present one cannot always control how people react. They may, however, be taught and that became a chief aim of Wimber. The Holy Spirit would be allowed to move and manifest Himself but believers would be taught how to respond to His presence as appropriately as possible without quenching His work. Wimber's passion was to stay open to what "God was doing." The revival that followed the Frisbee meeting particularly touched young people and spread to the campuses of area schools. The church mushroomed and by 1982, thousands were attending.

Yet another strand to this story has to do with Ken Gulliksen, a young tongue speaking Lutheran, who associated with Calvary Chapel and was ordained as a pastor in 1971. After a stint of ministry in Texas, Gulliksen returned to California and started a church he called "Vineyard" in the home of Jesus movement musician Chuck Girard in 1974. The church grew and spun off several other churches in the Southern California area, also called "Vineyards," each associated with the Calvary Chapel churches, while not carrying its name.[16] Gulliksen attended the occasional meetings held by the Calvary Chapel association of churches and got to know Wimber well. Both men respected each other's ministries.

It isn't surprising that the events at Wimber's Yorba Linda church caused a stir among other Calvary Chapel pastors. In a "fateful meeting in 1982"[17] with Chuck Smith and other leaders with the group, Wimber was questioned about the practices at the church.[18] After some discussion it was agreed that Wimber's church, given its emphasis on healing and spiritual gifts, ought to drop "Calvary Chapel" from its name. Wimber decided on "Vineyard" given his friendship with Gulliksen. That simple decision birthed a separate church movement from Calvary Chapel. While Wimber was not asked to leave, it was obvious to him and everyone else that he held a much different view on the present working of the Holy Spirit.

Within months Gulliksen, not wanting to continue leading the eight or so Vineyard churches that had grown out of his leadership, turned them over to Wimber. Soon some thirty other Calvary Chapels, pastored by leaders wanting more emphasis on the Holy Spirit, left their previous association to join with the association of Vineyard churches. By early 1983 Wimber was no longer the leader of only one church but a thriving group of forty churches.[19]

Another milestone in 1982 for Wimber was an invitation by Peter Wagner to teach a course at Fuller Seminary's School of World Mission. With Wagner as the professor of record, Wimber was primary teacher. The course called "Signs, Wonders, and Church Growth," or simply MC510 as it became widely known, was a sensation at the seminary and brought national attention in the media. It quickly had the highest enrollments in the seminary's history. Wimber not only taught on healing and other spiritual gifts but offered "clinics" or "laboratories" where students got to practice what they were taught. The class went on for nearly four years and was finally stopped after controversy developed over the course's Charismatic emphasis. After review by administration and faculty it was reinstated but not taught by Wimber.

The publicity over MC510 brought Wimber into the national spotlight. His balanced approach to healing and his concerted effort to ground spiritual gifts theologically helped him gain a large audience among mainline Protestants, and strategically among evangelicals as well. The years of teaching the MC510 course helped Wimber articulate an approach to spiritual gifts that congealed better with evangelical theology. Wimber never emphasized either Spirit baptism or speaking with tongues; instead, he put the emphasis on what he called "power evangelism," declaring that healings, miracles, and spiritual gifts made people more ready to receive the gospel of the kingdom of God. The bulk of the content of the MC510 course was contained in Wimber's widely distributed 1986 book by that title, *Power Evangelism*.[20]

For Wimber, a self-described conservative evangelical, Spirit baptism was not necessarily an event subsequent to salvation. The Pentecostal demand that baptism with the Holy Spirit is a distinct and separate experience has often caused heated debate. Wimber realized that many evangelicals use the term baptism with the Spirit to describe regeneration and he sought to avoid using the term to describe a distinct subsequent experience. He believed, according to his understanding of Scripture, that the Spirit was initially received at conversion but could be followed by subsequent fillings. His approach was most compatible with many evangelicals.

By 1984, Vineyard Christian Fellowship had a Sunday worship attendance of over three thousand and had moved to a nearby Anaheim high school to make room for the increasing throng. That same year they held the first of a series of annual conferences on power evangelism, which over the next few years were attended by thousands of young pastors and leaders. Wimber's down-to-earth spirituality and more evangelical approach to spiritual gifts drew spiritually hungry non-Pentecostals to his events. The conferences were nevertheless "Pentecostal-like." The worship was enthusiastic and during prayer times people spoke in tongues, prophesied, were healed and the like. Wimber's mainstream appeal and manner, joined with his emphasis on evangelism and church planting helped draw many university and seminary trained leaders into the expanding movement.

During the mid- and late 1980s Wimber and a traveling team made many trips to Europe, with frequent visits to the United Kingdom where the Vineyard movement made a lasting impact. A number of already Charismatic Anglican churches hosted his conferences which helped bring a new wave of renewal among Anglicans and other mainline and evangelical groups. The emphasis on church planting by the Vineyard also resulted in a number of churches being planted in the UK.

Over the coming years Wimber continued to look for what "God was doing" which led him to welcome the prophetic ministry of a number of contemporary prophets who were associated with Kansas City Fellowship, a Missouri-based independent church pastored by Mike Bickle. Prophets Paul Cain, Bob Jones, and John Paul Jackson were gaining attention for rather specific prophecies. Jack Deere, formally a professor at Dallas Theological Seminary, introduced Wimber to Paul Cain. After arranging dates for Cain to visit Wimber, Deere told John that Cain said there would be an earthquake the day he came to California for the meeting with Wimber. When there was a small earthquake that day in nearby Pasadena, Cain had Wimber's attention.

At the 1989 annual Vineyard conference, Wimber invited Cain and other "Kansas City prophets" to speak, which ushered a season of emphasis on prophetic ministry among Vineyard churches. Mike Bickle also brought his Kansas City congregation into Vineyard as an associated church. In 1990 controversy swirled over the prophets when accusations were brought alleging false teachings in the Kansas City group. Although Wimber and most Vineyard churches were not the main focus of the charges, he was thrust into the middle of it all because of his very public identification with Bickle and the other prophets.

After Wimber and Bickle had to discipline one of the prophets for moral failure, the strain caused a number of churches and key leaders to leave Vineyard, feeling it wasn't consistent with their vision and values. In 1995 Wimber admitted at a pastors' conference that he regretted embracing the prophetic movement. It was a difficult season for Wimber and the Vineyard as they came under increasing criticism.

John Wimber encountered health problems beginning in 1986 with a heart attack. In 1993 he was diagnosed with sinus cancer and its treatment weakened him severely; a stroke in 1995 added to his struggles. In typical fashion Wimber was forthright about his health problems and acknowledged that he couldn't fully explain why others were healed through his ministry and yet he was not. This kind of honesty is part of what endeared him to many. In 1997 Wimber died of a brain hemorrhage after a fall in his home. The movement didn't end with his death but has continued to grow, with over 800 churches worldwide in 2005.

What must not be missed in the controversy that sometimes surrounded Wimber and the Vineyard is his enormous influence in the evangelical world, especially among baby boomer pastors and leaders. His conferences, audio and video tapes, and books impacted tens of thousands. His steadfast refusal to adopt a Pentecostal or Charismatic moniker, particularly in the 1980s, helped him "Pentecostalize" many evangelicals by normalizing the practice of spiritual gifts without demanding the adoption of Pentecostal theology or nomenclature regarding baptism in the Holy Spirit. A large number of evangelical leaders embraced the Holy Spirit's supernatural work without considering themselves either Pentecostal or Charismatic. When Peter Wagner coined the term "Third Wave," he was identifying this group.

Something else made Wimber attractive to evangelicals. Despite some of the exotic and unusual Pentecostal-like phenomena associated with Wimber, he eschewed what he believed was unnecessary hype and unfortunate manipulation that sometimes occurred in the Pentecostal and Charismatic movements. For Wimber, spiritual gifts were not about being "hyper spiritual" but were ministered by everyday Christians, in everyday situations. He used the term "naturally supernatural" to describe ministry that was "normal," meaning that people did not have to act or talk differently for the Holy Spirit to work through them.[21] They could behave in a normal manner and God would still use them to bring healing and deliverance to others.

Wimber himself carried out his healing ministry in this same manner. There was no music at the end of services to effect a particular mood or atmosphere in the meetings he conducted. Instead he would explain that God would simply come in their midst if sincerely invited. Wimber then simply prayed, "Come

Holy Spirit" and ministered in healing, frequently calling out specific people through spiritual insight. Other times he would "see" God working in a person and call them out for prayer that followed with his "interview" with the person (he talked with them as he prayed) as the congregation watched.[22] Almost always after modeling prayer, he invited others to pray for each other, noting he didn't need to be the one to pray. This approach appealed to evangelicals who longed for healing but wanted to avoid the emotional excesses so often associated with Pentecostals.

THE TORONTO AND
BROWNSVILLE REVIVALS

In the wake of John Wimber and the Vineyard came an important revival that started at the Toronto Airport Vineyard Christian Fellowship in January 1994. John Arnot, the Toronto church's pastor, invited Randy Clark to conduct a series of renewal services beginning on January 20. Arnot had heard that Clark and the St. Louis Vineyard he pastored had experienced a season of refreshing. Clark's Toronto meetings turned into a remarkable revival. Almost immediately people were dramatically touched by the Holy Spirit, weeping, falling, shaking, dancing, and shouting. What captured the attention of the media was the phenomenon of laughter. People at the renewal meetings broke into uncontrolled laughter that doubled them over, leaving them laying on the floor laughing, sometimes for an hour or more.[23] Arnot asked Clark to stay for more meetings and by February the "Toronto Blessing" was fully underway. People traveled from around the world to witness and experience the revival. Nightly meetings were started that met six days a week.

The revival quickly outgrew the small Vineyard facility and a larger meeting place was secured. Attendance swelled to thousands in the evening meetings in the fall of 1994 and throughout 1995. By the end of 1995, 600 thousand people had visited Toronto from almost every nation on the planet. There were over nine thousand first time conversions in the renewal's first year.[24]

Both the secular and religious media covered the renewal largely because of the unusual manifestations that occurred among participants. In addition to the laughter, people shook violently or called out animal-like sounds some described as barking or roaring. Falling was another trait of the revival, with over half of the people being prayed for falling down, "slain in the Spirit." Some people compared the Toronto outpouring to the Azusa Street revival.

People who traveled to Toronto often experienced dramatic renewal and transformation. They testified to new devotion to Christ and a new love of the Scriptures. Couples said the renewal brought change that saved marriages. The renewal saw many powerful cases of healing and deliverance. Pastors and leaders were a particular focus in the Toronto revival and often experienced similar awakenings when they returned to their own churches after visiting Toronto.

For two years John Wimber and the Vineyard leadership generally endorsed the renewal in the Airport Vineyard, but encouraged Arnot and his leadership to not "biblicise" the more exotic or extra-biblical phenomena associated with the revival, such as the animal-like outcries. Finally in late 1996, Wimber withdrew his endorsement of the renewal, feeling that his cautions went unheeded. Not long after, the Toronto Airport Vineyard peaceably withdrew from Wimber's Vineyard association as did a number of other Vineyards that were in agreement with the renewal. From this disagreement a number of churches associated together in a new alliance of churches focused on the renewal and looking to Arnot and others for leadership.

With the Toronto revival still booming, another outpouring occurred at the Brownsville Assembly of God Church in Pensacola, Florida. Evangelist Steve Hill was invited by senior pastor John Kilpatrick to conduct revival services. At a Father's Day service in June, 1995, Hill, who visited the Toronto revival himself, finished his message and gave an altar call for repentance. As hundreds streamed forward the Holy Spirit fell on the people and like Toronto many people fell, shook, wept, and laughed as they encountered God's presence. Kilpatrick asked Hill to stay on—which he did for over two years—conducting nightly revival meetings that drew larger crowds than Toronto and some nights nearly five thousand people packed into the building. A mark of the Brownsville revival was the focus on conversion with over 100 thousand decisions in the first two years of the outpouring. Like Toronto it sparked revival fires as visitors took the revival back to their own churches in many instances.

The exotic behavior at both revivals, particularly because of broad media coverage, began to draw strong criticism. A particular vocal critic was Hank Hanegraaf of the Christian Research Institute, a watchdog group started by the late Walter Martin, a cult researcher. Hanegraaf used his daily national radio broadcast to blast the Toronto revival as well as John Wimber and the Vineyard movement. His 1997 book *Counterfeit Revival* was a best seller and a broadside of everyone associated with the renewal. Over time both in Toronto and Pensacola, some moderation was evident as leaders made efforts to teach people how to respond appropriately to the Holy Spirit's presence while at the same time giving way to His working.

THE EVER CHANGING SHAPE OF PENTECOSTALISM

As the 1990s progressed, the Charismatic Renewal faded in popular perception but its impact was not gone. Charismatics continued to work quietly in their churches working to bring renewal. Vinson Synan and other leaders had since 1984 sought to carry out the legacy of the historic 1977 Kansas City conference that brought together the diverse expressions of the Renewal. An umbrella group, the North American Renewal Service Committee (NARSC), was formed to sponsor a 1986 Charismatic Leader's conference and a 1987 believer's conference, both held in New Orleans. Other national Charismatic conferences were held in Indianapolis in 1990, in Orlando in 1995, and in St. Louis in 2000.

It became apparent though by 2000 that these events were

no longer drawing crowds as before. The renewal was too diffuse and pervasive. Increasingly, Charismatics were integrated into the regular life of the church instead of finding identity in separate, distinct renewal structures. This carried with it the risk of an erosion of the Charismatic distinctives, of course, but to many Charismatics it seemed the inevitable path if renewal was to penetrate denominations long term. There were other changes as well.

By the end of the century Classical Pentecostal denominations and independent Charismatics had established many enduring institutions in education, publishing, and broadcasting. Pat Robertson probably best illustrates this. Robertson's Virginia-based Christian Broadcasting Network (CBN) that started with one station in 1959 was a global network by the 1990s with state of the art broadcast studios. In addition he helped found CBN University in 1978 and by 2005 it included a full undergraduate program and eight graduate schools, all with full regional and professional accreditation.

The Family Channel, founded by Robertson and CBN was a cable network that provided family oriented programming. The Family Channel was acquired by Rupert Murdock and his Fox network in 1992 for several hundred million dollars. The proceeds of the sale of the Family Channel helped Robertson raise his University's endowment to three hundred million dollars, making it one of the highest endowed Christian universities in America. In 2003 Regent University's School of Divinity established the first Ph.D. program in the world exclusively focused on the study of the history and theology of the global Pentecostal and Charismatic movements.

Other Renewal teaching institutions such as Church of God Theological Seminary, Oral Roberts University, Kings Seminary, Assemblies of God Theological Seminary, and Asian Pacific Theological Seminary, are cultivating a rich soil for the study of modern Pentecostalism from the perspective of participant-scholars. Though some suspicion remains about the threat of scholarship to the vitality of Pentecostal faith, the need for academic dialogue and careful study of a movement reshaping world Christianity, is being recognized. Groups like the Society for Pentecostal Studies and its journal *Pneuma* are springing up around the world and gaining acceptance in the wider academic world.

While many of the Charismatic periodicals ceased as the Renewal grew and became more diffused, Strang Communications with its publication arm Creation House, and magazines *Charisma, Ministries Today*, and others are a growing force in Christian publication. *Charisma* magazine, with a circulation of a quarter million, celebrated its thirtieth anniversary in 2005, a remarkable achievement given the ever changing environment of the Renewal.

Although overall church growth in the United States has plateaued or declined in the last three decades, several Classical Pentecostal denominations are growing. Leading the way is the African-American Church of God in Christ with over 5.5 million members, making it the fourth largest Protestant denomination in the United States. There are now more mega churches (churches with a weekly attendance of two thousand or more) in America than ever before. These churches, particularly the larger ones, are "functionally nondenominational," in that they start churches and ministries, engage in media and publishing, and have extensive community and world impact. They also attract other pastors and leaders who want to align themselves with the pastors of these thriving church centers. A significant percentage of America's twelve hundred mega churches are Pentecostal/Charismatic in theological orientation.[25]

Independent Pentecostals

While the 1990s featured news of revivals like Toronto and Pensacola, almost unnoticed was the rapid growth among independent Pentecostal and Charismatic churches. As the Charismatic movement lost its cohesion in the late 1980s, the focus shifted to individual leaders and their ministry centers (often mega churches) that were either not a part of a denomination or the scope of their ministries eclipsed whatever association they had. Peter Wagner observed this and has written extensively on this new phenomenon.

Wagner's 1998 book *The New Apostolic Churches* featured a number of leaders not only from the United States but from around the world that he believed were contemporary apostles.[26] Around such leaders were growing networks, large and small, of what could almost be described as mini-denominations, except that they are organized relationally, not organizationally. These associations of pastors and churches under the apostolic leader are based on affinity rather than strict doctrinal statements or hierarchical structures. Wagner was simply observing something that was occurring. Denominational loyalty as an obligation is fading as many pastors look to leaders whom they see as sharing a common vision and who resource local pastors in relevant ways. These de-facto associations frequently mean more to leaders than any formal organizational ties they might have.

An example of such a leader is ORU graduate Ted Haggard, pastor of New Life Church in Colorado Springs, Colorado. His church, planted in 1985, has grown to over eleven thousand members. The independent congregation does not call itself a Pentecostal church but in all ways typifies a church moving in the fullness of the Holy Spirit. Around Haggard has grown a worldwide association of pastors and churches. Haggard does not call himself an apostle—though use of the title is becoming more common—but in Wagner's view is an example of one nonetheless. Haggard is widely respected and presently serves as president of the National Association of Evangelicals, further illustrating the reach of Pentecostalism after a century.

Wagner left his teaching post at Fuller Seminary and moved to the Colorado Springs area to establish a nontraditional ministry training school called the Wagner Leadership Institute. He continues to strongly affirm the present day expression of both apostles and prophets and started the International Coalition of Apostles to foster relationship and dialogue among apostolic leaders. Wagner is a part of Ted Haggard's congregation.

Also during the 1990s, and another example of Wagner's thesis, is the growth of African-American independent Pentecostal churches. Bishop T. D. Jakes is probably the most well known example. His media ministry has given him global prominence in the Pentecostal and Charismatic arenas. Since Jakes started the Potter's House Church in the Dallas/Ft. Worth area of Texas, he claims over thirty thousand members. A large network of leaders and churches has associated with Jakes and his ministry. The Potter's House is a dynamic ministry center that not only addresses holistic needs of church members but is impacting the Dallas/Ft. Worth community significantly. Both Haggard and Jakes are not unusual. Many other examples could be given and many church observers believe these independent Pentecostals represent the future of Pentecostalism in North America.

Global Growth

Although the focus of this book has been on the Azusa Street revival and its progeny in the United States, we've tried to keep in mind the global expansion of Pentecostalism. As Harvard's Harvey Cox has said, Pentecostalism is "religion made for travel."[27] Clearly we have seen that the Pentecostal embrace of the invisible is well suited for the worldviews in the developing nations. Its cultural adaptability has contributed to rapid indigenization. Almost silently, with attentions focused elsewhere the church outside the West has become increasingly Pentecostal.

While much credit is given to early Pentecostal missionaries, sometimes missed were the tireless efforts of indigenous pastors, leaders, and individual Pentecostals who were the essential keys to its astronomical growth. Only now are their stories becoming known, but they are just as surely heroes along with other missionaries. Consider the countless Pentecostals who suffered greatly under communism, preserving and quietly spreading their faith. After the fall of communism many Western ministries highlighted their outreach into Eastern Europe when the substantial work was being done by national leaders.

In Africa the growth of Christianity is primarily based in indigenous independent churches, most of which are Charismatic. The growth of Christianity in Africa is almost impossible to comprehend with Christians approaching fifty percent of the continent's overall population.[28] Even among African Christians, who make no claims of being Pentecostal or Charismatic, one finds their actual praxis very "Pentecostal-like" as they cast out demons, heal the sick, and believe in the fullness of the Holy Spirit. In the developing world and in the West it is no longer possible to easily distinguish who is Pentecostal by a church or denominational name.

Pentecostalism in Africa is extremely diverse in character and not easy to categorize. The significant work of Classical Pentecostal missionaries must not be ignored and they have left a lasting legacy on the continent. Much of the growth in the last thirty years, however, has come from African national leaders who are increasingly developing their own "brands" of Pentecostalism and spreading them far and wide.

Evangelists like German-born Pentecostal Reinhard Bonnke have touched Africa with the gospel of God's kingdom, his crusades attended by millions over the years, with as many as a million responses for salvation made in a single year.[29] Bonnke and other Western evangelists like T. L. Osborn have left an imprint of the supernatural on the African church. If demographic trends continue, by 2050, Africa will have more Christians than any other continent. While this is good news to those longing for the fulfillment of the Great Commission, it also forebodes a collision, when Sub-Saharan Africa, the heart of the emerging African Christendom, begins to reach into Muslim North Africa and other Islamic strongholds.

Latin America has also become a center for Pentecostalism over the last ninety years. Until the 1950s growth was steady but slow; since then it has exploded, with Pentecostals now making up eighty to ninety percent of all Protestants in Latin America. In Brazil alone the Assemblies of God have 22 million members compared to nearly 2.5 million in the United States. Chile has the world's second largest church, the Jotabechie Methodist Pentecostal Church in Santiago, with 350 thousand members.[30] This rapid growth has spurred Roman Catholics to be more Charismatic to retain members, moving the Latin American church more toward Pentecostal praxis. Pentecostalism resonates in Latin America as it touches deeply the needs of people that go unaddressed by other social institutions.

In Asia a similar story is developing. Leading the way has been South Korea, boasting the largest church in the world pastored by David Yongi Cho. The Seoul-based Yoido Full Gospel Assembly has a membership of over 840 thousand, larger than the city of San Francisco.[31] South Korea has several churches with membership over 100 thousand. There is also substantial Pentecostal growth in the Philippines, Indonesia, Singapore, and Malaysia. While statistics are hard to estimate, the rapid growth of Christianity in China is primarily Pentecostal in character.

PERSPECTIVE

Many were shocked in 1955 when Henry P. Van Dusen, of Union Theological Seminary, called conservative Christianity, especially Pentecostals, the "third force in Christendom."[32] Van Dusen later said: "I have come to believe that the Pentecostal movement with its emphasis on the Holy Spirit is more than just another revival. . . . It is a revolution comparable in importance with the establishment of the original church and with the Protestant Reformation."[33] Van Dusen's words were clearly prophetic looking back from today's perspective.

In just one hundred years Pentecostalism has moved from the margins of Western society to become the most dynamic, diverse, and expansive expression of the Christian church globally. While far from perfect itself, more than in any other branch of Christianity, it has challenged ethnic, gender, and other cultural barriers. Most dramatically, Christianity, once the faith of the white, Western world, is now growing fastest in Africa, South America, and Asia. In a shocking, tectonic shift, the Christian center is moving. The challenge for North American Christians is whether we will stand and serve this unprecedented transition.

This global change in fact fulfills the simple but profound vision of William Seymour, who just a century ago longed for a church that embraced the Pentecostal message. It was not just a message of speaking with tongues but a message of God's love for all humanity and his desire to include all people in his redemptive purposes. Wasn't that the promise? "I will pour my Spirit on all people" (Acts 2:17). As we commemorate that historic revival at Azusa Street we can now see that Seymour's dream was God's dream for His Church, and despite man's failings His will has been inexorably moving forward.

Waves of renewal that started at the beginning of the twentieth century have not ebbed but continue to revitalize and reshape, not just Pentecostals, but the entire Church. There is no reason to think they will stop. The challenge is obeying the apostle Paul's call to live a life of Holy Spirit fullness (Eph 5:18).

BROUGHT TO THIS MOMENT:

To Decide Our Response to the Spirit's Century-long Workings

To look at the closing of The Charismatic Century is to observe a trail of men and women who have responded to a call—a call to both a broader and deeper dimension of spiritual ministry. The words "deeper dimension" are not an arrogant statement of condescension toward non-charismatic faith, when the individual's faith is in Jesus Christ as Savior, and founded on the Word of God. But it is to put an emphasis on "ministry" as defined by the full-orbed ministry of Jesus Christ and His workings through His people in the first century Church.

The growth of so broad a sector of Christianity as represented in these pages which describe the Church's "twentieth century reformation"—an ever-spreading awakening to the works, gifts and power of the Holy Spirit—has not been institutional: it has been incarnational. The "charismatic" sector of the Church has grown because of its commitment and effectiveness in cultivating the "ministry of the Body"—the incarnation of the ministry of Jesus Christ through ordinary people everywhere.

As millions of Christians have opened to the presence and power of the Spirit globally, the Church is moving daily beyond the walls that house their assembled times of worshipping God and learning His Word. Then, nurtured by their worship and fellowship, by the natural flow of their daily lives, they spread into the marketplaces, workplaces and neighborhoods of the world, which become salted through and through with people for whom faith has begun to manifest beyond "belief in a system," to "believing for the presence of Jesus—in my life, on my job, in my circumstance, and toward those I know, meet, work with and care for."

This is the reason for and meaning of The Charismatic Century!

It is a summons from heaven, reminding us that above all systems, the Church is about people—people who know who Jesus is. It is with and through them He has willed to "build My Church"; enfranchising them with "keys of the kingdom of heaven"—with Holy Spirit power, gifts, signs and enabling boldness to "minister" in His Name (Matthew 16:13-19).

It is a statement from God's Word, pointing us to the last times—that He who said He "has given you the former rain faithfully" will cause "the latter rain" to come, bringing with it restoration and redemptive graces; bringing the Bride of Christ to a place of purity (without spot), fidelity (without blemish), integrity (without wrinkle), and maturity ("a glorious Church")—all this enhancing Her (the Church's) "ministering" presence (Ephesians 5:24-27).

It is a surging stream from God's eternal temple, breaking forth like a river that brings divine life wherever it comes, and bursting out in every place hearts that welcome the Holy Spirit's power, like "streams of living water" bring refreshing newness to first time recipients, refilling for established believers—transforming barren places from deadness to vital blessing as God's grace rivers to the world via spiritually functional believers (Ezekiel 47; John 7:37-39; Isaiah 44:3, 4).

The Century's significance is not in its phenomena but its people!

The astounding statistical increases in the global Christian Church are not touted as a boast of human achievement but as a gift of divine grace. Just as seasons of refreshing have been experienced throughout the centuries, the century just traversed has been another—but by every indicator, possibly the one ushering us to the last moments of our world as we know it. The Apostle Peter said,

Repent therefore and be converted, that your sins may be blotted out, so that times of refreshing may come from the presence of the Lord, and that He may send Jesus Christ, who was preached to you before, whom heaven must receive until the times of restoration of all things, which God has spoke by the mouth of all His holy prophets since the world began.   Acts 10:19-21

Both a promise and a portent beckon us to hear that call again—the promise of "Last Days Outpouring" (Acts 2:17-18) and the portent of The End (Acts 2:19-21). The message is clear—repentance, that is a respondent heart and willing mind, open the way for God to make each of us—you and me—a vital part of this "moment" to which we have all been brought.

As we have navigated these pages, the Holy Spirit's decade-to-decade workings in the Church have highlighted divine values—pointing us toward those things that call for our availability to His divine ways. Chapter by chapter defines points at which any one of us may be called to humble our hearts to experience in our days what broke forth a hundred years ago, renewing what began two thousand years ago. We have been brought to this moment:

- which uniquely invites us to say, "Come, Holy Spirit—I am open to the Savior's salvation's forgiveness and to Your overflowing fullness,"
- which faces us with the Spirit's summons to permit Him to capacitate us with power by reason of a passionate quest, not passive questionings;
- which seeks to draw us past self-righteous distancing from revival by using human failure seen there as our excuse for apathy and criticism;
- which echoes Jesus' call to each of us, "Receive the Holy Spirit—and you shall receive power after He has come upon you!" (John 20:21; Acts 1:8);

- which demands we face-up with honesty to the fact that "tongues" are not trivia, but a Bible-based spiritual resource to be prayerfully employed;
- which urges the Church to rise beyond any residue of entrenched male chauvinism regarding public spokespersons and leaders in its ranks;
- which promises the healing presence of God as an accompanying grace from God to empower believers to touch with power and compassion;
- which teaches us to balance passion with discernment, walking wisely in paths that unite God's Word of Truth with His Spirit's works of power;
- which defines "charismatic" in the Bible's way, refining our perspective to open to God's purpose, means and methods for empowering us today;
- which submits to Jesus' primary desire for each of us—to make every one of us disciples who not only know His Word, but who receive His directive to do His works— drawing upon His TRUTH which sets us and others free, and His POWER which will enable us as ordinary people to serve and minister with extraordinary abilities—filled and flowing, alive in Christ and loving the world in the same way He did.

It was sixty years later . . .

It wasn't the twentieth century, it was the first. And at a moment when the Church looked feeble in some places, impure in others, and generally weakened by Her dependence on human ways, works and wisdom, Jesus made a personal appearance to one man exiled to a remote island. To this day, the Revelation which John relayed from Jesus' own lips stands as a holy watchword: "Behold I come quickly!"

But matching that word of anticipation, Jesus speaks seven times saying, "He that has ears to hear—Listen to what the Holy Spirit is saying to the churches!" In short, any thought about the second coming must be preceded by our sensitivity to His Word about the Spirit's coming—and continuance among us! By our Lord's own emphasis, our steadfast hearing, opening to and obeying the Holy Spirit is the Church's only hope for vitality, fiery devotion, purity, faithfulness and fruitfulness.

That's the objective of our having studied the past century, and our quest to summarize the lessons of that century have not been an afterthought to each span of year, but to provide forethought and provoke ready hearts that respond to the Spirit's voice as He seeks to overflow and lead us to effective ministry today.

It is "unto that" that we have been brought "unto now."

Carpe diem!!

A Closing Personal Tribute

Having had an active part in leadership in the Church for the past fifty years, I feel indebted to those who God used to shape my life and ministry. Six men and one woman had profound influence upon my life, both as a believer and as a leader. Two of these were my mother and my father—Jack (Sr.) and Dolores Hayford—both of whom, as with the next two, have passed into the eternal presence of God in heaven. Vincent Bird, Clarence Hall and Kenneth Erickson—my first bishop, my college dean and the pastor who most affected my view of shepherding Christ's flock (respectively)—fathered values in my life which I've recorded elsewhere. Only two are widely known, and just as they impacted me so did they innumerable others—Oral Roberts and Billy Graham.

In the past twenty years of my life I have been privileged to know both men, being honored by their evident trust shown toward me in different ways. A few years ago, I was recipient of a literary award for an article in a national journal which I wrote about Billy Graham in 1995. Similarly, I more recently wrote concerning Oral Roberts, and because of the subject of this book, I have thought it worthy to include that article.

TIME FOR AN "ORAL" REVIEW

Though still honored in most charismatic circles today, "Brother Roberts," as he was earlier referenced by most until the last twenty years, it is an unfortunate fact that Oral is generally slighted by much of the larger Christian community. And, while not disregarded within classical Pentecostal traditions, open acknowledgment of his role in shaping the history of the whole Spirit-filled movement is not given, and sometimes seems to be either neglected or marginalized.

The history of the twentieth century is in place now, and without self-congratulation (for few of us living had anything much to do with this fact) the "Spirit-filled" community—the Pentecostals-Charismatic movement—has been universally declared to be the century's most penetrating, shaping and fruit-begetting global Christian influence. In that light, and from the vantage point of a half-century of overview myself, let me offer a review of the traits of Oral's ministry that initiated his influence on the whole Church.

In 1951, Oral Roberts was not a household name in America. But his preaching-healing ministry had already begun drawing thousands to his tent meetings—simultaneous with the tent-revivals beginning to draw throngs to hear Billy Graham. It is as unnecessary as it would be unwise to make a comparison of the two men's ministries. Billy's straight-ahead soul-winning crusades won the hearts and trust of us all, and it is doubtless that he has personally ministered to more people than any evangelist in history to date. But while Graham crusades moved multitudes and made headlines around the world, it was Oral's unfettered-by-fear "Full Gospel" ministry that changed the direction of the Church.

In post–WWII America, the flame of Azusa Street's Pentecostal revival was waning among those denominations and fellowships born in its heat. Even though the breezes of the "Latter Rain" movement stirred eddies of spiritual renewal in a few places, the broad stream of Christian ministry was not impacted. For the most part, traditional evangelical ministry defined the public's expectation of Bible-centered Protestantism, and "ripe-pickings" awaited anyone launching a ministry or planting a church—as long as it maintained a plain-vanilla approach to the Gospel.

Well do I remember the "soft-peddling" of Pentecostal distinctives (especially "tongues" and "healing") at that time—the season of my own training and entry to ministry. But Oral shook the landscape with the inescapable reality and practicality of Jesus' whole ministry—"teaching . . . preaching the gospel of the Kingdom, and healing . . . sick people who were afflicted with various diseases and torments, and those who were demon-possessed, epileptics, and paralytics—and great multitudes followed Him" (Matthew 4:23-25). And he was unstinting in his posture as a full fledged "Pentecostal"—as a man for whom "speaking in tongues" was neither a silly or optional practice. But while standing solidly for the fundamentals of the "Full Gospel," he was a breath of fresh air and a tower of strength at once—manifesting both the simplicity and the dynamism of a pure New Testament ministry in the power of the Holy Spirit.

A Focused Ministry With Substance

The campaign services of Oral Roberts rarely find a counterpart today, for not only was the whole scope of teaching, preaching, healing and deliverance ministry taking place at once in his meetings, there was also a notable downplay of sensation or the dramatic. His was a no-nonsense, straight-from-the-shoulder, full-orbed-power-of-God presentation that provided a focused ministry with substance.

The Word of God was preached with a strong development of the text of the scriptures (not merely a few clever ideas or a superficial glossing of a passage). Though the evangelistic pulpit-platform style of the era in all sectors of the Church was usually bombastic, to listen to Oral was to witness a white hot passion that was focused on drilling truth into hearts with no time or space for mere histrionics or spasms of "style."

Biblical order was maintained, with governance that clearly gave place for the dynamic moving of the Holy Spirit but disallowed the intrusion of fanatical distractions or the indulgence of supposed "Holy Ghost prompted" activities then frequently presumed as necessary among many Pentecostals.

Evangelism was given foremost priority, and a typical response to Oral's altar call brought hosts of souls forward to receive Christ. His call to salvation was not muddied by a generic appeal geared to maximize the possibility of filling the altar area, even though he did call the backslider to return home as well as the unconverted to repentance.

Every service contained two parts—the teaching-preaching, and the ministry of healing. Both resulted in verifiable miracles—(a) in souls being born again to eternal life, and (b) in bodies and minds being healed and delivered from physical and spiritual bondage. Again, the evangelist's style was pointed and manifestly powerful, but there was a complete absence of "flair" or "showmanship," and an unmistakable focus was kept on Jesus above all.

It was this kind of balance between pure Pentecostal passion, penetrated with his personal lifestyle of laser-like targeting of pursuing a Christ-like ministry of healing and miracles (sans capitalizing on crowd appeal or sensation), that awakened the mid-century generation to the multi-dimensioned power of God. Without question, it was Oral's ministry that confronted and restored focus and passion to the Pentecostal movement and laid the groundwork for what became the global spread of Spirit-filled life and experience in the 1960s and 70s.

No Oral—No Movement?

It may seem the rendering of an undue degree of influence to suggest it, but it is dubious to me that if God had not, in His sovereign will, purpose and power, raised up the ministry of Oral Roberts, the entire Charismatic moment might not have occurred. This is not to glorify the man, but to acknowledge the Holy Spirit's strategic timing and workings.

Without revisiting the nuances or commending the worth of the several acknowledged "voices" which rose in that renewal—birthed amid (1) the healing revival-evangelists of the late 1950s, (2) the spread of the Full Gospel Businessmen's fellowship, (3) the influence of Dave Wilkerson's and John and Elizabeth Sherrill's books, *The Cross and the Switchblade* and *They Speak With Other Tongues*, and (4) the awakenings on Duquesne's and Notre Dame's campuses—I believe an honest review recommends acknowledging Oral Roberts as the human "daddy" who God used to seed the charismatic movement.

Oral's teaching and concepts were foundational to the renewal that swept through the whole Church, internationally and interdenominationally—some even noting that he may be the one to coin the word "charismatic" in the theological-experiential sense it came to be used. He taught concepts that spread throughout the world and both simplified and focused a spiritual lifestyle that is embraced by huge sectors of today's Church.

To merely note the slogans Oral Roberts used in his teachings, or to miss the real biblical truths he taught by linking his original approach to shallow or sensationalized shadows of those truths too often clouding biblical clarity among some "charismatic" sectors today, is to trivialize what he actually taught and to cheapen what he offered at the time. For example, whatever today may have been done to the idea of "seed faith," in circles where it may seem to be advocated as a self-serving easy-way-to-wealth, Oral's foundational teaching and coinage of the term opened hearts to understand the life-giving, life-multiplying power of God's Word. Even his verbal logo, "God is a good God," was a bludgeon against legalistic patterns of thought that riddled the Church at the time, oppressing the souls of innumerable millions. This simple but Gospel-true statement became a song and a salutation, opening the doorway of hope to multitudes that the Father's heart had a place for them!

The elaboration of Oral's ongoing influence would take pages more, but this personal acknowledgement of mine is offered here as a tribute, which I conclude with this practical observation.

When the disciples described to Jesus their attitude and actions toward a ministry they saw as "different," but which functioned in Jesus' Name, they disclosed their opposition and prohibition. Jesus' answer came back as a strong corrective: "Do not forbid him, for no one who works a miracle in My name can soon afterward speak evil of Me. For he who is not against us is on our side!" (Mark 9:38-40).

Having been brought to the Church's present moment and the Holy Spirit's continuing unfolding of Jesus' purposes through us all, let us heed that well. For some, perhaps, joining me in commending Oral Roberts' influence through the past sixty years would be a worthy beginning place.

J.W.H.

A Prayer of Invitation

It seems possible that some earnest inquirer may have read this book and somehow still never have received Jesus Christ as personal Savior. If that's true of you—that you have never personally welcomed the Lord Jesus into your heart to be your Savior and to lead you in the matters of your life—I would like to encourage you and help you do that. There is no need to delay, for an honest heart can approach the loving Father God at any time. So I'd like to invite you to come with me, and let's pray to Him right now. If it's possible there where you are, bow your head, or even kneel if you can. In either case, let me pray a simple prayer first and then I've added words for you to pray yourself.

My Prayer

Father God, I have the privilege of joining with this child of Yours who is reading this book right now. I want to thank You for the openness of heart being shown toward You and I want to praise You for Your promise, that when we call to You, You will answer.

I know that genuine sincerity is present in this heart,

which is ready to speak this prayer, and so we come to You in the name and through the cross of Your Son, the Lord Jesus. Thank you for hearing.

And now, speak your prayer.

Your Prayer

Dear God, I am doing this because I believe in Your love for me, and I want to ask You to come to me as I come to You. Please help me now.

First, I thank You for sending Your Son, Jesus, to Earth to live and to die for me on the cross. I thank You for the gift of forgiveness of sin that You offer me now, and I pray for that forgiveness.

Forgive me and cleanse my life in Your sight, through the Blood of Jesus Christ. I am sorry for anything and everything I have ever done that is unworthy in Your sight. Please take away all guilt and shame, as I accept the fact that Jesus died to pay for all my sins and through Him, I am now given forgiveness on this earth and eternal life in heaven.

I ask You, Lord Jesus, to please come into my life right now. Because You rose from the dead, I know You're alive and I want You to live with me—now and forever.

I am turning my life over to You and from my way to Yours. I invite Your Holy Spirit to fill me and lead me forward in a life that will please the heavenly Father.

Notes

Chapter 1: The New Shape of Christianity

1. Patti Gallagher Mansfield, *As By a New Pentecost: The Dramatic Beginning of the Catholic Renewal* (Steubenville, OH: Franciscan University Press, 1992), 8: Val Gaudet, "A Woman and the Pope," *New Covenant* (October, 1973), 4-6.
2. "The Rise of Pentecostalism," *Christian History*; Vinson Synan, "Pentecostalism: William Seymour," *Christian History*, no. 65 (Winter 2000): 17.
3. David B. Barrett, George T. Kurian and Todd M. Johnson, *World Christian Encyclopedia*, 2nd ed. (New York: Oxford University Press, 2001), 19.
4. We should mention that Oneness Pentecostals affirm the essential unity of God and are not Trinitarian but believe that God merely "manifests" himself in various "modes" as Father, Son, and Holy Spirit.
5. Grant Wacker, *Heaven Below* (Cambridge, MA: Harvard University Press, 2001). Wacker's primitivism/pragmatic interpretive paradigm is most insightful and based on an exhaustive reading of primary sources.
6. Stanley M. Burgess and Edward M. van der Maas editors, *The New International Dictionary of the Pentecostal and Charismatic*

Movements *(NIDPCM)*, Rev. ed. (Grand Rapids, MI: Zondervan, 2002), xv-xxiii.

7. Frank Greer, telephone interview with author, January 30, 2006.
8. Barrett, *World*, 13.
9. This demographic shift has fueled religious conflict in Nigeria between Christians and Muslims.
10. Phillip Jenkins, *The Next Christendom: The Coming of Global Christianity* (New York: Oxford University Press, 2002), 7.
11. See Vinson Synan, *The Holiness-Pentecostal Tradition: Charismatic Movements in the Twentieth Century* (Grand Rapids, MI: Eerdmans, 1997), 88; Barrett, *World*, 1772.
12. Synan, *Holiness-Pentecostal*, 88; Barrett, *World*, 1772.

Chapter 2: The Road to Topeka

1. Vinson Synan, *The Holiness-Pentecostal Tradition: Charismatic Movements in the Twentieth Century* (Grand Rapids: Eerdmans, 1997) 1.
2. Mark A. Noll, *Turning Points: Decisive Moments in Church History* (Grand Rapids, MI: Baker Books, 1997), 223–24.
3. Mark Galli, "Revival At Cane Ridge," *Christian History* (Issue 45, 1995), 14.
4. Barton Stone, "Piercing Screams and Heavenly Smiles," *Christian History* (Issue 45, 1995), 15.
5. "God's College and Radical Change," *Christian History*, 20, 27.
6. Robeck, "Frank Sanford," *NIDPCM*, 1037.

Chapter 3: The Enigma of Charles Fox Parham

1. Quoted in Jim Goff, *Fields White Unto Harvest: Charles Fox Parham and the Missionary Origins of Pentecostalism* (Fayetteville, AR: University of Arkansas Press, 1988), 66.
2. Goff, *Fields*, 67.
3. Goff, *Fields*, 68.
4. Goff, *Fields*, 69-72; William Faupel, *The Everlasting Gospel* (Sheffield, UK: Sheffield Academic Press, 1996), 175-176.
5. Goff, *Fields*, 73.
6. Faupel, *The Everlasting Gospel*, 161.
7. Edith L. Blumhofer, *Restoring the Faith* (Urbana, IL: University of Illinois, 1993), 46.
8. *The Apostolic Faith*, January 1900.
9. Charles Parham, *A Voice Crying in the Wilderness*, 3rd ed. (Baxter Springs, KS, previously published, n.d.), 138. Cited in Blumhofer, *Restoring the Faith*, 45.
10. Sarah Parham, *The Life of Charles Fox Parham*, 3rd ed. (Birmingham, AL: Commercial Printing, 1977), 48. Cited in Blumhofer, *Restoring the Faith*, 47.
11. Goff, *Fields*, 74.
12. Goff, *Fields*, 73.
13. Goff, *Fields*, 75.
14. Goff, *Fields*, 67–68.
15. Robert Mapes Anderson, *Vision of the Disinherited: The Making of American Pentecostalism* (New York: Oxford University Press, 1979), 54.
16. Gary D. McGee, "Tongues, The Biblical Evidence: The Revival Legacy of Charles F. Parham," *Enrichment*, Summer 1999.
17. Goff, *Fields*, 76.

18. Parham, *The Life*, 79.
19. Blumhofer, *Restoring the Faith*, 53.
20. Faupel, *The Everlasting Gospel*, 181.
21. Faupel, *Everlasting*, 183.
22. Blumhofer, *Restoring the Faith*, 54.
23. Blumhofer, *Restoring*, 54.
24. Goff, *Fields*, 165.
25. Anderson and Hollenwegger, *Pentecostals After a Century* (Sheffield: Sheffield Academic Press, 1999), 42–43.

Chapter 4: William J. Seymour and the Azusa Street Revival

1. Cecil M. Robeck Jr., "William J. Seymour and 'The Bible Evidence'" in Gary McGee, *Initial Evidence* (Peabody, MA: Hendrickson Publishers, 1991), 72. Much of this chapter depends on the work of Robeck.
2. The name Asberry has been spelled various ways in the accounts of the Azusa St. Revival. We are choosing the spelling according to Seymour scholar Cecil M. Robeck.
3. *The Apostolic Faith*, September 1906, 1.
4. William Faupel, *The Everlasting Gospel* (Sheffield: Sheffield Academic Press, 1996), 202.
5. The *Los Angeles Daily Times*, April 18, 1906, 1.
6. The *Los Angeles Daily Times*, April 19, 1906, 1.
7. Frank Bartleman, *Azusa Street Meeting* (South Plainsfield, NJ: Bridge Publishing, 1980), 43
8. Bartleman, *Azusa*, 43.
9. C. M. Robeck, "Azusa Street Revival," *NIDPCM*, 345.
10. *The Apostolic Faith*, September 1906, 1.

11. *The Apostolic Faith*, September 1906, 1.

12. Bartleman, *Azusa*, 58–59.

13. *The Apostolic Faith*, November 1906, 1.

14. Robeck, "Azusa Street Revival," 346.

15. Robert Owen, *Speak to the Rock* (New York: University Press of America, 1998), 65.

16. Bartleman, *Azusa*, 56.

17. Bartleman, *Azusa*, 54.

18. Bartleman, *Azusa*, 58.

19. *The Apostolic Faith*, September 1906, 1.

20. *The Apostolic Faith*, September 1906, 1.

21. Bartleman, *Azusa*, 62.

22. Edith L. Blumhofer, *Restoring the Faith* (Urbana: University of Illinois, 1993), 57.

23. Robert Mapes Anderson, *Vision of the Disinherited* (New York: Oxford University Press, 1979), 64.

24. Blumhofer, *Restoring*, 57.

25. Vinson Synan, *The Holiness-Pentecostal Tradition* (Grand Rapids, MI: Eerdmans, 1997), 86.

26. *The Apostolic Faith*, September 1906, 1.

27. *The Apostolic Faith*, September 1906, 1.

28. Faupel, *Everlasting*, 208.

29. Blumhofer, *Restoring*, 61.

30. *The Apostolic Faith*, December 1912, 4–5.

31. *The Apostolic Faith*, December 1906, 1.

32. Robeck, "William J. Seymour," *NIDPCM*, 1036.

33. Robeck, "Azusa Street Revival," 347.

34. Robeck, "William J. Seymour," 1057.

Chapter 5: The Pentecostal Explosion

1. *The Apostolic Faith*, September 1906, 4.
2. *The Apostolic Faith*, September 1906, 1.
3. Gary McGee, "The Calcutta Revival of 1907 and the Reformulation of Charles F. Parham's 'Bible Evidence' Doctrine," *Asian Journal of Pentecostal Studies*, 124. We wish to express our debt to Gary McGee's valuable research on the history of Pentecostal missions. This chapter relies heavily on his work.
4. McGee, "Calcutta," 128.
5. Gary McGee, "Garr, Alfred Goodrich. SR." *NIDPCM*, 660.
6. Gary McGee, "Minnie F. Abrams: Another Context, Another Founder" in James R. Goff and Grant Wacker, *Portraits of a Generation: Early Pentecostal Leaders*, 87.
7. Gary McGee, "Ramabai, Sarasvati Mary (Pandita)," *NIDPCM*, 1016.
8. McGee, "Minnie F. Abrams," 99.
9. J. Edwin Orr, *The Flaming Tongue* (Chicago: Moody Press, 1973).
10. E. A. Wilson, "Brazil," *NIDPCM*, 35.
11. William Faupel, *The Everlasting Gospel* (Sheffield: Sheffield Academic Press, 1996), 232.
12. Faupel, *Everlasting*, 218.
13. Edith Blumhofer, "William H. Durham: Years of Creativity, Years of Dissent," in James R. Goff and Grant Wacker, *Portraits of a Generation: Early Pentecostal Leaders*. Much of the account on Durham draws on this excellent essay by Blumhofer.
14. Blumhofer, "Durham," 123.
15. Edith Blumhofer, "The Finished Work of Calvary," *AG Heritage*, Fall 1993, 10.
16. Blumhofer, "Durham," 133.

17. Vinson Synan, The *Holiness-Pentecostal Tradition* (Grand Rapids, MI: Eerdmans, 1997), 108.
18. Synan, *Holiness-Pentecostal*, 114.
19. Donald W. Dayton, *Theological Roots of Pentecostalism*, 21. More than any other researcher, Dayton has given scholars great insight into the theological roots of Pentecostalism.
20. William Durham, *Pentecostal Testimony*, n.d., 1.
21. Blumhofer, "The Finished Work," 10.
22. Bartleman, *Azusa Street Meeting*, 150.
23. Bartleman, *Azusa*, 151.
24. Faupel, *Everlasting*, 249.
25. Faupel, *Everlasting*, 249.
26. Vinson Synan, *The Century of the Holy Spirit* (Nashville: Thomas Nelson, 2001), 372.
27. Faupel, *Everlasting*, 278.
28. Synan, *Holiness-Pentecostal*, 160.
29. Faupel, *Everlasting*, 258.

Chapter 6: Aimee, America, and Pentecostalism

1. Grant Wacker, "Travail of a Broken Family: Evangelical Responses to Pentecostalism in America, 1906–1916," 23-49 in *Pentecostal Currents in American Protestantism* (Urbana, IL: University of Illinois, 1999). Wacker's essay is an excellent appraisal of the radical evangelical attack on Pentecostalism that fairly assesses some of the possible reasons for their responses.
2. Torrey, *The Baptism of the Holy Spirit*, 17.
3. Vinson Synan, *The Holiness-Pentecostal Tradition* (Grand Rapids, MI: Eerdmans, 1997), 146.
4. Wacker, "Travail," 513.

5. Edith L. Blumhofer, *Restoring the Faith* (Urbana: University of Illinois, 1993), 101.

6. Donald W. Dayton, *Theological Roots of Pentecostalism* (Grand Rapids: Zondervan, 1987), 21-23.

7. C. Neinkirchen, "Albert Benjamin Simpson," *NIDPCM*, 1069.

8. Blumhofer, *Restoring the Faith*, 105.

9. The narrative on Aimee relies heavily on the scholarship of Edith Blumhofer, particularly: Edith L. Blumhofer, *Aimee Semple McPherson: Everybody's Sister* (Grand Rapids, MI: Eerdmans, 1993).

10. Daniel Epstein, *Sister Aimee: The Life of Aimee Semple McPherson* (New York: Harcourt, Brace, Jovanovich, 1993), 182–183.

11. Epstein, *Sister Aimee*, 205.

12. Epstein, *Sister Aimee*, 205.

13. Matthew A. Sutton, " 'Between the Refrigerator and the Wildfire': Aimee Semple McPherson. Pentecostalism and the Fundamentalist-Modernist Controversy," *Church History*, March 2003, 159–188. Sutton provides a helpful survey and discussion on McPherson's ecumenical struggle.

14. Synan, *Holiness-Pentecostal*, 201.

15. Robeck, *Aimee, NIDPCM*, 857.

16. Robeck, *Aimee*, 857.

17. Sutton, "'Between the Refrigerator and the Wildfire,'" 16.

Chapter 7: Oral Roberts and a New Wave of Renewal

1. An outstanding discussion on the subject of racial tension in Pentecostalism is: Cecil M. Robeck Jr., "The Past: Historical Roots of the Racial Unity and Division in American Pente-

costalism" in *Pentecostal Partners: A Reconciliation Strategy for the 21ˢᵗ Century* (Memphis, TN: n. p. October 1994), 1–71.

2. Robeck, "Historical Roots," 69–70. A. J. Tomlinson split from the Church of God (Cleveland) in the mid-1920s to form the Tomlinson Church of God, a group that was organized interracially.

3. We are deeply indebted to the work of Auburn University historian David E. Harrell for much of the biographical narrative on Oral Roberts' life that follows. Harrell has written the definitive biography on Roberts that is both sympathetic and scholarly. David E. Harrell, *Oral Roberts: An American Life* (Bloomington, IN: Indiana University Press, 1985); David E. Harrell, "Oral Roberts: The Quintessential Pentecostal," paper submitted at the 15th Meeting of the Society of Pentencostal Studies; David E. Harrell, *All Things Are Possible: The Healing and Charismatic Revivals in America* (Bloomington, IN: Indiana University Press, 1975).

4. The narrative on Branham leans heavily on Douglas Weaver's biography on Branham. C. Douglas Weaver, *The Healer-Prophet William Marrion Branham: A Study of the Prophetic in American Pentecostalism* (Macon, GA: Mercer University Press, 1987).

5. Weaver, *Healer-Prophet*, 36.
6. Weaver, *Healer-Prophet*, 36.
7. Weaver, *Healer-Prophet*, 45.
8. Harrell, *All Things*, 30.
9. Weaver, *Healer-Prophet*, 47.
10. Harrell, *All Things*, 33.
11. Harrell, *All Things*, 49.
12. Harrell, *All Things*, 25.
13. Harrell, *All Things*, 25.
14. Harrell, *All Things*, 44–45.

15. Harrell, *Oral Roberts*, 100.
16. Harrell, *Oral Roberts*, 105.
17. Harrell, *Oral Roberts*, 101.
18. Harrell, *All Things*, 147
19. Harrell, *All Things*, 101.
20. Harrell, *Oral Roberts*, 207.
21. Harrell, *Oral Roberts*, 207, 212.
22. Harrell, *All Things*, 153.
23. Harrell, *Oral Roberts*, viii–ix.
24. Harrell, *Oral Roberts*, ix.

Chapter 8: Dennis Bennett and the Charismatic Renewal

1. Dennis J. Bennett, *Nine O'Clock in the Morning* (Plainfield, NJ: Logos International, 1970), 61.
2. Bennett, *Nine O'Clock*, 61.
3. Bennett, *Nine O'Clock*, 63.
4. Bennett, *Nine O'Clock*, 2.
5. Bennett, *Nine O'Clock*, 12.
6. Bennett, *Nine O'Clock*, 14.
7. Bennett, *Nine O'Clock*, 16.
8. Bennett, *Nine O'Clock*, 20.
9. Bennett, *Nine O'Clock*, 20.
10. Bennett, *Nine O'Clock*, 23.
11. Michael Harper, *As at the Beginning: The Twentieth Century Pentecostal Revival* (Plainfield, NJ: Logos International, 1965), 63.
12. Vinson Synan, *The Holiness-Pentecostal Tradition* (Grand Rapids, MI: Eerdmans, 1997), 229. Richard Quebedeaux, *The New Charismatics II* (San Francisco: Harper & Row, 1983), 63.

13. *Time*, August 15, 1960, 53–55; *Newsweek*, July 4, 1960, 77.
14. Synan, *Holiness-Pentecostal*, 230.
15. Bennett, *Nine O'Clock*, 82.
16. Vinson Synan, *Under His Banner* (Costa Mesa, CA: Gift Publications, 1992), 40. This narrative on FGBMFI relies heavily on Synan's book.
17. Synan, *Under His Banner*, 51-53.
18. Synan, *Under His Banner*, 53.
19. J. R. Zeigler, "The Full Gospel Business Men's Fellowship International (FGBMFI)," *NIDPCM*, 653–654.
20. Zeigler, "The Full Gospel," 653.
21. Synan, *Holiness-Pentecostal*, 224.
22. Harper, *As at the Beginning*, 47.
23. David du Plessis, *A Man Called Mr. Pentecost* (Plainfield, NJ: Logos International), 158.
24. Du Plessis, *Man*, 172.
25. R. P. Spittler, "Du Plessis, David Johannes," 589–592.
26. Spittler, "Du Plessis," 591.
27. Spittler, "Du Plessis," 592.
28. Spittler, "Du Plessis," 592.
29. Peter D. Hocken, "The Charismatic Movement," *NIDPCM*, 481.
30. Hocken, "Charismatic," 481.
31. Peter D. Hocken, "Bredesen, Harald," *NIDPCM*, 442.
32. Hocken, "Bredesen," 442.
33. Vinson Synan, *In the Latter Days*, 96.

Chapter 9: Catholic Charismatics and the Three Rivers of Renewal

1. Kevin & Dorothy Ranaghan, *Catholic Pentecostals* (Paramus: NJ: Paulist Press Deus Books, 1969), 22. Much of this narrative is drawn from the Ranaghans' account of the Duquesne weekend.
2. All of the quotes in this paragraph are taken from Patti Gallagher Mansfield, *As by a New Pentecost: The Dramatic Beginning of the Catholic Charismatic Renewal* (Steubenville, OH: Franciscan University Press, 1992), 41.
3. Vinson Synan, The *Holiness-Pentecostal Tradition* (Grand Rapids, MI: Eerdmans, 1997), 246.
4. It is worth noting that not everyone in the chapel was caught up in it all. A few students felt nothing and wondered if there was something wrong with them. One young woman even walked out and started for home until another member of the group went after her.
5. Gallagher, *New Pentecost*, 41.
6. Ranaghan, et al., *Catholic Pentecostals*, 10.
7. Ranaghan, et al., *Catholic Pentecostals*, 14.
8. Ranaghan, et al., *Catholic Pentecostals*, 15.
9. Ranaghan, et al., *Catholic Pentecostals*, 15–16.
10. Peter Hocken, "The Catholic Charismatic Renewal" in Synan, *Century of the Holy Spirit*, 211.
11. Synan, *Holiness-Pentecostal*, 243.
12. T. P. Thigpen, "Catholic Charismatic Renewal," *NIDPCM*, 460.
13. Ranaghan, et al., *Catholic Pentecostals*, 42.
14. Synan, *In the Latter Days*, 112.
15. Synan, *Holiness-Pentecostal*, 248.
16. Synan, *Holiness-Pentecostal*, 251.

17. Quotations in the previous paragraph and all subsequent are from Vinson Synan's unpublished and still-in-process autobiography and a telephone interview on January 21, 2005.
18. Vinson Synan, *Charismatic Bridges* (Ann Arbor, MI: Word of Life, 1974), v.
19. In an interview with Kevin Ranaghan, he emphasized McDonnell's perspective as part of what motivated the Charismatic Catholics in participating in efforts toward unity. In fact, Ranaghan pointed out the Christian communities formed under his leadership in South Bend, and the communities in Ann Arbor under the leadership of Ralph Martin and Steve Clark, were truly ecumenical communities and not limited to Catholics. Kevin Ranaghan, interview with author, December 17, 2003.
20. Michael Harper, *Three Sisters* (Wheaton, IL: Tyndale House, 1979), 104.
21. "Dennis Bennett, Mainline Charismatic: An Interview," *Christian Century*, September 27, 1972, 952–955.
22. Jim Hamann, "One City, One Church," *New Wine Magazine*, February 1974, 26.
23. Hamann, "One City," 25.
24. Hamann, "One City," 26.
25. Francis MacNutt, interview with S. David Moore, December 10, 2003.
26. MacNutt, interview.
27. Don Basham, *True and False Prophets: Confronting Immorality in Ministry* (Grand Rapids, MI: Chosen Books, 1986), 189. The elderly Pentecostal minister was David du Plessis.
28. MacNutt, interview.
29. Under the leadership of Francis MacNutt, the meetings continue today as the Fellowship of Charismatic Leaders and remain

genuinely ecumenical with Catholic Charistmatics, Protestant Charismatics, and Classical Pentecostals in attendance. As the Charismatic movement faded as a clearly identified movement in the 1990s, the group no longer is comprised of the most influential Pentecostal leaders. Nevertheless, it is the one annual leaders meeting that reflects the passion for dialogue and unity so central to the Charismatic movement in its heyday.

30. The "Glencoe" name came from a small community near St. Louis where the leaders gathered at a Catholic retreat center.

31. Through documents and interviews with Kevin Ranaghan and others, I discovered that the Kansas City conference, inspired by Synans' suggestion to Ralph Martin in 1973, was originally planned by the group that had planned the 1975 National Shepherds Conference known as the "ecumenical council" or "national council." This group was comprised of Catholics Ranaghan, Clark, and Martin, Lutherans Christenson and Don Pfotenhauer, and Don Basham, Ern Baxter, Bob Mumford, Derek Prince, and Charles Simpson, the five Bible teachers who led the Shepherding movement. Realizing the controversy over Shepherding could complicate plans for the conference, the group recommended that Ranaghan propose the conference to the Glencoe group. See S. David Moore, *The Shepherding Movement: Controversy and Charismatic Ecclesiology* (London: T&T Clark, 2003).

32. Bob Mumford, telephone interview with S. David Moore, April 7, 1992.

33. While there were many instances of spiritual abuse, the Shepherding movment has often been unnecessarily vilified by critics. Not everyone in the movement was hurt, and many people were helped by their emphasis on personal pastoral care. The extreme independence they sought to challenge was a true

problem among charismatics. Further, the unique ecclesiology of the movement deserves fuller study. For balance and objective history of the movement, see S. David Moore, *The Shepherding Movement: Controversy and Charismatic Ecclesiology*.

34. Moore, *The Shepherding Movement*, 92-96.
35. Richard Quebedeaux, *The New Charismatics II* (San Francisco: Harper & Row, 1983), 142.
36. Vinon Synan, *The Century of the Holy Spirit* (Nashville: Thomas Nelson, 2001), 358.

Chapter 10: John Wimber and the Third Wave(s)

1. Carol Wimber, *The Way It Was* (London: Hodder & Stoughton, 1999), 75–76.
2. John Wimber with Kevin Springer, *Power Healing* (San Francisco: Harper & Row, 1987), 3–4.
3. Wimber, *Power Healing*, 27.
4. Wimber, *Power Healing*, 29.
5. Bill Jackson, *The Quest for the Radical Middle* (Cape Town, South Africa: Vineyard International Publishing, 1999), 55–56.
6. Wimber, *Power Healing*, 34.
7. Wimber, *The Way It Was*, 117–118.
8. Wimber, *Power Healing*, 45.
9. Wimber, *The Way It Was*, 119.
10. Rich Nathan and Ken Wilson, *Empowered Evangelicals* (Ann Arbor, MI: Servant Publications, 1995).
11. Donald E. Miller, *Reinventing American Protestantism* (Berkeley: University of California Press, 1997), 32.
12. Wimber, *Power Healing*, 51–52.
13. Wimber, *The Way It Was*, 147.

14. Wimber, *The Way It Was*, 148.
15. Wimber, *The Way It Was*, 148.
16. Donald E. Miller, *Reinventing American Protestantism* (Berkeley: University of Berkeley Press, 1997), 32–51.
17. Miller, *Reinventing*, 48.
18. Miller, *Reinventing*, 48.
19. Miller, *Reinventing*, 49.
20. John Wimber with Kevin Springer, *Power Evangelism* (San Francisco: Harper & Row, 1986).
21. Bill Jackson, *The Quest for the Radical Middle* (Cape Town, South Africa: Vineyard International Publishing, 1999), 99-107.
22. Jackson, *The Quest*, 114-116.
23. The laughing that was such a defining feature of the Toronto revival had been observed for a few years before 1994, often associated with evangelist Rodney Howard-Browne.
24. Vinson Synan, *The Holiness-Pentecostal Tradition* (Grand Rapids, MI: Eerdmans, 1997), 276.
25. http://hirr.hartsem.edu/org/faith_megachurches_FACTsummary. html#theology. Accessed 1/5/06.
26. C. Peter Wagner, *The New Apostolic Churches* (Ventura, CA: Gospel Light, 2000).
27. Cox, *Fire from Heaven* (Reading, MA: Addison-Wesley Publishing, 1994), 102.
28. David B. Barrett, George T. Kurian and Todd M. Johnson, *World Christian Encyclopedia*, 2nd ed. (New York: Oxford University Press, 2001), 13.
29. H. V. Synan, "Bonnke Reinhard Willi Gottfried" *NIDPCM*, 438-439.
30. Synan, *Holiness-Pentecostal*, 287.
31. "Annual Growth of Membership," Yoido Full Gospel Church Handout, 2002, 1.

32. "The Third Force of Christendom," *Christian Century*, August 17, 1955. Van Dusen was echoing the words a year earlier (1954) when Bishop Lesslie Newbegin had called Pentecostals the "third force."

33. Quoted in John Sherrill, *They Spoke with Other Tongues*, 27.